The Government of Money

A volume in the series

Cornell Studies in Political Economy

EDITED BY PETER J. KATZENSTEIN

A full list of titles in the series appears at the end of the book.

The Government
of Money

MONETARISM IN GERMANY AND
THE UNITED STATES

PETER A. JOHNSON

CORNELL UNIVERSITY PRESS

Ithaca and London

b25092078

First published in 1998 by Cornell University Press

Library of Congress Cataloging-in-Publication Data

Johnson, Peter A. (Peter Andrew)
  The government of money : monetarism in Germany and the United States/Peter A. Johnson.
    p.   cm.
  Includes index.
  ISBN 0-8014-2835-1 (cloth : alk. paper)
    1. Monetary policy—Germany.   2. Monetary policy—United States. 3. Banks and banking, Central—Germany.   4. Banks and banking, Central—United States.   I. Title.
  HG999.5.J64   1998
  332.4'943—dc21   98-38346

Printed in the United States of America

Cornell University Press strives to use environmentally responsible suppliers and materials to the fullest extent possible in the publishing of its books. Such materials include vegetable-based, low-VOC inks and acid-free papers that are recycled, totally chlorine-free, or partly composed of nonwood fibers.

Cloth printing   10   9   8   7   6   5   4   3   2   1

For my parents, Ruth and David Johnson

Contents

Preface

Monetarism, among the most uncompromising free market doctrines to have acquired a substantial following in recent politics, is at the same time a significant contributor to, and even a proponent of, state power. At the most superficial level it argues that a state agency, the central bank, should heed no counsel other than its own and should pursue a policy of unflinching monetary discipline. Though monetarist doctrine no longer preoccupies the writers of editorials and political speeches as it did only a few years ago, the problems that monetarism addresses can never be permanently resolved. If they are to avoid the problems of inflation and recession, governments must always ask how money works and how it may best be controlled. Answers to these questions can never be permanent because capitalism constantly evolves. Monetarism is of great interest, both because it provided—indeed, continues to provide—answers to these questions, and because it confronts the deeper problem of how governments think about policy questions: What can governments know, and on whose behalf can they know it?

As more societies around the globe adopt the institutions and principles of market organization, they are in many cases also adopting the institution of independent central banking, and the pursuit of price stability, at whose birth monetarism was the (largely inadvertent) midwife. But in many of these countries, the speed with which the new institutions have been imitated from the established models, especially Germany and the United States, has meant that some of the most important features of that birth have been forgotten. Above all, there is a perception that independent central banking and anti-inflationary shock therapies are ends in themselves, required by Western trading partners, investors, or donors of aid. In this view, central banking and low inflation exist apart from democratic politics.

This book hopes to correct that perception. In the United States and Germany, monetarism was once far more "political" than it is today— it was almost as much a political philosophy as an economic doctrine. Most significantly, it asked how governments could reconcile institutional accountability with social stability, at a time when the world was less inclined than it is today to assume that narrow institutions automatically served broad goals, or that capitalism and democracy could happily coexist. That such coexistence is much more accepted today has much to do with the political and intellectual battles fought and won by monetarists in the arena of democratic politics. Today, however, in failing to remember those issues of statecraft that underlay the monetarists' success, we risk repeating the errors of twenty years ago. As monetarists have always insisted, economic doctrines and institutions must be judged by how they promote the higher purposes of democratic governance.

I and this book owe much to many people. My first and least repayable debt is to those present and former central bank governors and their staffs, government officials, bankers, union leaders, academic economists, journalists, and representatives of interest groups too numerous to mention who allowed me to interview them for this research. These interviews were conducted between 1988 and 1996. As I promised virtually all of them anonymity, I cannot thank them by name, yet my gratitude is deeply and personally felt. Although I have used my interviewees' recollections and insights mostly to fill in gaps left by the written record, I believe the book is much richer for the freedom that many of my interviewees gave me to quote their words and *aperçus*. And of course, I, and not my sources, am responsible for the content of this book.

The primary bases for this research are the memoirs, speeches, official reports, memos, newspaper accounts, and other documentary sources by or about the participants themselves. To obtain access to both these and my interviewees, I have relied on several fellowships, grants, and institutions. Direct financial support for the research was provided by Michele Sicca, DAAD, and SSHRC fellowships. Dr. Beatrix Brandi-Dohrn of the DAAD was very helpful, both in providing additional research money to conduct interviews in Germany and in assisting with travel arrangements. Manfred Körber, Siegfried Guterman, and especially Wolfgang Ploch, of the Bundesbank's Press and Information Office, were exceptionally courteous and generous with their time, with the information resources of the Bundesbank, and in helping me arrange interviews with staff and directors both in Frankfurt and at many offices of their Landzentralbanken. I knew that I had accomplished something human in that sometimes austere institution when I found myself invited to Wolfgang's wedding in Portugal.

I am likewise indebted to Joseph Coyne and his staff at the Board of Governors' Press and Public Relations office in Washington, D.C., and particularly to Susan Vincent and Judy Back of the Federal Reserve's Research Library, both for their ever-friendly assistance and for the abundant library access they afforded me. At the Library of Congress Bill Martin provided me with an office during my stay in Washington. The final writing of this book was accomplished in Vienna, Austria, at the Institute for Human Sciences (IWM). I thank Krzysztof Michalski and his associates at IWM, Jochen Fried and Traude Kastner, for the serene yet stimulating ambience they have established overlooking the Danube Canal. In Germany I benefited greatly over the years from the academic counsel and hospitality of Manfred Schmidt, Wolfgang Fach, and Fritz Scharpf. And my research in Germany would have been neither so successful nor so enjoyable without the hospitality of Dieter, Gabi, Julia, and Christoph Jung in Heidelberg and Matt Weiller in Bonn.

The argument of this book is much improved by the readings, commentary, and conversation provided by numerous individuals, all of whom I am honored to call colleagues; many are also friends from the Department of Political Science at Columbia University. They include Ira Katznelson, Helen Milner, David Baldwin, Peter Hall, Andrew Moravscik, Douglas Chalmers, Richard Nelson, Brigitte Nacos, Lewis Edinger, Robert Lieberman, Patrick Wolf, Markus Kreuzer, Pat Jackson, Kasia Stanclik, Michael Turner, and Tony Marx. As the book neared completion, I profited greatly from several colleagues' reading of key parts of the manuscript. Robert Aiello, Janusz Grzelak, János Kovács, John K. Glenn III, Jochen Fried, John Symons, and especially Christine Di Stefano and Michael Harvey were stalwart advisors to the end.

I am deeply grateful to the superb teachers whose company and guidance I enjoyed at Cornell University, where this book began. This book originated with a paper I wrote for Theodore Lowi's course on politics and public policy. Readers who are familiar with his theory of "arenas of power" may hear echoes of it here. Such echoes should not be surprising. That course, and the ideas which informed it, may be the most efficient engine yet devised for sparking exciting inquiry into the workings of politics. Quite apart from that marvelous intellectual experience, Lowi was always an enthusiastic backer of this project, especially in its formative phases, as were Jonas Pontusson, Martin Shefter, Benjamin Ginsberg, and Werner Dannhauser.

From the first research proposals to the last revisions for publication, Peter Katzenstein's imprint is everywhere on this book. So many of his grateful colleagues and former students have written about his inspiration, selflessness, rigor, and professionalism that almost the greatest intellectual challenge of this book has been to find new words to express my admiration and fondness for him. So let me mention one virtue that has come to mean more to me than any other: his loyalty—not only to me personally, but to this project, whose good ideas he stubbornly supported, even when I myself began to think better of them. Roger Haydon of

Cornell University Press gets special thanks, for more than his fine editorial skills: he proved to have a special knack with deadlines, which for the sake of future authors I will not disclose, and for which I am most grateful. Thanks, too, to three anonymous readers for the press, whose suggestions, while not always taken, were always helpful in making me aware of areas for improvement.

In the protracted business of bringing to light a book such as this, one leans heavily on the patience and love of friends who have nothing whatever to do with monetarism. In particular, I wish to thank Tony Marx, Peter Shapiro, and especially Elisabeth Beron for their encouragement and companionship. And special thanks to my dear, dear friend and dramaturge, Elizabeth Margid, who helped make this book's closing act a grand finale.

Finally, to my parents, Ruth and David Johnson. You did everything right: you gave me years of love, and the confidence to follow my own compass. Yet you have wondered how my first pursuit of Plato produced, of all things, a book on central bankers. Well, there really is a path from one to the other, and if this preface hasn't convinced you of that, I hope the pages that follow will. If in the end, however, you take this book to express nothing other than my love for both of you, and my thanks for your friendship and support, then I can count myself a successful author indeed.

PETER A. JOHNSON

Vienna, Austria

Abbreviations

ABA	American Bankers Association
AEI	American Enterprise Institute
BDI	Bundesverband Deutschen Industrie (Confederation of German Industry)
CBM	Central Bank Money
CBO	Congressional Budget Office
CDU	Christliche Demokratische Union (Christian Democratic Union)
CEA	Council of Economic Advisors
CPI	Consumer Price Index
CRS	Congressional Research Service
CSU	Christlich Sozial Union (Christian Social Union)
DANAT	Darmstadter und National Bank
DGB	Deutscher Gewerkschaft Bund (German Trade Union Confederation)
DIW	Deutsche Institut für Wirtschaftsforschung (German Institute for Economic Research)
EMS	European Monetary System
EMU	European Monetary Union
FDP	Freie Demokratische Partei (Free Democratic Party)
FOMC	Federal Open Market Committee
FRG	Federal Republic of Germany
GAO	General Accounting Office
IMF	International Monetary Fund
MCA	Monetary Control Act
NPD	National Partei Deutschlands (German National Party)
OECD	Organization for Economic Cooperation and Development
OPEC	Organization of Petroleum Exporting Countries
OTA	Office of Technology Assessment
PEPAB	President's Economic Policy Advisory Board
SEEPC	Shadow European Economic Policy Committee
SOMC	Shadow Open Market Committee

SPD	Sozialdemokratische Partei Deutschlands (Social Democratic Party of Germany)
SVR	Sachverständigenrat (Council of Economic Experts)
WSI	Wirtschafts und Sozialwissenschaftlicher Institut des Deutschen Gewerkschaftsbundes (Economic and Social Scientific Institute of the German Trade Union Confederation)

The Government of Money

CHAPTER ONE

The Problem of Economic Policy
Innovation in Democracies

"The independence of central banks is only justified if it is used to take unpopular measures." —Milton Friedman

In this book I investigate how the policy processes of Germany and the United States translated the innovations of academic monetarism into the monetary targeting practiced by the Deutsche Bundesbank and the U.S. Federal Reserve during the 1970s and 1980s. My purpose is to understand the capacity of democratic governments to stabilize their societies through the timely and successful implementation of new economic policies. The demise of Germany's Weimar Republic in the aftermath of hyperinflation and a deep economic depression in the 1930s is often held to be the paramount demonstration of the lesson that democracies may live or die by their ability to change course economically. But what, precisely, is the content of this lesson? On the one hand, some lay the blame for the collapse of Weimar at the door of the hyperinflationary policies pursued by the politically dependent Reichsbank in the years immediately after World War I. They conclude that independent policy institutions are necessary to provide an objective basis for policymaking and to resist the ill-considered demands of politicians and the public. On the other hand, their opponents point to the catastrophic policies of the Reichsbank after it had been made independent in the 1930s. They argue that the Riechsbank's failure to provide countercyclical support to the German economy during the Great Depression led directly to the massive unemployment that in turn facilitated the Nazis' takeover. They conclude that political independence may produce erroneous, destructive, and unaccountable policy. In short, every democracy that grasps the potentially crucial role of economics in the stability of its regime must confront the tension between independence and accountability in its economic institutions. The contrasting and paradoxical experiences of Germany and the United States with the adoption of monetarist-inspired policies during the economically chaotic 1970s and 1980s shed light on this tension, especially concerning the precise contributions of institutional independence and democratic processes to the timing, implementation, and consequences of this major policy change. These experiences show that the tensions between independence and accountability are ultimately reconciled by expertise, in this case embodied in the theories of monetarism.

Monetarism may be defined as the economic doctrine which argues that central banks should steer the national money supply so as to provide steady growth in a specified monetary aggregate (the so-called monetary target), in order to minimize the risks of inflation and recession and thereby maximize the long-term performance of the economy. The monetarist economists who advocated these programs of monetary targeting saw them as especially suited to combat the pronounced rise in prices and lengthening unemployment lines that beset both Germany and the United States in the 1970s. Yet the policy processes of both countries—especially their famously independent central banks—proved unequally congenial to this advice. Germany's monetarism was early, gradualistic, consensual, and durable, whereas the introduction of monetarism in the United States was late, sudden, conflictual, and transitory. Yet, as I suggest in this book, the reasons for these differences are not those usually attributed to the role of the two central banks. To begin to account for these differences, and to understand how they challenge some of our received notions about the roles that institutional independence and democratic politics play in macroeconomic policy change, it is helpful to sketch some of the salient contrasts of these two monetarist experiences.

Though the Bundesbank has since become internationally recognized as perhaps the world's premier practitioner of monetarism and monetary targeting, the ultimate acceptance and durability of its monetarism were at first scarcely discernible. For many years two factors discouraged the adoption of monetarism: a commitment to international fixed exchange rates and the export interests of politically powerful industries and commercial banks. In response to inflationary pressures that grew during the early 1970s, a majority coalition of Keynesians, supporters of Bretton Woods, and dirigistes grouped around president Klasen of the Bundesbank began implementing a series of ever more "authoritarian" measures that were the antithesis of monetarist prescriptions, including legislation that would have transformed the Bundesbank itself into a more statist and less independent institution. But in March 1973, under the leadership of the Bundesbank's vice-president Otmar Emminger, monetarists within the bank secured a majority in favor of an early break with the fixed exchange rate system and adopted monetary targeting as an administrative and technical "experiment." The Bundesbank introduced monetarism to the German public in an annually announced series of monetary targets, beginning in late 1974. In consequence, monetary targeting and monetarism became the main instrument for coordinating macroeconomic policy among the central bank, the federal government, and major private-sector interests. As the success of this program in curbing inflation and recession gradually strengthened the Bundesbank's hand politically, the central bank's influence among monetarists and so-called supply-siders in Germany contributed to a moderate conservative reorientation in fiscal policy beginning in the early 1980s. This reorientation brought the public deficit more into balance, but it did so essentially without touching the welfare state, so that there were benefits for Germany's unionized workforce. Although the cost of such status quo politics turned out to be high and protracted unemployment, Germany's rates of unionization increased, as did average real wage levels and the scope of the social safety net. Moreover, Bundesbank monetarism was a remarkably cooperative and consensual affair. Senior officials of the trade union movement said that their organization was in "far-reaching agreement" with the Bundesbank's policy of monetarist gradualism. Even the father of academic monetarism, Milton Friedman, cited the Bundesbank's experience as the first and most successful application of his ideas. To this day, the Bundesbank's "experiment" with monetarism remains a cornerstone of its policy.

By contrast, the surprisingly late monetarist regime change after 1979 in the United States proved much more contentious. As early as 1970 the presence of key monetarists or their sympathizers in positions of influence in the Federal Reserve and the White House led many to believe that the United States would be the first major country to implement a thoroughgoing monetarist reform. In fact, although the United States followed the monetarist prescription to end the convertibility of the dollar into gold in 1971, the Federal Reserve resisted committing itself to a domestic monetary target. Over the ensuing eight years, inflation worsened and the dollar was buffeted on international currency markets. Despite the proselytizing scholarship of American monetarists, the Federal Reserved exhibited an entrenched antipathy to monetarist thinking throughout most of the 1970s. Until 1979, its board of governors and its principal policymaking body, the Federal Open Market Committee (FOMC), made only minor cosmetic concessions to the challenges posed by Milton Friedman and his colleagues. In frustration, monetarists looked to alternative channels to promote their ideas. They founded their own pressure group, the Shadow Open Market Committee (SOMC). They established a political beachhead for monetarism in populist-led congressional banking committees. In the middle 1970s, Congress passed legislation requiring the Federal Reserve to publish and meet quarterly targets for a number of monetary aggregates. Yet prior to Paul Volcker's appointment as Federal Reserve chairman in the summer of 1979, not even legislation could persuade the Federal Reserve to pilot the economy by monetarist lights.

But with a seriously deteriorating economic climate, the Federal Reserve at last made a radical switch in its attitude toward monetary targeting. In October 1979, Volcker's Federal Reserve committed itself for the first time to key elements of the monetarist position, targeting M1 and controlling nonborrowed bank reserves.[1] In the months and years to follow, monetarism would be a doctrine in the eye of an economic storm. The Federal Reserve discovered that its delayed adoption of monetarist ideas had inadvertently caused an anti-inflationary backlash which saw radicalized monetarist economists from the SOMC join forces with militant supply-siders in the Reagan administration. Their volatile policy mix of tax cuts, increased defense spending, and support for Volcker's monetarism would push interest rates and the federal deficit to unprecedented levels. A deep recession, sought by neither monetarists nor their opponents, would elevate unemployment to levels not seen since the Depression. And inflation, the curse of the 1970s, would abruptly subside. All this occurred within the space of little more than two years.

By the middle of 1982, against a backdrop of worldwide financial instability, the Federal Reserve would significantly curtail its own "experiment" with monetarism—but not before industry and workers in the Northeast and Midwest, the heartland of the New Deal coalition, were devastated by high interest rates and the strong dollar. The implementation of radicalized monetarism increased the pressure to roll back the welfare state and left a weakened and demoralized American labor movement mobilizing a smaller proportion of the workforce than at any time since Roosevelt. And in contrast with his approval of German monetarism, when Milton Friedman was asked in 1982 by a congressional committee whether the label "monetarism" accurately described the recent policy of the Federal Reserve, he declared, "If this be monetarism, then I am not a monetarist."[2]

These differences in the American and German experience, which the *Financial Times* aptly characterized as "Big M" versus "little m" monetarism,[3] point up the two central questions which this book addresses: why these common programs of monetary targeting should prove to be implemented so differently, and what lessons we should draw about economic policymaking in democratic societies. Contrary to the initial assumptions of those who debate the choice between unpopular measures by independent institutions and responsive policy from democratic institutions, I will suggest that with the adoption of monetarism, the greater social responsiveness found in Germany was attributable to economists influenced by, and sympathetic to, Germany's unique banking institutions, whereas the unpopular measures associated with American monetarism were undertaken at the behest of economists-turned-populists animated by a profound theoretical skepticism about banks in general and independent central banks in particular.

EXPLAINING VARIATIONS IN MONETARY TARGETING

Variations in monetary targeting can be explained by looking at three factors: the policy (decision-making) culture of the central bank, the degree of "universality" of its financial and other economic institutions, and the patterns by which economists are mobilized into the central bank's policy culture. The greater rapidity and moderation with which the Bundesbank adopted monetarism initially depended on the greater collegiality of its policy culture relative to the Federal Reserve. This greater collegiality and openness in turn reflected the external incentives and constraints provided to Bundesbank policymakers by the more universalistic economic organizations in the German monetary policy environment, particularly the presence of universal banks, in contrast to the policy environment of the Federal Reserve, which was constrained by the presence of highly fragmented specialized banks.

To see why the German and American experience with monetarism involves these three factors—the central bank culture, the external bank structure, and the mobilization of expertise—one must begin by recognizing that the key resource which central banks control, money, plays a unique mediating role in organizing relations among economic agents in advanced market economies.[4] This mediating function creates unique policymaking dynamics for central banks, which I call the "dilemma of learning while governing." Because money is the sea in which all economic agents swim, raising or lowering interest rates (or controlling the money supply) affects the balance of power between buyers and sellers, borrowers and creditors, employers and employees, and—perhaps above all—citizens and the state. The manipulation of money transforms central banks into policy arenas where the stakes are not ordinary political conduct or outcomes per se, but rather the *manipulation of the environment of such conduct,* in which entire classes of economic and social agents will be affected by the decisions of the monetary authorities. This represents the "governing" component of the monetary policy dilemma: the control of money constitutes a form of political governance with universalizing implications perhaps unrivaled in any other domain of public policy.

Conversely, the "learning" aspect of this dilemma stems from the fact that central banks do not set interest rates or determine the money supply arbitrarily or in isolation. Central banks are purposive institutions with long-term policy objectives, an operational (or intermediate) set of short- or medium-term targets to guide them toward those ultimate objectives, and a set of conceptual tools for monitoring the attainment of those objectives. All of this culminates in a set of decision-making procedures to govern the application of their policy instruments. Central banks must constantly assess the appropriateness of their goals and the extent to which their policies meet those goals. To determine the proper aim and execution of monetary policy, they must constantly monitor and analyze their interactions with developments in the ever-changing modern economy. Such developments result from the actions of businesses, financial institutions, unions, governments, and households. Again, because monetary policy is so comprehensive in its impact, all these economic actors have a strong incentive to participate in the decisions that will affect them, and will try to identify their private interests with the public interest. Yet since the raising or lowering of interest rates that results from these investigations must, by definition, produce losers as well as winners, no policy can satisfy all these claims. Consequently, policymakers must attempt to limit or exclude such claims. Thus central banks are forever caught in the dilemma of "learning while governing," with the widest possible implications for the entire economy and the balance of economic and social power in the polity at large.

"Learning while governing" is an acute case of the central problem of economic policymaking in modern liberal democratic states. Claus Offe identified its key features when he wrote:

> In an advanced industrial economy, interest organizations have the power to interfere with public policy making in highly dysfunctional ways; hence the need to "keep them out." At the same time, however, such representative organizations are absolutely indispensable for public policy because they have a monopoly of information relevant for public policy and, most important, a substantial measure of control over their respective constituents.[5]

Especially in the case of central banks, this has increasingly fostered the subordination of normal patterns of political representation (party politics, interest groups, etc.) in favor of one of several more or less efficient patterns of *epistemic mobilization* to resolve the "learning while governing" conundrum by recruiting economic expertise and incorporating it into the policymaking process. Important similarities and important differences between the German and American monetarist experiences can be understood by noting how efficiently central bank cultures, the structure of financial institutions, and economists themselves mobilize expertise to manage the unique power of monetary policy.

Central Bank Cultures

As the following chapters will show, the Bundesbank's greater success in mobilizing monetarist expertise for its decision-making process had much to do with its more collegial and bifurcated corporate culture, which allowed monetarists, who had previously been in a minority among its senior officials, to wage and win an intellectual battle against a heretofore dominant Keynesian and dirigiste alliance from inside the central bank. This action allowed the monetarists to redefine the intermediate goals of the central bank away from its received notions—to say nothing of its legal obligations—to support the fixed exchange rates of Bretton Woods and toward stabilizing the domestic economy through monetary targeting. By contrast, the far more hierarchical (although styled "consensual") decision-making culture of the Fed, in which the chairman came to hold disproportionate power, afforded less internal access for monetarist ideas; around the Fed's policy table, there were simply fewer meaningful seats for any alternative programs. Years of stubborn adherence to an old institutional mission that increasingly lacked an economic rationale (essentially, to stabilize interest rates for commercial banks) by the Fed chairmen Arthur Burns and William Miller met little effective resistance from other governors or district bank presidents. Consequently, monetarists mobilized from outside the central bank, through the political avenues of interest groups, partisan coalitions, and a new advisory infrastructure.

To understand the workings of the corporate culture within a policy-making body such as a central bank, it is important to distinguish between its procedural and substantive aspects, even though they are by no means completely separable. Substantive culture consists of those shared formal and informal rules and assumptions which define the institution's ultimate objectives and the intermediate policy targets which it must pursue in order to fulfill its long-run objectives. By contrast, the procedural culture consists of those formal and informal rules by which the institution goes about the routine business of gathering and evaluating data, sets it immediate policy instruments (for instance, votes on raising or lowering interest rates), and administers those decisions (buys or sells securities in the money market, for example). These two types of culture taken together make up the institution's corporate or policy culture.

In both the Bundesbank and the Federal Reserve, the arrival of monetarism involved a redefinition of the relationship between the central bank's ultimate objectives and its intermediate policy target. In both cases, an intervening target (fixed exchange rates in Germany, stabilization of interest rates in the United States) was rejected as no longer compatible with the central bank's ultimate objective (essentially, to stabilize the business cycle). But as noted above, the flexibility needed to change the substantive culture depended on the collegiality of procedural

7

culture. In Germany, not only are senior officials of the central bank (the members of the Central Bank Council) formally endowed with equal power (each is entitled to one vote, each enjoys a long tenure in office, and so forth), but each councilor also has substantial de facto power as well. Among the directors at the Bundesbank headquarters in Frankfurt, this stems from their role as line managers of operational departments, and the access to the informational resources this affords. The presidents of the Land Central Banks (the regional bank headquarters) not only enjoy similar powers of knowledge and administration but also profit from substantial democratic legitimacy owing to their appointment by their respective Land governments. For all members of the Central Bank Council, a high level of expertise was both a functional and a statutory requirement, enforced by a vote on new members' qualifications taken by the Council itself. This balancing of power at the procedural level thus led, in some degree, to a balancing of economic theories and perspectives at the substantive level, as Bundesbank councilors representing different departments or states, or appointed by governments of different ideology, coalesced into loose but opposing factions.

In terms of formal powers and organization, opportunities for a collegial distribution of power and influence within the Federal Reserve system at the outset of the 1950s resembled those of the German Bundesbank. Formally, of course, each member of the Federal Open Market Committee (FOMC) is entitled to one vote; and governors, who are a majority on the FOMC, enjoy fourteen-year terms of office, a full six years longer than Bundesbank directors. However, in the ensuing years the accretion of informal practices and rules has increasingly served to tilt the Fed's decision-making culture ever more firmly toward a dysfunctional hegemony of the chairman. A survey of scholarship over the years reveals this trend. In the 1950s, the literature on the Fed noted the disproportionate but not excessive power of its chairman as CEO. Then, in the 1970s, ex-governor Sherman Maisel attributed the greatest percentage influence—35 percent—on Fed policies to the chairman. Most recently, David Jones described the corporate culture of the Fed as "chairman-centered," arguing that the chairman had attained "nearly absolute powers in internal administrative matters and Fed policy formulation."[6] Monetarists themselves noted in the 1970s that there was clearly something wrong with a multimember FOMC that, no matter how ambiguous or controversial the issues that divided it, always voted unanimously or nearly so for measures which the chairman supported.

How did this come to pass? This decay in the Fed's procedural culture stems partly from its formal organizational structure. The literature on corporate governance in America has frequently stressed the weakness of (outside) directors in their dealings with corporate CEOs.[7] Indeed, as

Chapter 4 will show, in the Fed, the chairman as CEO is formally responsible for staffing, governors do not have managerial responsibilities, and the procedures for nominating Federal Reserve district presidents deny them democratic legitimacy. Yet, as noted, at the height of the Fed's success under Martin's chairmanship, collegiality was relatively high. For a more thorough explanation of corporate culture we must look outside the institution itself. Donald F. Kettl, in one of the relatively few full-length treatments of the Federal Reserve to showcase the unusual power of the chairman, understood it as a positive development, arguing that "the Fed's power has depended on the chairman's leadership."[8] This view, I shall show, is gravely mistaken. The chairman's predominance within the Fed is, on balance, more baneful than beneficial, and like the president's role within the Bundesbank, is a symptom, not a cause, of the central bank's relations with its external policy environment.

Universal Financial Institutions

Clearly, the formal attributes of different central bank cultures do not by themselves adequately explain the discrepant receptivity to monetary targeting in the two countries. The fundamental reason is that policy cultures of central banks are redefined over time by the institutions through which, and on which, they exercise their power. Observers of bureaucratic behavior have long noted a tendency of constituents or clienteles of agencies to shape the goals and activities of the institutions established to regulate them.[9] For central banks, the clientele is the banks of the monetary system. At different points in their histories, the central banks of both Germany and the United States understood their mission as preserving the safety, the soundness, and even the profitability of the banking system they managed. However, history endowed these central banks with very different banking systems. This difference consisted in the degree to which the banking system was characterized by the presence of universal banks. The more the central bank exercised its monetary control through a banking system in which financial intermediaries are essentially undifferentiated by type of portfolio, type of business, geographic locations, or type of clientele—universality—the more likely it is that the central bank will be able to use money effectively to stabilize the economy. Moreover, the presence of powerful savings institutions as universal banks creates a counterweight to the traditional presence of commercial banking and a constituency for domestic stabilization not previously represented in central banks' policy environment. These patterns, when reinforced by other universally organized social institutions (notably industrial unions and parliamentary government), enhance the balance of power among decision-makers within the central banks themselves.

Many commentators have noted the presence of universal banks in Germany's "organized capitalism."[10] The features that have drawn most attention are the close connection between private commercial banks and German private industry—what I call the "vertical" features of the universal bank system. German banking law permits banks to own and vote shares in private nonfinancial corporations in ways that have been illegal in the United States since the 1930s. This has permitted them to appoint bankers to the supervisory boards (Aufsichtsräte) of firms—an opportunity which Germany's so-called Grossbanken ("Great Banks")—Deutsche, Dresdner, and Commerz—exploited to the fullest. This vertical intermingling, when combined with the significant underdevelopment of the German stock market, was said to enthrone these "big three" commercial banks as so-called prefects of the German economy. Their power was thought sufficient to organize the modernization of German production through a process of "bank-led adjustment," particularly through the promotion of exports. From this starting point, many have drawn the implicit conclusion that the monetary policy of the Bundesbank has essentially been dominated by this constellation of universal banks, industry, and exports.

The following chapters, however, will suggest that this misconstrues the real significance of German universal banking for the Bundesbank's monetary policy. The postwar period proved more significant for the blossoming and consolidation of what I call the "horizontal" aspects of universal banking. First, during the period after the occupation, the German government removed the restrictions on interstate banking that had been imposed on the big three banks by the U.S. military. One of the principal aims of the Adenauer government was to ensure the integrity of German banking as an instrument of monetary policy. German legislators came to believe that a system of universal banks which permeated all regions of the country and therefore all branches of the economy would more effectively smooth out inevitable seasonal and cyclical liquidity crises.

The second and more important aspect of the "horizontal" feature of German banking was the growth of the German savings institutions (Sparkassen) as rivals of the traditional commercial banks and as universal banks in their own right. The rise of the Sparkassen created a domestically oriented constituency for stabilization which counterbalanced the traditional export orientation of the more strictly commercial banks. The Sparkassen are analogous to thrift institutions in the United States in that their principal role has been to facilitate saving in the household sector, often to finance the purchase of homes. The German Sparkassen blossomed during the postwar period to such an extent that by the time of the adoption of monetary targeting, they had far outstripped their traditional big three rivals in total share of banking business. Unlike the thrifts, however, the Sparkassen were not limited to household deposits and home mortgages. As full universal banks, they enjoyed all the rights and duties shared by the big three, and they too were subject to the Bundesbank's monetary control (reserve requirements). Their regional giro institutions, the Landesbanken (provincial banks), became as large as the big three by the 1970s. These giro institutions, moreover, were partly owned by the Land (provincial or state) governments in which they were located, and as such, became the de facto central banks for the Land governments. Because of their intimate connection with their Land governments, the Sparkassen became enormously influential with their local Landzentral Bank (Bundesbank provincial headquarters), whose president was also a Land-government appointee.

Over the twenty-five years after the war, the Sparkassen and their middle-class clientele created a new constituency for domestic stabilization within the Bundesbank's policy environment that played an important role in helping the Bundesbank redefine its culture away from its traditional orientation toward maintaining an undervalued deutsche mark (DM) in the Bretton Woods system. The Sparkassen, but *not* the commercial banks, were among the earliest and staunchest supporters of monetarism.

The bifurcation of German banking into two powerful sectors with conflicting interests but similar regulatory status was replicated elsewhere in the political economy. In particular, the centralization of the German workforce into (in my sense) universalized industrial labor unions after 1949 reinforced the pressure to domesticate monetary policy, especially when, as in the 1960s, Germany achieved de facto full employment and the mobilization potential of the unions was at its peak.

This pattern of universalistic economic institutions contrasts markedly with the American policy environment, and especially with the regulatory specialization of banking. In the United States, regulatory fragmentation has deep historical roots stretching back to the populist crusades of the nineteenth century, when American banking was first divided between state-chartered and nationally chartered banks, and interstate banking was prohibited. During the 1930s, however, the collapse of the stock market and the failure of thousands of banks led Congress to impose a massive supplementary set of regulations on the banking system. Under these new "pluralist" regulations, commercial banking was divided from investment banking, and the thrift institutions became a separate, parallel financial system outside the Fed's system of monetary control. In exchange for an implicit guarantee of their soundness, the commercial banks were subjected to regulated interest rates (regulation Q). By the 1960s, in response to political pressure from the commercial banks, the thrift institutions were also made subject to interest-rate regulation.

This pluralist development created a set of incentives and constraints within the Fed's policy environment that were very different from the Bundesbank's. First, regulatory fragmentation diverted the banks' and thrifts' lobbying away from the content of monetary policy and towards issues of regulatory change. In particular, the thrift industry failed to emerge as the representative of its savings clientele within the Federal Reserve because, regulated by the Home Loan Bank Board, it stood outside the purview of the Federal Reserve system: it had no reserves on deposit with the Fed, and so it did not participate directly in the Fed's monetary policy. Second, and perhaps more important, further regulation of the thrifts created, in the late 1960s, a new, fragile system of monetary control loosely termed "credit crunches." When, in 1966, the Federal Reserve raised interest rates in the money market to curb inflation, the principal victims were the thrifts, whose depositors withdrew their funds to invest in the new higher rates in the money market. The thrifts were forced to call in billions of dollars worth of mortgages, and the result was that monetary restriction was confined almost exclusively to the household sector. This produced a political backlash and fear of financial instability that made future efforts to stabilize the price level much more tentative than they otherwise would have been. These two weaknesses—the lack of an institutional constituency for anti-inflationary policy and the fragility of monetary control—would propel the monetary system into a series of financial and political crises which chairman Burns in particular would use to consolidate power in his own hands, creating the dysfunctional corporate culture of the Fed in the 1970s.

Embeddedness of Expertise

The delayed effects of universalistic institutions on the central bank culture meant that even in the case of the Bundesbank, the adoption of monetarism did not result from central bankers' simply changing their minds in response to pressure or persuasion. On the contrary, in both Germany and the United States the adoption of monetarism was effected by a mobilization of a new set of experts, bringing into the central bank and its immediate policy environment a new definition of monetary policy expertise. These mobilizations of expertise—efficient and internal in the case of the Bundesbank, less efficient and external in the case of the Fed—not only shaped the character of monetary targeting but affected the tenor of politics in each country.

Although Germany's academic economists were less numerous than their American colleagues, less advanced theoretically, and less entrepreneurial, they nonetheless found it easier to make the leap from academia to policymaking than their American colleagues did. As I show in the following chapters, this had to do with the greater *embeddedness* of economic advisory pathways in German policymaking. This denotes two characteristics. First, German economists, unlike their American counterparts, profited from a set of preexisting advisory institutions that allowed for a more direct pathway from academia to advising, and from advising to governing. To a much greater extent, American monetarism, like other wings of American conservatism, required the *creation* of advisory institutions (e.g., the innumerable think tanks that sprang up during the 1970s). Second, the process of selecting experts and their ideas—sorting out *which* of these would move from academia to advisory institutions, and from advisory institutions to policymaking—was influenced by the different organizational arrangements of research and advisory bodies in the two countries. In Germany, expertise was more likely to be organized according to sponsoring social institutions, whereas in the United States it was more likely to be organized according to earlier policy problems or to the interests of individual political office-seekers. This difference meant that in Germany, certain experts and their theories were more quickly identified as having a constituency among one of the universalistic economic interests. This was much less the case in the United States, where the very abundance of research institutes amplified the lack of coherence among economic interests. American policymaking was thus more discordant, and it forced the experts themselves to organize a constituency for their ideas among the public at large.

These differences suggest something important, indeed paradoxical, regarding an old and unnecessarily unproductive debate in the social sciences. The decades-old literature on the sociology of knowledge and the more recent literature on the influence of ideas on public policy converge on the question of the relationship between ideas and interests. The former seeks to show—though more typically, simply assumes—that ideas do not matter because they are reducible to interests. The most idealist dispensations of the latter have asserted *in extremis* that interests do not matter because ideas constitute (that is to say, *construct*) interests. The experiences of monetarist economists suggests that these all-or-nothing positions are unhelpful. At least insofar as expertise is concerned, rather than seeing interests and ideas as mutually exclusive, in certain political circumstances there is actually good reason to expect them to be complementary. A political role for experts and expert knowledge is often the political residue, and a sublimation, of more overt competition among powerful social interests. The Enlightenment's centuries-old project to decant the contests of politics from violence into reason becomes more urgent the more organized the contestants and the more substantial their interests. Thus the varied intellectual bridges that experts construct between governments and societal interests contribute to how fluidly expert knowledge will be integrated into public policy. Paradoxically, it appears that greater embeddedness helps identify ideas which matter for governance *and* contributes to the status of those ideas as disinterested expertise.

Once our attention is drawn to the role played by the embeddedness of expertise in the adoption of monetarism, we can discern two distinct patterns affecting monetarist mobilizations. The first and more efficient of these—the German—I call *scientific corporatism*. Contrasting economic theories have been institutionalized in German political life since the inception of the Federal Republic. Weimar made the Germans acutely aware that economic issues were of vital importance. This recognition invested economic science with special political significance and reinforced a national esteem for science in general that was as prevalent on the political left as on the right. For every Ludwig Erhard, the neoliberal father of the postwar "economic miracle," there was a Karl Schiller, the Keynesian father of Concerted Action; for every research group of the Bundesverband Deutschen Industrie (Confederation of German Industry), there was a WSI research institute of the union movement. Each major political party maintains its own policy research foundation with government funding. Governments and universalistic social institutions jointly selected the professors who would make up the highly regarded Council of Economic Experts, and the council's annual report required an official response by the economics ministry. Between reports, the five quasi-public economic research institutes with their distinct intellectual profiles sustained a running commentary on economic affairs.

This pattern of balanced but embedded expertise began to have its most pronounced effect on the Bundesbank after the first moves toward monetary targeting in 1973. As Chapter 3 shows in detail, the spread of scientific corporatism to the Bundesbank paralleled the demise of the de facto corporatism represented by Concerted Action. Once it became clear that the Bundesbank would be the new locus of economic policy-making, outside interests wanted it to be governed by their own experts. Thus, unlike the standard patterns of neo-, liberal-, or societal-corporatist representation with which political science is familiar, the independence of the Bundesbank meant that there could be no direct representation of private-sector economic interests within the Bundesbank Council. Instead, there came to be proxy representation by coalitions of economists. This represented a marked departure from the domination of the Bundesbank Council by bankers. Indeed, between 1973 and 1976, members of the Central Bank Council waged a struggle over the definition of the statutory expertise appropriate for Bundesbank officials, as retiring bankers sought to resist their replacement by economists. While these new economists sitting on the Bundesbank Council were first regarded with suspicion by the bankers they replaced, eventually it came to be understood that the economists' intellectual affiliation with a wider network of economic theory, policy research institutes, and, ultimately, the philosophic perspectives of Germany's universal economic institutions lent them a legitimacy they would not otherwise have enjoyed. Bundesbank officials recognized that economists of different schools reduced the likelihood that the Bundesbank would misinterpret new economic developments or misread the behavior of outside economic actors. Ultimately, the negotiated form of monetarism constructed by scientific corporatism reduced the incentive for outside policy experts to move beyond advocacy to activism, and their ideas were thus more pragmatic and less ideological. Scientific corporatism fostered monetary corporatism.

The second and less efficient type of advisory pattern, found in the United States, can be called *scientific populism.* In the United States, public policy research and advocacy is plentiful, but only haphazardly heeded by policymakers. The fact that American research and advice on public policy are more likely to be organized around (preexisting) problems or politicians rather than (universalistic) social constituencies means that experts interested in new policy problems often have to create their own infrastructure *de novo.* The result is that in any area, public policy is likely to be derived from only a single paradigm—even in institutions with an otherwise collegially organized board. Policymakers apply the traditional prescriptions until they are replaced by new officials. Among outside policy experts, a plethora of policy institutes, prescriptions, theories, and paradigms vie for attention. The propensity of policymakers to ignore or overlook important new perspectives sometimes leads these outside experts to enter partisan politics. Externally mobilized policy expertise is likely to undergo radicalization as it adjusts its prescriptions to suit a more political, less scientific arena. For this reason, policy implemented by experts mobilized in this way is more likely to be late, controversial, and even revolutionary.

This pattern is exemplified very clearly by the United States' experience with monetary policymaking. American economic advisory institutions are kaleidoscopic in their diversity. The American Council of Economic Advisors is too often excessively partisan; American political parties, lacking the research foundation support of their German counterparts, are intellectually decapitated; and independent research institutes (such as Brookings) that were established to deal with such problems as public administration, defense, poverty, or race often proved ill-prepared to address the problem of inflation. Monetarists found they could not persuade the Federal Reserve of the merits of their policies while confined to academe; they turned, in the 1970s, to the creation of the Shadow Open Market Committee (SOMC) and numerous other libertarian research and advocacy organizations. These new organizations would supply the personnel for the revolutionary monetary populism of the Reagan administration.

THE POLITICAL SIGNIFICANCE OF MONETARIST MOBILIZATION

The differences between monetary corporatism and monetary populism point to the significance of patterns of mobilizing experts. In the introduction of new economic ideas, expert pathways shape policy in two major ways. First, the timing of the introduction of monetary targeting can influence the overall tenor of politics. Earlier introduction of monetary targeting through more embedded and efficient pathways reduces the inflationary or recessionary forces that lead directly to social mobilization. Second, more embedded pathways also reduce the tendency of economic ideas to become radicalized.

To see how differing pathways shaped the content of monetarist policies, one must contrast the less radical version of monetarism in Germany with the version found in the United States. These differences turn on the implications of monetarism for other areas of economic policy, especially fiscal policy. Because monetarists favor the free market, they strongly prefer small government. Some scholars have therefore suggested that balanced budgets and neutral fiscal policy represent the monetarist norm.[11] While this adequately characterizes continental European monetarists, it does not apply to American monetarists. As I will show in Chapter 5, the external mobilization of American monetarists led them to argue that fiscal policy and deficits did not (or need not) matter. As Beryl Sprinkel, former Treasury undersecretary for monetary affairs and the preeminent Reagan monetarist, once put it: "Control the money supply and everything else falls into place."[12] For American monetarists, it was government spending as such that represented a burden on the private sector. The means by which governments chose to pay for this burden (formal taxes, borrowing, or inflation) left the citizenry equally poorer. It was only the *quantity* of money, not whether it was spent by the private or public sector, that had empirically demonstrable effects on inflation (or the business cycle). As Friedman would frequently insist, to worry about the budget "deficit" in a misguided belief that it had inflationary consequences was to fetishize a bookkeeping entry as if it were a policy problem. So long as the central bank did not accommodate government spending by monetizing the deficit, then inflation would be low and growth steady, even if the deficit represented a claim on future taxes or crowded out private-sector borrowing through higher rates of interest. By adopting the extreme view that only monetary policy affected inflation, monetarists in America created the possibility of a policy alliance with tax-cutting supply-siders that allowed Republicans to campaign with a clear economic conscience on the platform of lower inflation and lower taxes.

American monetarists hoped, however, that by prioritizing monetary over fiscal control they would do more than simply restore stable prices. They hoped, in addition, that the resulting deficits would shock voters and politicians into trimming expenditures, thereby achieving their long-run goal of smaller government. Yet this strategy involved an explosive intellectual and political contradiction. "What is most important and most dangerous about the monetary rule," argued the noted Keynesian economist Arthur Okun, "is its implicit precept: ignore fiscal policy. Carried to its ultimate conclusion, the monetarist position would justify a totally unconstrained federal fiscal policy."[13] As it turned out, a single administration could not accommodate both the old Republican tradition of balancing the budget and the new doctrine that deficits did not matter for inflation. If deficits truly did not cause inflation, then it was hard to see how they could be used to frighten politicians into spending cuts. The coalition of monetarists and supply-siders erased decades of unpopular Republican policies ("root canal therapy") and helped win a powerful mandate for the Reagan administration, but it saddled the United States with a massive deficit that would linger for years. Only in the late 1990s, when memories of the radical monetarist doctrine faded, would politicians again be willing to tackle the deficit.

By contrast, Otmar Emminger, the Bundesbank official who was most instrumental in implementing monetarist policy in Germany, was among those Germans who were most scandalized by the way American monetarism courted fiscal profligacy. The Bundesbank tolerated an initial explosion in the public-sector deficit at the time that monetarism was adopted in 1973, but subsequently the Bundesbank was able to make budget balancing a litmus test of sound economic policy. This view was generally shared by German monetarists in academia. Deprived of a radical monetarist constituency, the conservative Kohl government in the early 1980s proceeded to raise taxes while Reagan lowered them, with all of the consequences for the welfare state that this difference entailed.

With these differences in mind, it is important not to make hasty judgments about the political implications of monetarism *tout court*. On the one hand, to be sure, monetarists in the United States provided much of the intellectual infrastructure and the political will behind the Reaganite revolution. But this was primarily due to the later introduction of monetary targeting via new, less embedded pathways of scientific populism, in which the hostility of American monetarists to independent central banks played a not inconspicuous role. In Germany, on the other hand, the early introduction of monetarism by the more embedded pathways of scientific corporatism helped preserve the welfare state by permitting the flexible adaptation of unions and fiscal policy and by intellectually demobilizing neo-conservative radicalism.

Indeed, the contribution of advisory pathways in which central banks are embedded to effective stabilization policy provides the larger perspective of this book. In Chapter 6 I explore the claim that central banks are, or can be, stabilizers of democracy. One of my principal conclusions is that monetary stabilization was adopted not simply for narrow economic reasons but responded to broader political concerns. Monetary targeting, especially in the case of the Bundesbank, was an act of "statesmanship" which rendered timely service to an anxious and untested democracy. Monetarism even cured America's malaise of the late 1970s. Although the German and American experiences with monetarism had pronounced differences, in the end they shared one fundamental trait: as I show in Chapters 3 and 5, both countries ultimately mobilized a new set of experts for monetary policy, to implement monetarism and to curb the problems of governance created or exacerbated by inflation's "price revolution." Not all countries were able to do this. In the concluding chapter, I explore more fully the implications of epistemic mobilization and an independent central bank for democratic stability.

Indeed, perhaps even more than the German state itself, the principal beneficiary of its efficient mobilization of expertise was the prestige of the Bundesbank. While American monetarists failed to alter the independence of the Fed, the Bundesbank converted the next generation of economists to the cause of independent central banks, albeit with a foreshortening of political vision that comes from over emphasizing independence as the crucial factor for success. This legacy in enhancing the prestige of independent central banks among economists on opposite sides of the ocean illustrates the powerful influence that epistemic politics can have on researchers themselves. It would be naive to suppose that the greater success and durability achieved by monetarism (especially in the Bundesbank) has not also had an impact on analysts of comparative public policy. Thus an increasingly popular "rationalist" interpretation invokes the seemingly irresistible power of money and markets—indeed, of independent central banks themselves—to give these events a cast of historical inevitability. As our last task, therefore, we must consider the explanations that have come to dominate the field after the triumph of monetarism and examine to what extent they are consistent with the actual history and contingency of monetarist events.

ALTERNATIVE VIEWS: "MARKET RATIONALISM" VS. "POLITICS AS USUAL"

My explanation for the different timing and implementation of monetary targeting may be clarified by contrasting it with some of the most common alternatives. These generally claim that the differences I have identified can be understood by considering the impact of market forces and the self-interest of domestic political actors and institutions in the different countries. Particularly with regard to the power of markets, the pervasive rationalist interpretation inspired by the new political economy (of which monetarists were founding members) now overwhelmingly colors the reading of these events in the minds of academicians and practitioners alike. In this view, the adoption of monetarism was chiefly driven by the exposure of individual countries to international market forces. This, it is argued, was especially true for Germany, with its dependence on exports and its exposure to international currency markets. Conversely, it is held that the greater isolation of the United States from international market forces (owing to its size, the unique role of its currency, and its patterns of trade) gave its politicians and political interests greater scope to ignore deterioration in the performance of their monetary policy and to use monetary policy as a vehicle for their own short-term interests. These arguments share the supposition that the rise of monetarism can be understood largely without reference to the processes that mobilized monetarists and their ideas into the central banks.

The first argument marshaled by the rationalist model to explain the demise of neo-Keynesianism and the rise of monetary targeting focuses on the power of independent central banks themselves. The rationalist model typically argues that the more central banks are effectively endowed with the attributes of formal-legal independence—including lengthy tenure for their officials, self-financing, and statutory mandates to pursue stable-money policies independent of government instructions—the more such central banks are likely to resist the demands of government and the public for inflationary financing of public expenditures and to pursue the kind of anti-inflationary policy that monetary targeting implies. In other words, *formal* independence is thought to be necessary for *behavioral* independence or institutional *autonomy*. Scholars working in this tradition have designed a number of measures for both formal independence and behavioral independence, and they have generally concluded that the Bundesbank is both formally and behaviorally more independent than the Federal Reserve.[14] The preponderance of research in this vein shows reasonably strong statistical correlations between independent central banks and low inflation rates.

But what accounts for the greater independence of central banks? The second line of argument advanced by the rationalist model sometimes relies on singular events: Germany's history of hyperinflation in the 1920s, and again after World War II, allegedly created a social consensus supportive of tight-money policies, as well as the original grant of independence to its central bank. Indeed, when applied to Germany, the rationalist model seems to envision tight-money policies descending in an unbroken line from Hjalmar Schacht's resolution of the hyperinflation crisis in 1923 through Ludwig Erhard's currency reform of 1948 to the Bundesbank's monetarism itself.[15] By contrast, it is said that the United States, never having experienced such crises, has a historical tolerance for inflation that is not found in Germany.

Far more fundamental to the rationalist interpretation, however, is the power of financial markets to impose an independent central bank on an unwilling government or public. These market-based explanations for the rise of monetarism are virtually indistinguishable from rationalist explanations of the demise of Keynesian policies. The power of markets is the bone of contention as regards Keynes's two chief legacies—management of domestic demand through fiscal policies and the international system of fixed exchange rates. Essentially, the rationalists argue that the more nations are exposed to powerful markets, especially for capital, the more a credible threat of a capital strike leaves finance-hungry governments little choice but to guarantee tight-money policies by granting central banks de facto independence. Although this argument in its original incarnation rested heavily on the presence of domestic markets for goods, services, and capital, it has more recently stressed the power of economic globalization and especially the power of international financial markets.[16]

According to the original domestic version of this argument, monetarism and independence of the central bank came into play because Keynesian (or neo-Keynesian) policies for managing demand were so rigid that they were doomed to failure. These policies were originally designed to permit flexibility in government outlays to stabilize the private sector. In fact, according to this argument, they proved vulnerable to unrelenting demands for increased government spending, which steadily ratcheted fiscal deficits upward. As government borrowing increased, so too did its dependence on financial markets. Simultaneously, private sector markets grew in unforeseen ways, creating new products and services while discarding old ones, undermining the assumptions on which government planning and fiscal stimulation rested. Cyclical unemployment became difficult to distinguish from structural and technological unemployment. As old industries declined, union membership and left-leaning voting patters declined with them, while social-democratic governments alienated their remaining electorates by trying to defend and reconcile too may incompatible constituencies, creating a crisis of governability.[17]

This culminated in a weakening of the social democratic or New Deal coalitions and parties which had originally created Keynesian policies.[18] In the 1970s, governments turned to monetarism as the simple solution to demand overload. As Lindberg, Scharpf, and Englehardt expressed it:

> All that is necessary for [the monetarists'] success is the strict limitation of the money supply, which in the extreme case could be enforced by the central bank acting alone and even in the face of very high government deficits. Furthermore, union collaboration . . . is rather unimportant for monetarism. With or without union collaboration, wages eventually will be forced down by rising unemployment. Thus monetarist requirements for policy co-ordination among separate institutions are minimal when compared to those of neo Keynesianism.[19]

Here again, Germany is thought to have a structural advantage over the United States because its commitment to Keynesianism was thought to be weaker and of more recent origin.[20]

Over time, these market forces translated divergent national fiscal policies, particularly in the United States, into a breakdown of the Keynes-influenced system of international fixed exchange rates known as Bretton Woods.[21] So long as the international treaties had fixed international currency parities, the independence of central banks from domestic governments was secondary to their dependence on the Bretton Woods system. But here too, according to the rationalist interpretation, the Keynesian vision proved too rigid to cope with innovations unleaded by markets. Offshore banking, Eurodollar markets, electronic transfer of funds, new financial products not envisioned by the old Keynesian rules—all these undermined the capacity of governments to stipulate currency parities by international treaty. With fixed exchange rates no longer possible by the mid-1970s, heightened exposure to international capital and currency markets accentuated the tilt toward monetary targeting that the failure of domestic Keynesianism had initiated. Germany, with its smaller, more internationally open economy, was simply the first of many countries that would be driven by international trade and capital flows to adopt monetarism.

Finally, rationalists also tend to believe that the ease and consensus with which monetarism was adopted in Germany are largely consistent with its overall postwar politics of consensus. Germany has often been characterized as pursuing "the policy of the middleway," suggesting that German politics has generally had both the will and the skill to fluidly adapt its policy institutions to new circumstances across a whole range of issues.[22]

In contrast to the cooperative spirit with which German policy is said to be made, rationalists find in the United States a far greater tendency toward self-seeking policymaking.[23] For example, Robert Weintraub has argued that the president gets the monetary policy he wants, and thus that we can predict monetary policy by knowing who the president is. Hibbs has shown that inflation tends to be higher and unemployment lower during Democratic administrations, suggesting that the Fed adopts the monetary policy congenial to the president's electoral coalition.[24] John Woolley has argued that the president is rarely unhappy with the monetary policy he gets. This theory of self-seeking emphasizes the electoral consequences of monetary policy for political officeholders, especially the president. Many observers say that the president's chief objective while in office is reelection—for himself and his party first of all, but also to reward his supporters. In this view, the Fed is not independent at all but is, wittingly or not, part of an electoral monetary cycle operating at the president's behest. Voters seem to hold presidents accountable for the nation's economic performance: there is a fairly strong statistical evidence that economic conditions affect the outcome of presidential elections. This would seem to give the president an electoral motive to manipulate monetary policy in ways that are conducive to electoral success. Precisely this sort of manipulation is alleged to have occurred in 1972, when an overly stimulative Federal Reserve policy seemed to help reelect President Nixon. Moreover, Congress is likewise considered by those who study it to be an extraordinarily adept reelection machine. The frequency of elections and the weakness of party discipline make members of Congress especially inclined to promote their own reelection through spending programs for voters and interest groups in their home districts. Institutional self-interest, then, would seem to account for governmental aversion to monetarism in the United States.

Yet, for all the analytic sweep of this rationalist interpretation, and its status as a kind of received wisdom in certain financial circles and finance ministries, in few countries with independent central banking does this argument apply less than in Germany and the United States. In reality, the question why the Bundesbank, with its allegedly more independent central bank, adopted monetarism more rapidly and smoothly than the Federal Reserve is more puzzling and much more interesting than is recognized by the rationalist model. It can be seen that the rationalist model errs in two fundamental ways. First, it reads the known outcomes of the 1980s and 1990s backward into the events of the late 1960s and 1970s. In general, this results in overstating the independence and anti-inflationary predispositions in the case of the Bundesbank, and understating them in the case of the Federal Reserve. Second, it severely underestimates the willingness of policymakers in both countries, including businesspeople and bankers, to misread and even oppose the dictates of the marketplace.

To see this, it is necessary to recover empirically the relationship between institutions, interests, and goals in each country *as the principal actors understood them to be*, before, during, and after the monetarist episodes. In other words, the beliefs of actors must not be deduced from what we assume to be true today. This necessarily entails what I call a historical-hermeneutical approach. This differs from "historical institutionalism" in that it does not assume that history determines norms or institutional imperatives once and for all.[25] Quite the contrary. The historical hermeneutical method, properly conceived, recognizes that institutions are contestants for power and prestige. As such, the historical hermeneutical method approaches institutional mythology as written (or rewritten) for partisan purposes, not to preserve the truth.

Armed with this historical awareness, we can begin to recover actual institutional politics by noting that in neither country did the emergence of inflation as a problem automatically entail the choice of a particular (monetarist) solution in the minds of decision makers in the early 1970s. This was not for lack of anti-inflationary zeal. Contrary to the assumptions of the rationalist model, inflation had been identified by publics and officials as the number-one economic problem in both countries, perhaps even more in the United States than in Germany. By 1971, Americans were telling pollsters that inflation was the paramount national problem, a status that it was to retain for the rest of the decade. And monetarists were far from alone in proposing solutions. The monetarist prescription for a monetary and market-oriented approach was long overshadowed by a more established neo-Keynesian orthodoxy, which had its own remedies. The neo-Keynesian anti-inflationary prescription tended toward what one German author called an "authoritarian" or dirigiste approach that advocated increasingly stringent regulation of the free market.[26] This was no less true in Germany than in the United States. The Bundesbank's postwar legal mandate "to maintain the value of the currency" was originally understood to refer to the DM's *external* value; to the extent that fear of inflation played a role, it did so by binding German central banking ever more tightly to international agreements. The Bundesbank inherited its legal mandate directly from its postwar predecessor, the *Bank Deutscher Länder,* the creation of the American military occupation, whose originators understood that this clause tied the German currency to the dollar by international treaty. In fulfilling its mandate, the Bundesbank was, to be sure, "independent of instructions of the government." But this writ ran only as far as its international commitments; Bonn's legal primacy on questions of international exchange rates gave it leverage over the central bank that the Bundesbank accepted almost without question, even during periods of floating. The Bundesbank invented the new version of its mandate—to preserve the internal purchasing power of the DM—only after it began shirking its legal obligations under the Bretton

Woods system. This newer domestic reading appeared for the first time in its reports of 1972 and has never been universally accepted outside the Bundesbank.

As I describe in Chapter 3, from 1969 through 1973 Germany's commitment to fixed exchange rates and its memories of the political consequences of recession led key figures in the Bundesbank and government to try to stem the tide of inflation with highly regulatory measures. On its own initiative, the Bundesbank proposed dramatic changes to its own governing legislation. These would have brought it into line with its much more dirigiste counterparts elsewhere in Europe. A political clash between Karl Klasen, the dirigiste president of the Bundesbank, and the free-market finance minister, Schiller, ended in Schiller's defeat. These moves culminated in a government-sponsored and Bundesbank-endorsed effort to limit the independence of the central bank itself. Although the monetarist viewpoint was gaining favor among certain Bundesbank directors and (especially) presidents of the Landzentral-banks, only in 1973 did a fortuitous set of circumstances let this minority assert itself. With the principal proponents of market controls sidelined by illness, the minority monetarist faction made the Friedmanite prescription of a free float and monetary targeting a *fait accompli*. For many months, however, Bundesbank monetarism appeared to have no visible effect, reinforcing perceptions of the Bundesbank's powerlessness. But eventually, the measures worked, and worked more effectively than even many Bundesbank officials dared hope, bringing to an end efforts to change the bank's status. Thus, monetarism in Germany was less a tour de force than a fortuitous discovery. In Germany, *monetarism fostered the central bank's independence, not vice versa.*

Similarly overdrawn is the claim that Germany's memory of two episodes of postwar hyperinflation makes it more willing to restrain the social demands of workers and interest groups that might contribute to inflation. The myth of the "lessons of hyperinflation" has always been rivaled by another memory that found a broad reception in the late 1960s—the role of the independent Reichsbank in triggering and aggravating the Great Depression. While the hyperinflation of 1923 certainly contributed to Weimar Germany's social ferment, it cannot be overlooked, as the Bundesbank is now inclined to do, that the active complicity of Hjalmar Schacht and the independent Reichsbank in the Great Depression helped bring Hitler to power. As I discuss in Chapters 2 and 3, historiographic research shows that ordinary Germans in the late 1960s were as fearful of recessions and mass unemployment—both in their own right, and as threats to the life of their young democracy—as they were of inflation. Chapter 3 reminds us that we cannot understand the political reaction to Germany's recession of 1966—the votes for neo-Nazi parties, the panicky formation of a "grand coalition" government, sweeping economic and social reforms—unless we bear in mind both sides of the history of the German central bank. As subsequent chapters reveal, it was the lesson of depression and recession, not of hyperflation, that animated the majority faction of the Bundesbank after 1967. For this reason, the Bundesbank's monetarism had to be far more gradualist and consensual than the rationalist model predicts. Even after the Bundesbank's monetarism elevated it to the status of an icon in the 1980s, the bank's version of the "lessons of Weimar" has never been fully accepted by the German public. The Bundesbank's own strictly confidential polls indicated that the German population, defying the bank's mythology, continues to worry more about unemployment than inflation. (Indeed, Bundesbank polls indicate that many Germans may not even recognize the difference between the Bundesbank and the Deutsche Bank, the largest of the private commercial banks.) In some ways, the real discovery of German monetarists was that the Bundesbank could trigger recession and unemployment while bolstering the regime, something not previously believed.

How did German monetarists make this discovery? They did so by allying their doctrine to fears for the political health of German democracy. German monetarists were the first to argue that inflation was the cause, not the effect, of the interest-group conflicts, popular mobilizations, and widespread strikes besetting Western societies in the late 1960s and early 1970s. Curbing inflation, they learned to argue, would stabilize German democracy. They could make this argument because of a crucial innovation in anti-inflationary doctrine wrought by monetarists: the separation of stable prices from balanced budgets. Monetarists told government officials that to reduce inflation, they need not curb their spending programs. Had the monetarists not made this argument, they would have confronted far more political resistance than actually proved to be the case. And indeed, the combination of price stability with high levels of government spending proved a political blessing, as strikes in Germany subsided dramatically even while governments were using deficit spending to placate disaffected groups and win back voters. This discovery was repeated in America in the later 1970s. As a general rule, in fact, the adoption of monetarist arguments and practices has almost invariably *caused* an explosion of government deficits, not resulted from such deficits.

This counterintuitive relationship between deficits and monetarism surprises only those unfamiliar with the typical taxation policies of most major governments in the postwar era. With only some exceptions, these relied on inflationary automatic revenue escalators such as unindexed progressive income tax brackets. Eliminating inflation while maintaining spending generated deficits more or less automatically simply because of a dropoff in anticipated inflation-driven revenue. I have already suggested that this logic was necessary for the adoption of monetarism. But it also had advantages for workers and other beneficiaries of the welfare state because the early stabilization of inflation helped to consolidate its political base, rather than turning popular opinion against it in a wave of antitax resentment. It has been forgotten that in the late 1960s, German and American unions mobilized virtually identical proportions of their workforces. The differences in unionization rates that we see today result from the weakening of the union movement in the United States, but not Germany. This is why the rationalist contention that monetarism followed in the wake of a weakened social-democratic or New Deal constituency misstates the actual relationship. Indeed, what is most striking, perhaps, is the fact that monetarism in both countries was initiated during the tenures of parties which had traditionally been most sympathetic to the aspirations of workers. The political alienation of the working class from the welfare state, the erosion of support for unions, and the collapse of the left's electoral base are complicated phenomena; but timely adoption of monetarism seems to have forestalled the right-wing revolution which attacked the welfare state and implemented later, harsher versions of monetarism. Monetarism, properly timed, helped mitigate or even prevent these developments, not initiate them.

The American history of monetarism now suffers from similar historical blind spots. With the current Bundesbank serving as their model, too many scholars now take it for granted that the Federal Reserve would have difficulty fighting inflation. This was not the view in 1970. At that time, most informed observers expected the Nixon administration and the Federal Reserve to be the first to implement monetarist policies, especially when Arthur Burns—Milton Friedman's former teacher and a long-time opponent of wage and price controls—was appointed chairman of the Federal Reserve in 1970. That his tenure witnessed both the imposition of wage and price controls and the worst inflation seen in the United States since World War II defied what almost everyone knew about the Fed's behavior and Burns's beliefs. As I describe in Chapter 4, it has been forgotten that even though the United States experienced no hyperinflation, the dominant interpretation of the stock market crash of 1929 was the functional equivalent of hyperinflation. In the 1930s, Congress and the Democrats laid the blame for the crash on loose monetary policies pursued by a Fed that was too close to greedy Wall Street speculators. Thus, the reforms of the Fed and the banking system, undertaken as part of the New Deal, were designed to ensure economic stability by providing for independence from both politicians and financiers. Formally, the Fed's independence now reached its zenith. It is true that the Fed's governing statutes lack any specific mention of either price stability or independence from the government. But these were taken as unquestioned givens, implied by the gold standard itself, and were thought to be guaranteed by the fourteen-year term of office of the Fed governors—tenure which far outstrips that of the Bundesbank directors', who serve for only eight years. The Fed's independence flowered after the war, when chairman Martin and his fellow governors became the very soul of financial rectitude, achieving inflation rates that for years were consistently the equal of, or better than, those achieved by Germany's central banks. Presidents Eisenhower, Kennedy, Johnson, and Nixon dealt with Martin as with a foreign sovereign. And, as I show in Chapter 2, it was this refurbished Fed that served as the model when the U.S. military occupation originally designed the first postwar German central bank, the Bank Deutscher Länder.

In fact, as I argue in Chapter 4, the whole idea that politics has more short-term, self-seeking influence on the Fed is belied by both a lack of corroborative evidence and a manifest lack in Congress and the White House of the expertise necessary to formulate the kind of monetary policy they want in the long run, and their lack of influence over monetary policy in the short run. The statistical evidence for an electoral monetary cycle has been found to be extremely weak, and its popularity depends mostly on the anecdotal evidence of the Nixon landslide.[27] In particular, the fact that many presidents or incumbent party candidates have had to run against the economy (Nixon in 1960, Ford in 1976, Carter in 1980, Bush in 1992) suggests that presidential monetary cycles, if they occur at all, are far from automatic. Nor is there persuasive evidence that the Federal Reserve implements the policy desired by the President's supporters. Two Republican presidents, Nixon and Reagan, had a generally stimulative economic policy, whereas presidents Ford, Carter, and Reagan saw sharp recessions during their tenure. Polls indicated that although inflation was the nation's chief concern by 1979–1980, the Democratic voters preferred wage and price controls to a credit crunch; yet Carter preferred the latter, specifically invoking his authority to control credit in March 1980, and appointing a known conservative as chairman of the Federal Reserve. The very fragmentation of the American political system that in theory creates incentives to influence Fed policy is the same force that, in practice, prevents an effective anti-Fed coalition from forming.

Finally, what is perhaps most ironic about the rationalist model is that it has forgotten its roots in a monetarism that originally opposed independence for central banks. Originally, monetarists believed that independence for central banks was an obstacle to monetary targeting, not a means to it. Friedman and his followers, influenced by the theories of Becker, Stigler, Nordhaus, and other political economists, argued that these institutions' refusal to adopt a monetary rule reflected rent-seeking behavior by central bank bureaucracies and their constituencies. Only by restoring the power of national governments over such banks could monetarists hope to translate their academic doctrine into government policy. "Seventy years of Federal Reserve history," wrote Friedman of the Fed's long opposition to his ideas, "speaks with a single voice about the unwillingness of the Federal Reserve to adopt any policy which is clearly spelled out and capable of being objectively tracked by persons outside the system."[28] In the early 1970s, two monetarists modeled the likelihood that central banks would adopt targets and argued that it was *inversely* correlated with independence.[29] As recently as the 1980s, a monetarist historian of American monetary policy, Richard Timberlake, argued that an independent Federal Reserve "is no more logical than giving the same status to the State Department."[30] We have understood neither the politics of monetarism nor that of independent central banks until we have grasped how this original American monetarist opposition to the central bank's independence became today's unquestioned support. The weakness of the rationalists' interpretation of monetarism lies both in the history they construct and in their self-forgetting. A more satisfying alternative must acknowledge the impact of the concepts and choices of monetarists themselves.

OVERVIEW OF THE BOOK

Chapters 2 through 5 provide evidence for the theoretical contentions outlined above about the monetarist experiences of Germany and the United States. I have chosen to present this evidence by way of two separate national histories, each divided roughly into "before" and "after" chapters. The year 1970 represents a watershed in each case. When viewed in parallel over some forty years, these national narratives show in bold relief how the different patterns of mobilizing expertise shaped the responses of the two central banks to remarkably similar issues.

The origins of the more efficient German monetarist mobilization prior to 1970 are described in Chapter 2, particularly the centralization and rationalization of the German banking system, and the evolution of the Bundesbank's collegial policy culture. In Chapter 3, I describe the influence of this pattern on the switch to monetary targeting after 1970. In this chapter, several developments are particularly noteworthy: the division of the Bundesbank Council into two opposed policy coalitions and the unexpected defeat of the Keynesians by the erstwhile minority monetarist faction; the influence of the Sparkassen and other components of the policy environment on the evolution of the monetarist experiment; the political controversy that erupted as macroeconomists representing different theoretical paradigms began to displace traditional bankers on the Bundesbank Council, and the demobilization of monetarist radicalism by the early conversion of the Bundesbank.

By contrast, in Chapters 4 and 5 I describe the less efficient American mobilization of expertise. In Chapter 4 I show that prior to 1970, a long historical struggle between the forces of finance and populism left the U.S. government with a highly autonomous Federal Reserve, but one whose policy culture was increasingly undermined by pluralist divisions among the various sectors of the banking system. A sectorally vulnerable banking system and fragmented labor unions led to the Fed's excessive preoccupation with the fragility of the monetary system itself, fostering ever more insularity and deference to the power of the Fed chairman as the postwar years wore on. Chapter 5 shows the effects of this policy culture on the adoption of monetarism. Among other things, the chapter illustrates the recurring impact of the banking system on the Fed's continuing resistance to monetarism during the tenures of chairmen Burns and Miller. It describes the monetarists' turn to radicalization and populist mobilization to create new channels of access for their ideas, and it illustrates the interaction of these forces most dramatically during the Volcker-Reagan monetarist heyday.

Finally, the concluding chapter—Chapter 6—returns to the question of expert mobilization, independent central banks, and democracy. Does the rise of independent central banking which monetarism fostered mean that there is something inherently "unpopular," not just about monetarism but about all monetary policy? Chapter 6 explores this question by making four sets of comparisons. The first two are systematic comparisons of the strengths and weaknesses of German and American central banks, to see how powerful they are within their liberal democratic systems. On the basis of this review, I offer some possible reforms for both banks, but especially for the Federal Reserve. The third comparison is with other policy arenas. Previously, I hypothesized that central bank politics reflected an unusual property of money as the "environment of conduct" for economic interests, a status not shared by most other policy domains. But money is not quite alone in being an environment of conduct in liberal democracies. Another important environment is law. Drawing on the work of Talcott Parsons, I explore ways in which money and law share certain similarities as "media of influence." As such, they are fundamental for the large measure of bottom-up, spontaneous organization that is the hallmark of the most liberal features of liberal democracies. Generalizing about the institutions that manage money and law, I introduce the notion of *liberal stabilization* through "inductive bureaucracies" of banks and courts. There I suggest that a fundamentally similar organizing logic shapes the structures of banking systems and the judiciary. The chapter sketches how these institutions are likely to exhibit similar political attributes as they implement policies of liberal stabilization.

The final comparison in Chapter 6 is between economic regime changes that involve efficient expert politics and those that do not. This comparison emerges from the original recognition that some governments are much better at effecting timely economic stabilization than others. For all their differences, the governments of Germany and the United States were both eventually able to reorient their monetary policies to limit inflation and reestablish economic stability. Other countries have not been so agile and have paid more than an economic price. Examples range from the partisanship of Thatcher's adoption of monetarism to the authoritarianism of military rule in Chile after 1973 (which ultimately implemented a monetarist-inspired free-market revolution from the top down). As monetarists observed of such Latin American cases, governments left hyperinflation untreated for so long that it contributed to social chaos and demands for military intervention. Indeed, militaries imposed not just economic order but political order as well. Such comparisons return us to our original theme—that the timely introduction of new economic policies may be an issue not only of the "wealth of nations" but of the survival of democratic institutions. Thus, Chapter 6 considers to what extent the mobilization of economists may be a substitute for the mobilization of troops. But to put such speculation on firmer ground, we must first examine the historical details of the pathways through which expertise traveled in the case of monetarism in Germany and the United States. It is to this task we now turn.

CHAPTER TWO

The Origins of the Bundesbank's
Corporate Culture

In this chapter I describe the historical interactions of Germany's central bank with its policy environment prior to 1970. These interactions endowed the Bundesbank's corporate culture with a unique capacity to mobilize expertise and autonomously redefine its corporate mission in light of growing economic problems. Two influences were at work in this efficient mobilization of expertise. The first was external and involved the high degree of universality among German economic institutions, especially its banking system. The second was internal and institutional. Within the central bank, historical memories plus a collegial distribution of power created an unusual openness to the problems of the central bank's embeddedness in society. As Chapter 3 will show, the ease with which these two factors mobilized competing schools of expertise—especially monetarism—into the corporate culture of the Bundesbank facilitated the bank's renegotiation of its power and mission with the German political economy.

The Bundesbank's interpretation of its corporate mission is shaped by an economy whose major sectors are remarkably universalized yet have pronounced independent interests. This reflects Germany's rejection, in the postwar period, of the American military occupation's "pluralist" solution to the conflicts between private and public power in pre-war Germany. Instead of fragmenting social and economic interests by the restrictive regulation that the Americans attempted to impose on both banks and unions, the Germans effected a wide-ranging deregulation that permitted the emergence of universalistic institutions. Nowhere was this more true than in Germany's universal banking system. The Germans' deregulation of banking after the occupation created a powerful rival to the power of the traditional big three commercial banks in the rise of the Sparkassen. By the late 1960s, the German savings bank sector had grown to be substantially larger than the commercial bank sector; and although the savings banks were regulated as universal banks, their competitive advantage in domestic savings gave them a far greater anti-inflationary bias than the commercial banks. This alternative bank constituency reinforced the collegiality and theoretical openness that was already a greater structural feature of decision making in the Bundesbank than in the Fed. Germany emerged from the postwar period with institutions that were far more universalistic in their construction, and far more rooted in the lives of ordinary Germans, than the comparable pluralist institutions in the United States. And these more universalistic institutions would embed German central banking's adoption of monetarism in a larger awareness of its domestic—indeed, its democratic—responsibilities.

GERMAN CENTRAL BANKING: THE STATIST LEGACY

The reorientation of the Bundesbank's monetary policy toward the domestic or democratic purposes espoused by monetarism owes much to the long, failed history of central banks in Germany as unaccountable instruments of state power. Though these institutions were inevitably part of German national development, there could scarcely be any doubt on the part of students of Germany's monetary history that banking and central banking originally served not social but state purposes. Paramount among these purposes were financing wars and building a national industrial infrastructure. These goals required intimate links with government on the one hand and the private commercial banks on the other. Thus, for must of its history, Germany's central bank—the Reichsbank—was little different from other continental "statist" banks. Although the banking system and the central bank did not reach far downward from state to society, this occasioned little of the populist opposition so characteristic of American politics. Instead, those who opposed the privileges of the banks were more likely to reject the entire nexus of banks with capitalism and the existing state. Social democracy and Marxism would channel popular opposition to bank power into revolutionary directions. To prepare for the knitting together of state, central bank, and society that monetary targeting would represent, many alternative conceptions of the central bank's role would first have to be endured and discarded.

The Reichsbank

The first central bank to express German national power was the Reichsbank, founded shortly after the creation of the empire in 1875. The war that Prussia fought with France in 1870 was brief and victorious. The Germans demanded from their vanquished neighbor reparations in the sum of 5 billion gold francs. Much to Germany's surprise, this sum was delivered so quickly that a reorganization of its monetary and banking system was required to handle it. Thus the old Prussian State Bank was transformed into the new Reichsbank. The purpose of the Prussian bank had been to promote the circulation of money, make capital available to banks, support commerce and manufacturing, and prevent an increase in the interest rate. These goals were largely taken over by its successor. Prior to World War I, the bank was legally in private hands, but the authority to set policy rested firmly with the Reichschancellor. Though this signaled the central bank's subordination to state purposes, the Reichsbank lacked a monopoly over the issue of German currency. The Reichsbank shared this power with the treasuries of twenty provinces and thirty-three commercial banks whose rights predated the Imperial Federation. Nor could the Reichsbank require commercial banks to maintain reserves on deposit with it.

Instead, the Reichsbank was the house bank for the dynastic and industrial ambitions of the new Reich, empowered to grant huge credits directly to the imperial government, its client industries, and the four great universal banks in Berlin, the so-called *Grossbanken:* Deutsche Bank, Commerz Bank, Dresdner Bank, and Darmstadter und National (DANAT) Bank. These banks played an active role in cartelizing German industry through their nationally organized interlocking network of ownership and appointments to the supervisory boards of German industry. Under their tutelage, industrialization during the empire was extraordinarily rapid. Because of its dirigiste powers the Reichsbank was disinclined to conceive of its policy in what one might call social or democratic terms. It is not surprising then, that the most prominent German economist of this era, Georg Friedrich Knapp, should title his major work, *Der Staatlichen Theorie des Geldes (The State Theory of Money)*. This text represents the clearest expression of the idea that the state's role as guarantor of property rights, and therefore of value, ultimately determines a currency's worth.[1]

The full implications of the "statist" view of the central bank's power were revealed when the Reichsbank became the most important channel for inflationary monetary creation during and after World War I. Continuing the successful precedent set by the Franco-Prussian war, the German government of 1914 chose to finance the war by bank borrowing rather than taxation. As in 1870, this financial strategy presupposed a quick military victory that would reap sufficient reparations to redeem the loan. Unfortunately for the Reichsbank, this war was neither brief nor victorious. Germany's losses in men and material proved staggering, and the vindictive Versailles treaty made those losses exponentially worse. The Allies attempted to expropriate large parts of Germany's economic productivity and impose nightmarish financial reparations. To meet both foreign and domestic obligations, Germany's government turned to the Reichbank's loans and printing presses. The creeping inflation that had started during the war began to gallop after 1919. Before the war, a handful of marks bought an armload of bread; by 1923 an armload of marks bought only a handful of bread. The inflation rate accelerated so rapidly that in the latter months of 1923 shopkeepers changed their prices daily, often by simply adding zeros to price tags. Wages, if not spent on the way home, became worthless. To protect themselves from this surreptitious impoverishment, workers formed and joined unions by the millions to demand pay hikes. Strikes and protests washed across Germany at a tempo that matched the depreciation of the mark. Industry, finding itself unable to resist these demands, clamored for ever more money from the Reichsbank printing presses. To reduce the strain of labor conflict, more and more labor contracts indexed wage increases to the mark's dollar exchange rate, and more and more firms began to issue their own house currency or scrip.

It should not be concluded from these events that the central bank's policy was necessarily ill-considered or wantonly destructive. On the contrary, both general inflation and the granting of loans to government and industry had their uses. Part of this inflationary policy was deliberate, as the Reichsbank clandestinely printed marks to finance Germany's civil resistance to France's occupation of the Ruhr. But the Reichsbank was also acting to shore up weakened public authority. After the collapse of the old conservative empire, support for the new democracy was chiefly to be sought on the moderate left of the SPD and its working-class electorate. To stop inflation by means of unemployment that would hurt this constituency might have strangled the infant regime in its crib. Nonetheless, it cannot be denied that by 1923 the hyperinflation was arousing more discontent than it allayed. The prudent working and middle classes were embittered by the disappearance of their savings, although inflation wiped debts clean and gladdened the hearts of spendthrifts. Speculators like Hugo Stinnes amassed vast industrial holdings for a pittance. In November 1923, with inflation at the mind-boggling rate of 1000 percent per month and social disorder at its peak, Hitler attempted his military putsch (coup) in Munich. Though both the inflation and the putsch were soon suppressed, the connection between monetary instability and political revolution was now apparent.

Although the Reichsbank had been granted formal independence from the German government in 1922, not until late 1923 did a series of negotiations concerning reparations, French occupation of the Ruhr, and government budgetary deficits begin to curb the demand for money. The decisive move against inflation came when Haljmar Schacht, newly installed as president of the Reichsbank, became the first central banker to solve the problems of a German currency by legally abolishing it. Beginning in November 1923 the old mark was replaced first by the so-called Rentenmark, and then ultimately the Reichsmark. Here, too, we may detect the influence of the statist theory of money: the new currency was not backed by specie; it was money only because the public authority deemed it so. The credibility of the new currency rested on little more than a stringent tight-money policy (especially in 1925–1926) coupled with a pegging of the Reichsmark to the dollar. Short-term American loans, which now flowed into Germany in massive quantities, reinforced these measures.

The taming of hyperinflation launched the so-called golden years of the Weimar Republic. From 1924 to 1929, Germany's economic policymakers performed a precarious cabaret act of financial legerdemain and political tightrope-walking. As Germany's first fiat money depended to a large degree on American bankers, the long-term health of the currency and the economy depended on the delicate renegotiating of Germany's international financial obligations. During these years the Reichsmark's exchange rate with the U.S. dollar increasingly became the unchallenged benchmark of Reichsbank policy.[2]

After 1929, however, the antidemocratic possibilities of an independent central bank were revealed to their fullest. That year, the crash of the New York stock market began to reverse the flow of American loans. The Reichsbank's ultraconservative president, Schacht, who adamantly opposed fiscal expansion and social welfare spending, publicly voiced opposition to the Berlin government's efforts to reflate the economy to prevent a depression. Schacht's opposition helped foster a political debacle of parliamentary immobility in the face of worsening decline, and he was forced to leave the Reichsbank in 1930. His successor, Hans Luther, fought just as adamantly against using reflation to save the German economy from the looming abyss. Luther, together with Chancellor Brüning and President Hindenburg, "encouraged the new economic crisis to become a crisis of the Republic itself."[3] Out of office, Schacht used his prestige to undermine the credit of the Weimar Republic with foreign lenders, introduced Hitler into his social circle of the industrial elite, and solicited campaign funds for the Nazis.[4] The crisis reached its zenith in 1931 after the collapse of DANAT Bank, one of the big four Grossbanken. Here the Reichsbank's lack of a minimum reserve policy and its formal independence proved disastrous. The Reichsbank stood by impassively, neither willing nor able to act as lender of last resort. Indeed, the very weekend DANAT turned to the Reichsbank for financial assistance, the Reichsbank directorate raised its rediscount rate, knowing full well that this would force DANAT to shut its doors. Bank run upon bank run brought ruin to thousands of firms, artisans, and farmers. Economic downturn became financial collapse. In July, the government declared an unusual "bank holiday" during which all banks were restructured, and their majority ownership passed temporarily into state hands. Unemployment soon exceeded 25 percent, in an era of single-breadwinner families and little to no social welfare. Thus from 1929 to 1933, the Reichsbank and its sympathizers not only vigorously resisted the reflationary measures that would have spared millions of Germans their jobs, but actively promoted those forces of reaction that ultimately toppled democratic government itself. Germany's depression had international origins, but there can be little doubt that obstructionism by the Reichsbank worsened matters immeasurably. Some forty years later, Heinrich Irmler, one of the Bundesbank's Directors, would write in the Bundesbank's official history that the Reichsbank's policies had been "neither economically nor politically justified."[5]

Thus Hitler and the Nazis were enabled in no small measure to seize power by demogogically exploiting popular—and populist—outrage at the banking system, the depression, and capitalism in general. Although as early as 1920, the National Socialists had declared themselves opposed to "International Financial Capitalism" and *Zinsknechtschaft* (roughly, "interest-rate slavery"), Hitler's Nazis never enjoyed significant electoral support—not even after hyperinflation—until the onset of the Great Depression in 1929. As Gerald Feldman concluded in his monumental study of German hyperinflation and its consequences, "There is no contesting the fact that it was the Great Depression and not the inflation that was the driving force in making it possible for National Socialism to come to power in January 1933. The horrendous unemployment, wage cuts, and general impoverishment of the Great Depression proved a far greater danger to German democracy than inflation ever had," and, indeed, German inflation "saved German democracy during its early turbulent years by preventing precisely such conditions."[6]

With the collapse of the banking system in 1931, and the massive state support the banks received thereafter, many Germans—not just supporters of radical parties—assumed that the free-market economy was a thing of the past. This led directly to a populist campaign by the Nazis against the big commercial banks. Shortly after he came to power, Hitler declared that "National Socialism . . . is the strongest opponent of that liberal belief that the economy is to serve Capital, and the people to serve the economy."[7] In September 1933, a special investigative committee of the Nazi-dominated parliament held hearings on the excessive powers of Germany's great universal banks. The complaints rehearsed before the parliamentarians included that the banks "sought to become the masters of the economy, instead of its servants"; that too many of the banks had their headquarters in Berlin, where they became "bureaucratic and impersonal"; that they engaged in "pure speculation" and neglected the needs of small businesses. In recommendations that uncannily paralleled similar decisions taken by the U.S. Congress, the Reichstag committee advocated a wide-ranging "decentralization" of the power of the private commercial banks, a general lowering of interest rates, and the expansion of the Savings Institutions (Sparkassen).[8]

Nonetheless, this antibank sentiment was allowed to go only so far. Hitler had induced Hans Luther to resign the presidency of the Reichsbank by offering him the ambassador's post in Washington, and Hjalmar Schacht was brought back in as Hitler's man in the Reichsbank.[9] Choreographed by Schacht, a parade of rebuttal witnesses testified to the service, advice, and freedom that businesses both large and small enjoyed under the protection of the Great Banks. In the end, while the banks escaped nationalization, their freedom and powers were severely circumscribed by changes in the financial laws enacted in 1934. For the first time, the Nazis required commercial banks to place reserves on deposit with the Reichsbank. These laws also imposed interest-rate ceilings on the banks and limited the amount of money payable on stock dividends. These policies were meant to ease the German government's conversion of its short-term debt into long-term debt, secure a greater degree of control over the money supply, and with the resulting increase in the (less restricted) Sparkassen and cooperative banks, enhance the government's access to the increasingly large pool of ordinary Germans' savings. While the assets of the big commercial banks grew about 15 percent between 1932 and 1939, those of the Sparkassen more than doubled.[10]

Most remarkable, perhaps, is that with the Nazis' accession to power the Reichsbank's obstructionism ceased, even though the government now pursued a virtually unrestrained reflationary policy. As Feldman observed, "it was not the Nazis' ruthlessness that provided the key to . . . recovery, but rather the willingness to change policy."[11] Schacht freed the mark from both gold and dollar convertibility. To back his currency, he turned instead to one of his most infamous financial stratagems, rediscounting "MeFo" bills. MeFo bills were commercial paper which industry could issue against membership in a Metallische Forschungsanstalt, a front organization staffed by Reichsbank officials to disguise the financing of German rearmament in violation of the Versailles treaty.[12] Thus, the reflation Schacht withheld from a dying democracy he engineered for an emergent tyranny.

Schacht and the Reichsbank remained enthusiastic supporters of Hitler's reflation even when, in 1937, the Reichsbank was again made formally subservient to the wishes of the government in Berlin. Opposition, if it may be called that, came only in 1939, when Schacht and several of his fellow Reichsbank directors, fearing that debt financing of rearmament had reached its economic limits, wrote a memo to the Nazi government recommending a halt to further bond issues. Thereupon, Hitler removed Schacht and his colleagues from their posts. This episode is significant not so much because the Bundesbank and its supporters like to portray it as evidence of the central bank's resistance to tyranny, but because it provided the Bundesbank's own directors with something akin to a historical precedent for mass political resignation that would be at the back of many central bank officials' minds during the crucial switch to monetarism in 1973.

The Bank Deutscher Länder

The conclusion of the war provides Germany's second great example of monetary transformation. The years 1945 to 1947 represented not so much a second hyperinflation as simple economic collapse. A monetary overhang (substantial, though not comparable to 1923) was aggravated by a shortage of goods—due to the war's damage, hoarding, and the occupation's bureaucratic bottlenecks. Once Europe's economic powerhouse, Germany was reduced to barter, a cigarette currency, and a near-starvation diet. Naturally, this state of affairs could not continue. The German population, though defeated, grew restive while the Allies began to polarize over Germany's future.

Thus the next major change in the status of the central bank and currency was another of those landmark events signaling a major change in politics. In March 1947, the U.S. military occupation government established the new Bank Deutscher Länder (Bank of the German Provinces) to facilitate the introduction of a new currency, the DM. This bank is the immediate predecessor of today's Bundesbank. In June 1948, as in November 1923, an economy was salvaged by annihilating its currency. This move, inspired by Ludwig Erhard, the German economic adviser to the Allied occupation, is now celebrated as the dawning of the Federal Republic's postwar *Wirtschaftswunder,* or economic miracle. The new currency and the subsequent elimination of rationing and price controls restocked store shelves for the first time in years.

Although the currency reform was Erhard's, the design of the new central bank showed substantial American influence, particularly in its break with the centralized design of the old Reichsbank. The Americans pushed the Germans to design a more decentralized federal institution, resembling, in some respects, the pluralist structure of the U.S. Federal Reserve system. The central bank was made not only formally but informally independent of the central government. As David Marsh has pointed out, this was to some extent inevitable: the Bank Deutscher Länder predated the founding of the Federal Republic of Germany. But the Americans also envisioned the emergence of a new central government within the year, and it was their wish that the central bank not take instructions from it. To entrench this independence, the Americans insisted on organizational decentralization. The Americans designed the new federal central bank to be a confederation of independent central banks of the Länder of the Western zone with an administrative headquarters based in Frankfurt. The British, whose Labour government in London was strongly influenced by Keynesian theories of demand management, sided with Erhard and other Germans in opposing this decentralization, believing that it would inhibit the revival of the West German economy. The Americans, however, as Britain's creditor, used their financial leverage to impose their design on all of "Bizonia," and ultimately on the French-occupied zones as well. The Bank Deutscher Länder thus acquired a two-tiered decision-making structure. Day-to-day management was delegated to the directorate in Frankfurt. The highest decision-making body was a council formed of the presidents of Land central banks from the western occupation zone. The membership of this policy body was ultimately determined by the *Land* governments, with some limited supervision by the Allies.

This reform of German central banking extended beyond its internal organization to its techniques of monetary control. First, looking backward to the Reichsbank's rivalry with other banks of issue, the Bank Deutscher Länder now exercised a legal monopoly on the issue of all currency. Second, it retained fractional reserve banking from the Nazi era and began to use it actively. For the first time the creation of domestic credit by the banking sector could operate seamlessly within a single framework represented by the Bank Deutscher Länder's monopoly of money. Third, the Bank Deutscher Länder's was forbidden to lend directly either to governments or to private industry. The Reichsbank's statist or dirigiste functions were transferred to the new *Kreditanstalt für Wiederaufbau,* a surrogate German central bank whose role was to dispense Marshall Plan moneys. Finally, but not least important, the new currency was integrated into an international system of fixed exchange rates based on the dollar and pegged at a low, competitive rate. An undervalued exchange rate was essential to allow Germany's exports to compete in the United States and Western Europe. This competitive advantage was necessary not least to the central bank itself—without it the fledgling central bank could not have earned the hard currency necessary to build a coffer of reserves. The central bank's mandate, "to preserve the stability of the currency," thus appears in this historical context as a primarily *externally* oriented emphasis on maintaining a stable exchange rate during these early years.

THE RECONSTRUCTION OF THE MONETARY POLICY ENVIRONMENT, 1945–1958

In the aftermath of the war both the Germans and the Allies turned their attention not only to the physical reconstruction of Germany but to the reconstruction of relations among the German state, its civil society, and its economy. Apart from the Soviet zone of occupation, where Moscow imposed a command economy, Germany confronted a choice between two broadly contrasting plans for reconstruction. On the one hand, there was the American pluralist model, which sought to divide public power and fragment private power by confining economic actors within narrowly circumscribed limits as defined by regulation. On the other, there was the "universalist" model favored by German reformers such as Ludwig Erhard, together with German union leaders and the British occupation authorities. This model sought to reduce the risks of economic instability by rationalizing government through reform of the parliamentary system and by permitting the emergence of coherent, unified, and universalistic economic institutions. They hoped that these reforms would provide effective counterweights to the state in economic policy deliberations and the widest possible distribution of costs and benefits in the free adjustment of economic interests in the marketplace. The Americans succeeded at first in imposing their pluralist designs in the mid-1940s, but by the 1950s and the recovery of sovereignty, the Germans had rejected this model in favor of the universalist option. The key disputes concerned the universal bank system and the large industrial unions. Germany's rejection of American pluralism produced more organized and coherent banks and unions, which were capable of articulating clear policy preferences as well as responding flexibly to monetary control. These transformations, together with those of government and economics, would prepare the ground for the Bundesbank's remarkably collegial and embedded corporate culture.

Reconstruction of German Banking

No sector of German society would prove to be more material to the Bundesbank's understanding of its mission than the German financial system. Many observers have remarked upon the unique dominance by the big three commercial banks and their purported role as "prefects" of the German economy. It has long been noted that Deutsche Bank, Dresdner Bank, and Commerzbank exploited the provisions of German banking laws to own and vote shares in German corporations and name directors to firms' supervisory boards to a degree found almost nowhere else. The prominence of these banks in the vertical integration of German industry might suggest that they were the ultimate source of monetarist policies in the Bundesbank. But this misreads the true impact of the universal banking system that emerged after the war. While these vertical features of universal banking are not negligible, the *horizontal* aspects of the universal bank system have been much more important. These include the elimination of regional divisions imposed by the Americans after the war, the elimination of regulatory barriers among types of banking sectors, the removal of limits on interest rates, and the Bundesbank's mandate requiring all financial institutions to maintain reserves with it. These deregulatory measures reflect Germany's efforts to transcend the alien American pluralist institutions imposed on it after the war, in favor of a more liberal solution to the problem of state-economy relations.

In understanding the differences between German and American banking, it is important to recognize that classification by ownership is not the same as classification by regulatory status or function. Thus, in the United States after the war, almost all financial institutions were in private hands, but these institutions were sharply segmented into various regulatory or geographic compartments—thrift institutions, investment banks, commercial banks, federal, and state banks, to name just the most important. By contrast, German banking evolved to encompass major divisions by ownership (private versus public) but very few by regulatory specialization. Despite the visibility of the big private commercial banks, by far the largest sector of banking after the war came to be the publicly owned Sparkassen (savings banks) and the cooperative banks. The total assets held by the commercial banks in the late 1960s were only half the assets held by the savings bank system (584 billion DM versus 1,027 billion DM). All together, private commercial banks represented about 23 percent of German banks' volume of business in 1971; urban and rural cooperative banks, together with their 10 "central" banks, represented 15 percent, and public savings banks represented 39 percent of the total banking business by turnover. Most important, all these banks, whether private, public, or cooperative, would emerge by the middle of the 1960s as virtually indistinguishable nationally regulated universal banks, handling all deposits, loans, and investment business permitted to any bank under law. As such, all banks are required to hold reserves with the Bundesbank and are directly influenced by its monetary policy. While some specialist banks, such as the Kreditanstalt für Wiederaufbau, were not insignificant in the story of the postwar German reconstruction, they were largely eclipsed by the expansion of the Sparkassen as rival universal banks. The principal significance of this development is that, first, it affords the Bundesbank an unusual freedom to exercise monetary policy without regard for its selective effects on various sectors of the financial industry; and, second, it creates a constituency for domestically oriented stability policy that the big commercial banks did not previously represent.

The Allied occupation had attempted to impose the American pattern of pluralist deconcentration on German banking. Americans believed that concentrated private economic power—the trusts and cartels characteristic of the prewar German economy—had contributed to militarism and dictatorship. Although the so-called Morgenthau plan for the deindustrialization of Germany was never implemented, the Americans nevertheless sought economic deconcentration and decartelization. Apart from the federal fragmentation of the Bank Deutscher Länder itself and the breakup of the huge IG Farben chemicals conglomerate, their principal success was the treatment of the big three private commercial banks—Deutsche, Dresdner, and Commerz. During the immediate aftermath of the war, the American military occupation brushed aside the objections of the British, Erhard, and the banks themselves and imposed a significant decentralization whereby no bank was allowed to offer banking services outside its home state. Consequently, each of the big three commercial banks was split up into a minimum of eleven formally autonomous banks.

This system of decentralized banking never took hold, however, and the reasons advanced to defeat it reveal important differences in monetary policy in Germany. First, it must be acknowledged that at its birth the new pluralist banking system suffered from significant logistical problems. The occupation military government was never able to establish a proper legal foundation for the change. Many important issues—the ownership of the new institutions, their internal staffing and management, the division of their legal obligations among the successor institutions, and even their relationship to the trustee agencies that took over the "mother" banks—were left unsettled. This proved to be a severe handicap, especially in dealing with clients and foreign partners during the return to economic normalcy. Second, this deconcentration never won the support of such German reformers as Ludwig Erhard or the SPD: Erhard wanted less regulation, not more; and the SPD in its early years believed that the banks would eventually be renationalized in any case. Third, the Allies were divided among themselves. The British in particular increasingly sought a reunification of the banking system for their own economic and ideological reasons. The British, under the Attlee government, were now practicing Keynesian economics, and they believed that a centralized banking system was more suited to this ideology—an ideology that they assumed the Germans would pursue in due course. More important, however, is the fact that they were the biggest creditors of the banks from before the war. The British wanted to recoup their loans to these banks, and this was more likely to happen if they were allowed to reunite.

But the most compelling arguments for reunification came from the logic of the banks' own relationship to the wider economy and monetary policy. The interwar experiences had driven home to German bankers the very large extent to which the health of the economy was bound up with the soundness of the banking system. They felt that although the successor institutions were initially profitable, Germany's ability to cope with economic challenges would be limited if the economy experienced difficulties in the future. As one confidential memo from a former Deutsche Banker to the new finance ministry in Bonn put it, "A country's banking system is no stronger than its weakest commercial bank."[13] Universal banks operating in all branches of business and stretching from border to border would be able to diversify risks and smooth out regional liquidity imbalances and crises far more rapidly and at less cost than either decentralized banks or the government's central bank.

By 1952, the banks began to re-form across state lines, each consolidating into three regional successor institutions. The only substantial resistance they encountered, other than from the Americans, was from the Bank Deutscher Länder. Its federal council jealously guarded its new federal (i.e., provincial) powers and worried that the reunification of the commercial banks would necessarily require the reunification of the central bank, possibly including the diminution of the number of Land central banks. These objections were addressed, however, when the lobbyists for the banks and officials of the finance ministry assured the states that any necessary reorganization of the central bank would retain the principal of "one Land, one Land central bank" and ensure a substantial Land voice in its decision making.

Thus despite this apparent move toward recartelization of banks, Germany's program of reuniting the commercial banks actually reflected a *liberal,* deregulatory strategy. Erhard's free-market liberalism of the Freiburg school envisioned additional competition for the commercial banks by extending the universal banking principle throughout the entire financial sector. Among the important political beneficiaries were the six Banks für Gemeinwirtschaft. These banks had been set up by different unions and union movements during the pre-Nazi era, and their postwar status, given the subsequent unification of the union movement into the DGB in 1949, was uncertain. Erhard's policy allowed the union movement to consolidate its ownership of these powerful bank institutions, and thereby the commercial banks won crucial political support from the SPD and the left for their own reunification.

By 1956, the Bundestag's parliamentary committee on bank reform was prepared to endorse the reunification of the commercial banks. Its final report noted that the remaining regional constraints raised questions about the banks' soundness, their long-term competitive prospects, and their ability to supply the economy with credit. Moreover, the committee argued that there could be no question of an excessive concentration of power in the three big banks because they competed so vigorously with each other and above all with the newly powerful regional banks of the Sparkassen system. Soon, the last legal restrictions on national banking were lifted, and Deutche, Dresdner, and Commerz banks were re-united.

In permitting this bank restoration, German reformers acknowledged the problem that had motivated American policy—the concentration of economic power—but they provided an alternative solution that would allow the marketplace to create counterweights in new financial institutions. The long-run beneficiaries of this postoccupation liberal banking policy were the Sparkassen. Over the course of the postwar decades, they would be transformed into the largest single component of the German banking system by 1970. Originally, the public-sector savings bank system comprised some 600 local government-owned Sparkassen and their twelve regional giro institutions (the Landesbanken, typically jointly owned by the local savings banks association and the Land government, in each Land, and a central clearing bank). They had been created in the nineteenth century to attract the savings of the urban middle class. They acquired regional giro (check-clearing) institutions prior to the World War I, and (as was noted above) they and their depositors were among those most severely affected by the crises of the 1920s and 1930s. Financial liberalization during the 1950s and 1960s allowed these formerly sleepy Landesbanken to surge into powerful rivals to the big three. WestLB, the largest, had assets in 1970 which made it the equal of Dresdner and about one-third bigger than Commerzbank. Also among the ten largest German banks in the 1970s were the Bavarian Landesbank and the Hessische Landesbank.

A similar tale can be told of the third major grouping within the universal banking system, the cooperative banks. These banks were formed in the nineteenth century to provide credit to farmers and small artisans. Measured by number of branches, they have always been the largest component of the banking system; as of 1972 they had 19,000 offices. Originally, their principal significance, like that of the Sparkassen, was to attract savings deposits and provide credit for a segment of the population which had been neglected by the commercial banks. In the postwar period the cooperatives too were deregulated. Their "central" bank, the Deutsche Genossenschaftsbank (DG) was formed only in 1975. Nonetheless, it would quickly become one of Germany's ten largest banks, with a net balance of assets in 1976 of 35.9 billion DM. Finally, another major postwar innovation for German banking was the formation of the Bank für Gemeinwirtschaft, owned by the member unions of the Deutsche Gewerkschaftsbund. By 1970, it too would rank among Germany's ten largest banks, with a group balance sheet of 35.1 billion DM.

The rapid growth of the public savings banks and the cooperative banks was in part fueled by the early tight-money policies of the Bank

Deutscher Länder, and the commercial banks' slowness in recognizing an important new market. Savings institutions had always profited from the fact that their less volatile savings accounts were subject to smaller reserve requirements by the central bank. This gave them a competitive edge in mobilizing assets in their competition with the commercial banks, particularly in real estate, home ownership, and construction. Moreover, the big commercial banks had traditionally disdained a middle-class or lower-class clientele. Commercial banks had always primarily served the largest of Germany's industrial concerns, and perhaps a few of its wealthiest families. Deutsche Bank, for example, did not offer its first individual savings account in the modern sense of the word until 1928. In the Adenauer era, most of the business of the big three was directed to financing Germany's industrial rebuilding. Not until 1957 did they recognize that this market had essentially become saturated, and that the big growth was in retail banking. By this time, however, the Sparkassen had already come to dominate this field. In 1957, a court decided that the Basic Law's protection of *Gewerbefreiheit* ("right to conduct business or trade") applied also to the banking sector, and permitted the Sparkassen and the commercial banks to invade each other's territory. Finally, in 1965 and 1967 the remaining restrictions on interest rates were lifted, creating a financial arena very different from any that Germany had ever seen before, and very different from the United States, where restrictions on interest rates were being expanded. The German banking system had reasserted its universal character, but in doing so it had erected powerful new institutions with powerful new—and more egalitarian—clienteles.

Indeed, it would not be going too far to suggest that the Sparkassen and their middle-class depositors steadily displaced the big three commercial banks as the principal political constituency of post-war German central banking and political stabilization. With the growth in the power of the Sparkassen and the Landesbanken (their regional clearing institutions) came an increasing influence of Land government policies in the calculations of the Bundesbank. Landesbanken have a special role as the central bankers not only for their network of municipal Sparkassen, but also as the bankers to the Land governments, who are their part owners. This gives them a unique political significance, whereby their lending activities and business profile in their Land can very closely reflect the political orientations of the Land government. The chief executives of the Landesbanken are usually required to be skilled navigators of Länder politics, and while there can be a risk of conflict of interest between their role in raising capital and their role in supporting the financial activities of state and local governments, their ultimate accountability is to their vast clientele of middle-class depositors. The Landesbanken are in effect the central banks of the Land governments, and their relationship with the local Landzentralbank is often extremely intimate. It is not uncommon for

Landzentralbank presidents to become presidents of the Landesbanken, and vice versa.

Yet before the central bank could orient itself toward pursuing low inflation and protecting middle-class savers, and the Sparkassen, it would have to overcome the resistance of the traditional commercial banks. This difference in policy preference among the various constituencies of the German central bank is also reflected in the vertical aspects of German universal banking. In contrast with the new Sparkassen, Germany's traditional commercial banks had always identified their interests with industry and, particularly in the postwar period, with manufacturing growth and increased exports. This interest meant two things. First, commercial banks preferred that the currency be bound up with international agreements and at a rate that would permit German exports to flourish. Second, the commercial banks equated currency stability with the external value of the mark even when doing so risked domestic inflation.

German commercial banks' external and inflation-tolerant view of monetary policy stemmed from two key "vertical" aspects of universal banking that can be briefly sketched. First, there is the larger degree of financial dependence of German industry on German commercial bank loans and bonds. Second, there is the substantial proprietorial involvement by the banks, through their right to own and vote shares and name members of boards of directors *(Aufsichtsräte)*. Thus, while most German firms finance themselves primarily through retained earnings, expansion beyond the limits set by internal resources found firms with few sources of funding outside of banks. During the period of 1974–1978, for example, German firms raised 275 billion DM outside of what they retained from current income. However, German bank loans accounted for 136.1 billion DM of this total, whereas the stock market (stocks and bonds) accounted for only 19 billion DM. (The balance was raised from government loans, private loans, the money market, and foreign banks.) As these figures indicate, the stock market is not as central to German financial life as the banks. Germany is not a shareholding economy: various taxes and fees make participation in the stock market by private investors relatively unattractive, and the stock market system in Germany is divided among many small regional bourses. Finally, most of the shares owned and funded in the stock market are controlled by the banks, and the bond market is likewise administered by the banks.

As important as this financial dependence is, the second aspect of vertical integration is perhaps more crucial for coupling banks with firms' orientation toward exports. This stems both from the banks' significant direct ownership of shares and from their legal ability to vote proxy shares acquired from smaller shareholders *(Depotstimmrecht)*. Statistics from the late 1950s and early 1960s indicate that the universal banks (chiefly the commercial banks) controlled about 70 percent of the capital of the largest German firms, and that the proportion of votes controlled by banks increased with the size of the firm.[14] The big banks often use their voting power to increase their representation on the boards of directors of German firms. Shonfield reported in 1960 that of 318 listed companies, some 573 *Aufsichtsrat* (supervisory board) positions, or about one-third of the total seats available, were held by bankers.

As testimony to numerous parliamentary committees has repeatedly stressed, one of the most important reasons that banks and firms integrate in this manner is to enhance firms' performance in export markets. Especially for the big three, their wide diversity of business experience plus their knowledge of foreign markets is believed to be of vital importance to the success of their client firms as exporters. This was thought to be especially true in the postwar era. Traditionally, Germany had thrived on the export of capital goods that drew heavily on German craftsmanship in engineering. In 1913, its exports accounted for no less than 26 percent of world trade in manufactured goods, just a step behind Britain. But World War II left Germany's industry in ruins. Its share of world trade in manufacturing was a statistical nullity. But by 1950, it had returned to 7.3 percent, by 1958 it reached 18.5 percent, and in 1970 it would displace the United States as the world's single largest exporter of manufactured products, at 19.8 percent. More especially, no other nation would come to have as large a proportion of its GDP–one-third—derived from exports.

Therefore, in contrast to the concerns of the Sparkassen, the big banks sought fixed exchange rates for the mark that priced German goods competitively relative to those of their principal trading partners, even when this risked domestic inflation at home. Although some of the German recovery can be attributed to the Marshall Plan, the fact that the German economy developed a trade surplus in the 1950s owes more to the devaluation of the DM in 1949, which allowed it to compete in European markets and participate in the boom created by the Korean War. The original exchange rate for the DM had been 3.6 to the dollar, but following the devaluation of British sterling and the French Franc, the new Adenauer administration was forced to devalue also if Germany, now experiencing a budding recovery, was not to lose ground to its neighbors. Ludwig Erhard persuaded Adenauer and the rest of the cabinet that a devaluation of 20 percent would be appropriate. However, Hermann Abs, the spokesman for Deutsche Bank and the head of the Kreditanstalt für Wiederaufbau, argued in the cabinet that 20 percent would hurt German exports and risk unemployment; he persuaded the cabinet to opt instead for a stronger devaluation of 25 percent, even if the resulting increase in import prices—especially for food—risked a major increase in inflation.[15] Abs' position is all the more remarkable given that the new currency was already experiencing severe inflationary weakness; in November of 1948 German workers would go out on general strike to protest inflation rates of 33 percent and more. Although the American High Commissioner, John McCloy, eventually mandated the original 20 percent devaluation, the DM remained significantly undervalued for much of the 1960s and early 1970s.

Indeed, the relative undervaluation of the DM in the fixed exchange rate system soon became the cornerstone of German industry's export strategy.[16] As early as the 1950s, German businesses and their commercial bank patrons tolerated a series of tough tariff reductions that undermined their domestic market share but helped to defend the fixed exchange rate system. Then, in 1960–1961, Germany's principal representative of heavy manufacturing, the Bundesverband Deutschen Industrie (BDI), fearing an impending revaluation of the DM, championed an *Entwicklungs Anleihe* (development loan) to be offered by the Bonn government to the third world. Behind this apparent altruism lay an effort to alter capital flows sufficient to keep the DM from rising. Even as evidence accumulated that the DM would continue to be revalued upward, the motto of German industry and the big three commercial banks was "Fixed exchange rates or death" and would remain so until the 1970s, when the Bundesbank's monetarist policy taught them the superiority of floating.[17]

Reconstruction of Labor

The second major reconstruction after the war to shape the policy environment for German central banking was that of German labor. In Germany as in other countries, labor costs are, statistically speaking, the principal components of price behavior. Just as German monetary policy is conditioned by its universal banks, so too its labor movement emerged from the postwar years with a relatively universalistic organization. Representing an impressive 35 percent of the workforce, and having an iron grip on the workforce in Germany's vital industries, the coordinated power of German labor entered into the Bundesbank's policy deliberations as both an opportunity and a threat. German labor was too large to be ignored and too powerful to be easily disciplined.

As with the banking system, the power and autonomy of German trade union movement owe much to the lessons of the Nazi debacle, and to Germany's rejection of American pluralist reforms. Although numerically strong during the interwar years, German trade unionism fell victim to the Nazi's control and persecution in no small measure, owing to its internal divisions. During the Weimar period, over 200 individual craft unions were divided among three politically and philosophically opposed major movements: the socialist Allegmeine Deutscher Gewerkschaftsbund (German Trade Union Confederation, ADGB); the Gesamptverband Christlicher Gewerkschaften (Association of Christian Trade Unions), affiliated with the Catholic Zentrum (Center) party; and the liberal Hirsch-Duncker union movement. The earlier years of Weimar saw rapid expansion of union activism, especially in 1922–1923, when there was an enormous increase in strikes and union membership. But the onset of the Great Depression in 1929 brought increased fragmentation and defections under the pressure of massive unemployment and wage concessions. The leadership of the largest movement, the ADGB, was challenged by extremist Marxists on the far left in the Revolutionäre Gewerkschafts Opposition (Revolutionary Trade Union Opposition, RGO). The Nazis countermobilized with their own movement, the Nationalsozialistiche Betriebsorganisation (National Socialist Works Organization). After 1933, the Nazis rolled all these movements into one large organization, the Deutscher Arbeits Front (German Labor Front, DAF), which became an instrument of Nazi control. Non-Nazi trade union leaders were exiled, driven underground, imprisoned, or executed.

In the first few years after the war, trade union leaders who returned from abroad vowed to set aside their philosophical differences in favor of a movement with sufficient unity to guard workers' rights. Under the leadership of reformers such as Hans Boekler, and with the blessing of the Labour government in London, German unionists in the British zone of occupation in the north of Germany reorganized into a unified confederation comprising sixteen industrial unions. Unity was achieved by formally divorcing union membership from party affiliation. Gone too were most of the bitter rivalries among crafts. This unified model was eventually extended to all of the Federal Republic of Germany when initial French and especially American resistance to a revival of unions was overcome, and it was ratified at the Munich conference of the new Deutscher Gewerkschaftsbund (German Trade Union Federation, DGB) in 1949.

The early years of the Federal Republic codified into law most of the reforms secured by the new movement. Most important, the autonomy of trade unions and bargaining was enshrined in Germany's new constitution, the Basic Law. This ushered in a long era of relative labor peace and rapidly declining unemployment. By 1958, virtually full employment had been reached, and with the cessation of refugees from the East in 1961 came a growing manpower shortage. This shortage was met with the importation of millions of so-called guest workers from southern Europe and Turkey. But full unemployment also afforded an opportunity for the unions to take a more vigorous approach in wage bargaining. The DGB's membership attained 7.48 million in 1973, and enrolled (together with the union representing white-collar workers and government officials) about 36 percent of the working population. Reinforcing the unity of the movement are the organizational resources at its disposal. An annual income for the DGB of some 120 million DM in the early 1970s was augmented by extraordinary financial holdings. The DGB owned one of the ten largest banks, the Bank für Gemeinwirtschaft; the second largest insurance firm, Volksfürsorge; and an enormous housing concern, Neue Heimat. All together, the DGB's assets were estimated to exceed 3 billion DM in the early 1970s. Its financial resources supported the highly regarded WSI research institute and nine other educational institutions.

As with the banks, much of the significance of the union movement for German monetary policy derives from its universalistic organizational structure. The first consequence is the power this affords German unions. All workers in a given industry (or set of industries) can be represented by only one union, regardless of their craft or specialization. Thus, for example, IG Metall, which enrolled some 2.4 million members in 1973, exercises the legal monopoly to recruit membership within, and bargain on behalf of, workers in several crucial sectors—vehicle manufacturing, machine tools, the iron and steel industry, aerospace, and electronics. Unsurprisingly, the potential strike power of IG Metall has been described as the "nuclear weapon in the arsenal of the German labor movement." Wage contracts are set each year in negotiations by individual unions and one of several hundred employers' organizations. Although formally independent of one another, the DGB's seventeen affiliated unions exercise a remarkable degree of coordination in their bargaining strategies. Typically, IG Metall is designated to take the lead in negotiations. Its settlements with Gesampt Metall (the metal industry federation of employers) then provide the benchmark for negotiations by other unions. German unions are required to honor "social peace" during the life of contracts, and unauthorized wildcat strikes are prohibited. And not without reason. The greater power that Germany's univeralistic unions wield means that strikes and lockouts have the potential to disturb not merely the economy, but *in extremis* the polity itself.

As a corollary to their universalism, the principle of voluntary membership is extremely important to unions and is enshrined in law. Unions do not seek, nor would the law permit, closed shops where union membership is compulsory. This voluntary nature and the greater universalism of German unions have made for a greater degree of overlap between public opinion and union attitudes. To a greater extent than in the United States, they are one and the same. But in Germany universalistic union organization also implies a considerable statistical identity between wage settlements and price inflation. Wage bargaining under conditions of greater universalism and voluntarism place the unions and the central bank in a delicate tension. The focal point of the tension between them is the unions' standard negotiating formula. The union's wage demands comprises three key calculations: productivity increases, inflationary increases (both of which the union seeks to capture in full), and a redistributive component (i.e., can they transfer a portion of the national income away from profits to wages?) Whether union negotiators can obtain these things depends crucially on the membership's *Streikbereitschaft* ("willingness to strike" or "militancy"). Militancy is a complex phenomenon, comprising objective features such as the rate of unemployment but also more political components such as members' personal attitudes and ideologies. The question of inflation and inflationary expectations in wage bargaining is of most immediate relevance to the Bundesbank's monetary policy. Because the German working public is in effect a major potential cause of inflationary pressure, the Bundesbank has an interest in teaching it anti-inflationary attitudes. Conversely, because the industrial unions must justify their wage demands to both their mass membership and the general public, the unions are under a powerful compulsion to articulate their position in economic terms.[18] Thus the unions are led to argue with the Bundesbank over numbers, while the central bank is led to become an ideologist. Universalistic unions mean, in the end, that all major players in the German political economy (including the government, as Germany's largest employer) have an incentive to enhance their bargaining position by marrying economic data to a public philosophy.

The Reconstruction of the German State

The third major reconstruction in the monetary policy environment was the establishment of a new, sovereign Federal Republic in the 1950s. While some features of the new German state appear to have been adopted from the American system of checks and balances, especially its federal division of powers, in practice the Federal Republic sought a much more coherent decision-making regime. Above all, the authors of the West German constitution sought to reduce the opportunities for demagogic and populist attacks of the kind that brought down Germany's first experiment with democracy. Thus, in contrast to the divisions among the branches in the American system, German reformers sought to rationalize public power, creating effective but interlocking institutions centered on a streamlined parliamentary (cabinet) government. Among its many consequences, this streamlined state structure improves the opportunities for coordination between fiscal and monetary policy.

The founders of the Federal Republic of Germany looked back at the debacle of Hitler's rise to power and saw a republic that suffered from weak parliamentary government susceptible to demogoguery and populist agitation. By the early 1930s, paramilitary political parties were plotting coups, engineering crippling strikes, and turning the normal electoral process into chaos. Meanwhile the Reichstag, beset by strong proportional representation, succumbed to legislative paralysis as one cabinet after another fell and an increasingly isolated president and chancellor ruled by emergency decree. With this history in mind, the founders of the Federal Republic resolved to remove politics from the streets and place it in the hands of responsible parliamentary leadership. Executive authority, previously split between the chancellor and an elected president, was now centralized in the hands of the chancellor, who as head of government was made responsible to the lower house, the Bundestag. Henceforth, the chancellor would govern until replaced by a named successor in a "positive vote of nonconfidence." The centrifugal tendencies of proportional representation were constrained by a 5 percent threshold, which every party must surmount to obtain representation in parliament. The Bonn constitution further establishes strong protections for individual rights and an independent court system, policed by a powerful constitutional court, with the power to ban antidemocratic political parties. One of the most incendiary components of the Weimar constitution—the component Hitler first used to gain nationwide recognition—was the national plebiscite. This too was abolished under the Bonn constitution. Finally, a unique feature of German federalism gives primary responsibility for the execution of public policy to the Länder (federal states), while also giving them an autonomous voice in the formulation of crucial aspects of federal policy by sitting Länder delegates in the upper house, the Bundesrat.

Germany further insulates politics from the disruptive effects of electoral populism by facilitating parliamentary coalitions. From 1949 to 1965 (and again from 1969 to 1985) there were only three federal chancellors, and each of these was brought into power by a shift in preferences on the part of the junior partner in a coalition (usually the centrist Free Democratic party), or by internal party issues. Although each of these changes in governmental leadership was subsequently ratified by federal elections, it is remarkable how circumscribed electoral factors were. Particularly important for analysts of legislative politics is the theory that legislators seek to govern through "minimum winning coalitions," i.e., the smallest number of legislators or parties that can pass laws and programs. Given Germany's two more or less equally balanced dominant parties (the CDU and the SPD each have about 900,000 members and roughly 40–42 percent of the vote), and each with important regional bases of power among the Länder (and hence, the Bundesrat), the small, liberal Free Democratic Party becomes disproportionately powerful, even though it always hovers close to the 5 percent threshold. By exploiting the "politics of the last joiner" (since a party that threatens to leave a coalition can deprive it of its majority), the FDP often holds the whip hand in the formation of coalitions. As will be seen in Chapter 3, the German central bank has profited from the fact that the FDP's consistently anti-inflationary preferences should be so influential in parliament. The importance of coalition politics means that, in effect, the German electorate has never directly voted a government out of office at the federal level. Parliamentary government in this sense shields the Bundesbank from direct democratic or populist attacks on its autonomy and independence.

For all the constraints imposed by the vagaries of coalition politics, a coherent system of parliamentary government such as that adopted in Germany can in principle transform popular will into binding legislation more easily than can a congressional system. The Bundesbank must inevitably take this into consideration. The power of parliament suggests that a good case can be made for not projecting the independent, single-mindedly monetarist Bundesbank of the late 1980s backward into earlier, more politically ambivalent times. Constraints on the central bank's independence can be found as early as the Adenauer era. During the 1950s, Germany was governed chiefly by the Christian Union parties (CDU and CSU) led by Adenauer as chancellor. These center-right parties were formed after World War II by uniting previously divided Catholics and Protestants around a program of democratic stability, integration into Western Europe, and the "social market economy": a preference for liberal economics reinforced by a generous social safety net. The CDU has always been extremely close the export interests of German heavy industry and the commercial banks; Adenauer often invited Hermann J. Abs of Deutsche Bank to attend cabinet meetings even though Abs was not a member of the government. Abs's consistent advice to favor export performance even at the risk of greater inflation was a constant source of pressure on the central bank. Even without such pressure, coherent parliamentary government in Germany created ever more planning bodies and intergovernmental councils, which offered the Bundesbank proto-Keynesian opportunities to coordinate its policies with those of the government. The Konjunkturrat für die Öffentlichen Hand (Government Economic Planning Council) comprises representatives from the federal finance and economics ministries and representatives from each of the Länder as well as local governments. It meets at least twice a year to coordinate the economic policies of all governments that may affect the business cycle. A similarly constructed Finanzplanungsrat (Financial Planning Council) coordinates government fiscal policies. The Bundesbank came to take an active part in all such bodies by the late 1960s.

The most unequivocal demonstration of the power of parliament in these years came after Adenauer had passed the chancellorship on to Ludwig Erhard. During the mid-1960s, in an era of full employment but with signs of growing political restlessness, the Bundesbank induced Germany's first homegrown recession. This downturn, in 1966–1967, reduced economic growth to under 2 percent and produced a federal government deficit. The political reaction to this minor recession was dramatic (if not overdramatic). The CDU-CSU coalition with the FDP foundered on whether to raise taxes or lower expenditures to reduce the deficit. When Erhard opted to raise taxes, the FDP left the coalition. In elections in the state of Bavaria shortly thereafter, panic about the recession helped the extreme-right NPD to make dramatic gains; it won almost 8 percent of the popular vote and drove the FDP out of the Landtag altogether. Though in hindsight the extremist threat was negligible, headlines and the airwaves hummed with reminiscences of the Nazi takeover during the Great Depression.

Panicked by this historical spectre, Erhard's government resigned and was replaced by a "grand coalition" of the CDU-CSU and the SPD headed by Kurt-Georg Kiesinger of the CDU. The SPD now had a share of federal power for the first time since before the war, and this gave government economic policy a dramatic new tenor. As an economically moderate leftist party, the SPD enjoyed a hegemony, if not monopoly, on the representation of workers' interests in German politics. This did not translate into a unanimous Keynesian orientation among SPD politicians and activists; but as much of the SPD's constituency has been the working class and union members, it has always tended to be the party of fuller—if not full—employment. With the SPD's Karl Schiller as economics minister, the Bundestag ratified a special "stability and growth" law (*Stabilitäts und Wachstums Gesetz*), significantly neo-Keynesian in inspiration, designed to prevent the recurrence of unnecessary recessions.[19] This law imposed on all economic decision-makers, including the Bundesbank, an obligation to pursue a "magic quadrangle": price stability, sustained economic growth, full employment, and international equilibrium. The law created a quasi-corporatist "concerted action forum," in which all principal economic actors, including the Bundesbank, were to discuss and coordinate appropriate economic measures concerning prices, wages, and interest rates. The stability and growth law sent an important signal: unlike the Reichsbank, the Bundesbank did not have the unilateral authority to induce recessions without regard for the political consequences.

Indeed, by the late 1960s, it became clear that what Ralf Dahrendorf called Germany's ruling "cartel of anxiety" believed itself vulnerable to any form of economic instability, recessionary or inflationary. The collapse of the Erhard government and the rise of the extreme right (and later, in 1968, the "extra parliamentary opposition" on the extreme left) led to the question: was Bonn Weimar after all? From the observers of economic policy came the answer *Inflation und Rezession zerstören die Demokratie (Inflation and Recession Destroy Democracy)*. At the time when monetarism would come into the Bundesbank's field of vision, in other words, Germany's alleged single-minded fear of inflation, much trumpeted by later Bundesbank spokesmen, was overshadowed by a powerful fear of unemployment, which the same spokesmen now overlook. Karl Klasen, who became the Bundesbank's president in 1970, repeatedly stressed that Weimar Germany had been undermined not by inflation alone, but equally and more immediately by the Great Depression. Moreover, he referred circumspectly to the Bundesbank's "autonomy" rather than to outright "independence."

Taken together, the recession of 1967, the coordinating bodies of parliamentary government, and the concerted action forum created by the stability and growth law, left an important intellectual and political legacy which the Bundesbank, down to the present day, has had to acknowledge. The drafters of both the *Bundesbankgesetz* and the stability and growth law had an important influence in setting the central bank's intellectual poles: they reinforced the central bank's tendency to think about the implications of policy for both recession and inflation and, ultimately, the domestic political consequences.

Reconstruction of Economic Advice

Finally, in the twenty years following the war German economists and policymakers reconstructed and rethought the relationship between economic knowledge and policymaking. This produced transformations in the communication networks among economists and policy advisers that were more deeply embedded in the management of economic life in Germany than in the United States. To a great extent, this reflected the processes of organizational rationalization that we have already observed in the reconstruction of finance, business, labor, and the state. As we have seen, the greater degree of universalism in Germany's economic policy environment had already begun to push policymakers toward experiments with corporatism in the late 1960s. These same pressures served to structure the processes of gathering and analyzing economic data and advocating policy. This pattern of policy debate might be considered a kind of scientific corporatism. The emergent structures of the 1950s and 1960s help explain a key feature in monetary targeting in the 1970s: the greater ease with which economists of alternative theoretical persuasions were identified and mobilized into German monetary policymaking. To some extent, this was independent of the strictly academic standing of the economists within the discipline. If academics can be ranked by the degree to which they are organized by "hierarchy" or "markets," German economists appear to be much more representative of hierarchy.[20] German academic economists—especially monetarists—complained that their discipline was more hierarchical and parochial than its American counterpart, and that it lacked the structures of job mobility and publishing that make American academia so entrepreneurial.[21] The temptation is to expect this to inhibit the spread of new ideas. How then do we account for the relatively rapid incorporation of monetarism in official German policy? Certainly part of the explanation is to be found in the Bundesbank's long-standing pattern of internal policy polarity. But the rather Keynesian form of monetarism adopted, its gradual implementation, and the revolution in Bundesbank leadership from bankers to economists—events which I describe more fully in Chapter 3—owed much to this preexisting pattern of scientific corporatism among leading economists associated with powerful institutional interests in the German economy.

Many commentators have noted that military defeat and reconstruction by reform-minded American generals and German dissidents gave an unprecedented opportunity to apply economic theories to a slate wiped nearly clean by war. In his design of the new currency Ludwig Erhard was influenced by the Freiburg school's tradition of so-called ordoliberalism, particularly as developed by Walter Eucken. The impact of Eucken's ideas on Erhard, and thus on the entire program of postwar reconstruction, has been called an "unusually unambiguous example of the beneficent effects of economists' ideas on economic policy."[22] Eucken's doctrine was classically liberal in its insistence on the power of free markets to provide for the general welfare by efficiently allocating goods and services. As such, it advocated—and Erhard substantially delivered—a rollback of state intervention in the economy, relative not just to wartime conditions but also to prewar conditions. But the Freiburg school also borrowed a leaf from Knapp in arguing that efficient markets require a stable framework of laws and organizing institutions, chief among which were central banking and the judiciary, which it is the state's duty to provide. Monetary policy has a special place in Eucken's *Grundsätze,* as the essential framework of a successful social and economic polity. Eucken's ordoliberalism became a principal source of the "social market economy," the key notion adopted by the Christian Democratic and Social Democratic parties to characterize the postwar German economy.

The long-term influence of Eucken and the ordoliberals should not be overestimated, however. In particular, there is little evidence that they had a direct impact on the culture of German central banking or on the rest of the economics profession. First, Erhard lost the battle to create a unified central bank. Second, while the ordoliberals remembered the failure of the command economy as practiced by the Nazis, the majority of their colleagues remembered the failure of capitalism that preceded it. The majority of German economists in the postwar era were either Keynesians or socialists. A figure who was almost as influential as Erhard in the postwar era was Karl Schiller, perhaps Germany's leading Keynesian economist and actively involved with the SPD. Schiller, along with Erich Preisser, head of the Working Group of German Economic Research Institutes in Kiel, sat on the economic advisory council to the bizonal administration of the military occupation. When the bizonal administration later became the nucleus of the new federal government in Bonn, Schiller, Preisser, and others continued to argue (in the advisory council to the minister of economics) for demand (monetary) stimulus to promote capital formation through increases in retained earnings and lagged wage increases.[23] (Indeed, given that between 1950 and 1960 GDP increased 100 percent while wages increased only 75 percent, this is almost precisely what happened.) Schiller also played a key role in the parliamentary committee that drafted the Bundesbank law in 1957. From then until the early 1970s, the federal advisory council became more and more Keynesian. In short, in the late 1960s, as one who lived through those times put it, "monetarism was not widely accepted."[24] It had to be created in the 1960s, and would incorporate elements of both ordoliberalism and Keynesianism.

The pattern of bifurcated debate within the Bundesbank also reflects the structure of the German policy research community. During the postwar period, German economists set about constructing (or reviving, in one case) five premier private economic research institutes based in Munich, Berlin, Kiel, Hamburg, and Essen. Each developed its own separate research agenda, so that a broad spectrum of policy options were accounted for. More specifically, the Deutsche Institut für Wirtschaftsforschung (German Institute for Economic Research, DIW) in Berlin had a particularly neo-Keynesian perspective; the institute in Essen eventually became the most strongly monetarist; and the other three tended toward the middle. Apart from providing their own individual commentary on economic policy, they regularly pooled their resources to provide a joint critique of both fiscal and monetary policy. These critiques generally took the form of alternative interpretations of the government's or the central banks' numbers; occasionally, however, they either singly or jointly presented theoretical challenges to the central bank's conceptions of monetary policy.

The growing pressure for at least some sort of Keynesian or coordinating role led to the creation in 1963 of the Sachverständigenrat (Council of Experts, SVR). Here, too, we find a pattern of embedding but balancing different economic viewpoints; and it is here that the link to social interests is most visible. The SVR is composed of five leading university professors of economics. Of these, three are nominated by the government economics ministry, one is nominated by the employers' association, and one is nominated by the union movement. While this pattern of nomination sometimes means that the alignment of theoretical perspectives within the SVR can be four conservatives to one neo-Keynesian, it ensures a constant balancing of theories. Although the economist nominated by the unions is most likely to dissent from the majority report, it is nonetheless significant that the union movement has never nominated a member of the Marxist "Memorandum Group" of economists to the SVR.

The SVR is charged particularly with providing a year-end review of economic developments and providing nonpartisan policy advice to the government. The fact that the membership of the SVR changes slowly and is not partisan means that its advice can often be wider-ranging than the American Council of Economic Advisers (CEA) and that it is free of the political constraints which can often limit the CEA's analyses.[25] Consequently, the SVR takes a macroscopic view; it is concerned with both the business cycle and Germany's competitive position in the world economy. This attitude in itself creates a climate of intellectual give-and-take and provides moral authority also for those outside these networks to criticize the government. By law, the federal government is required, in its new year reports, to reply to the criticism and recommendation offered by the SVR. In 1964, in one of its first responses to the work of the SVR, the government took explicit notice of the dangerous relationship between the depression of the 1930s and political turmoil that brought the Nazis to power. To justify deficit spending, the federal government report argued that "Germany's fate after 1933 was connected by a causal sequence to the inability of the Weimar Republic to master unemployment."[26] Thus, these institutions, with their links to powerful and universalistic social actors, brought into the policy process a historical consciousness of the political significance of both inflation and recession for the wider German polity.

In the end, however, these various councils and advisory bodies may matter not just for the specific content of their ideas but also for the unique opportunities they provide for personnel mobility. They allow experts to translate academic credentials into public visibility and thus to develop credibility and authority with Germany's universalistic social actors, while maintaining the nonpartisanship necessary to the status of expert as such. Experts as different as Claus Kohler in the 1970s and Olaf Sievert in the 1990s would be recruited from these official decision-making bodies into the central bank council, ensuring both a high degree of professionalism and a sense of societal representation.

THE CORPORATE CULTURE OF THE BUNDESBANK

Since at least the 1980s, there has been a growing effort to claim that the circumstances of the Bundesbank's founding make the central bank "monetarist by law."[27] Whatever merit this characterization has for today's Bundesbank, it certainly distorts the reality of the Bundesbank in the years before monetarism. On the contrary, it is clear upon further examination that both the idea of a monetarist birth and the one-sidedly anti-inflationary historical mythology were embellishments by the post-1973 Bundesbank itself. The Bundesbank's original mission, as shaped by legislation and the incentives from its initial policy environment, was to stabilize the currency using an external criterion—the exchange rate. This interest in stability was counterbalanced by the Bundesbank's sympathies for the export interests of the big commercial banks. The Bundesbank was made even more sympathetic to policies of countercyclical demand management in the wake of the recession of 1966. Thus, the Bundesbank was much less receptive to monetarism than scholars now recognize or the Bundesbank now acknowledges. In this respect, therefore, the Bundesbank's corporate culture was, if anything, more open than the Federal Reserve under Chairman Martin to an activist anticyclical policy. Procedurally, however, the Bundesbank's corporate culture was markedly different. Its greater degree of procedural collegiality afforded many more opportunities than the Federal Reserve for those voices to be heard— monetarists, Keynesians, the commercial banks, the Sparkassen—that would later seek to redefine the Bundesbank's long-term goals and mission. It was these perspectives, in the various institutional power bases of the Bundesbank, that gradually gave final shape to the debate between monetarists and neo-Keynesians, and the early but moderate victory of the monetarists at the beginning of the 1970s. This can be seen by examining the central bank's founding statute, its procedural culture, and its substantive culture.

Statutory Mandate and Independence

The West German Basic Law (*Grundgesetz*), promulgated in 1949, notes a need to transfer the statutory basis for Germany's central bank from Allied ordinance to German legislation but does not specify the content of this legislation. In 1957, the CDU-led coalition government of Chancellor Adenauer, having determined that the central bank had amassed sufficient dollar reserves to be transferred to German control, proceeded to codify the status of the bank under the guidance of an expert commission. The resulting *Bundesbankgesetz* (law on the federal bank) thus encapsulates what German economists and policymakers had learned about the optimal relationship between the central bank and the central government, and its powers over the economy.

After a very thorough and contentious debate of the issues in the economic advisory committee, the Bundesbank law ultimately retained most of the key developments and assumptions in German central banking that had accumulated in the Bank Deutscher Länder. This is significant because it gave an external orientation priority in the central bank's mandate. This is apparent even in the language adopted. In its third article, the Bundesbank law carries over the Bank Deutscher Länder's duty to regulate the quantity of money and credit so as to safeguard the currency (*"Währung zu sichern"*).[28] The German term *Währung*, like the English term "currency," has a predominantly international connotation: a German would use the everyday term *Geld* (money) when speaking of domestic costs or prices. This international meaning of the Bundesbank's founding statute is perfectly plausible in the light of the DM's relatively new and untried status in 1957, and its legal ties to the dollar (the *Leitwährung*, or lead currency) in the Bretton Woods system. Many years later, this original international meaning would have to be overcome, if not explained away, in order for the Bundesbank to adopt a domestically oriented monetarist policy.

The legislation likewise stipulates that in its conduct of monetary policy the Bundesbank shall be independent of instructions of the government, but it adds in article 12, that the Bundesbank shall support the economic parogram of the government, so long as doing so does not impinge upon defending the currency. This is qualified by the government's right to postpone, for two weeks, any decision of the Bundesbank council to which it objects. The Bundesbank is required by law to advise the government on matters pertaining to its mandate. To make this possible, the Bundesbank president has authority to attend cabinet meetings when monetary policy is discussed. Similarly, cabinet ministers may attend meetings of the central bank's council and propose motions, though they cannot vote. The Bundestag, like the U.S. Congress, lacks many instruments of oversight: it cannot reauthorize the agency, nor does it hold the purse strings. The Bundesbank law strictly limits federal, Land (state), and business access to the printing press. The Bundesbank can lend to government only limited amounts (6 billion DM for the federal government) and only for short periods. It cannot hold government securities on its own account. The bank does act as a sales agent for government bonds, ensuring orderly market conditions at the time of sale. The government, as sole stockholder of the Bundesbank, receives its sometimes quite substantial profits.

However, not all the features of the Bank Deutscher Länder were retained. The new law reversed certain key organizational features imposed by the American occupation, which was pluralist in outlook and feared excessive financial concentration. The most important change was a shift in the balance of power between the presidents of the Land central banks and the Directorate at the headquarters in Frankfurt. German legislators recognized that the universal bank system required a comparably "universalized" central bank. The Land central banks, formerly independent entities organized within each Land, now became regional subsidiaries of a unified Bundesbank system. The former separation of powers between the old Directorate, which had played second fiddle to the Council of Land central bank presidents, was abolished. Now the Directorate and the Land central bank presidents would meet together every two weeks as a unified decision-making body called the *Zentralbankrat* (central bank council, CBC), with the president of the Bundesbank simultaneously head of the CBC and the Directorate.

One must also be careful not to exaggerate the Bundesbank's original independence. There are two major statutory sources of leverage on the Bundesbank that could be used by the central government. The first source of leverage is that the *Bundesbankgesetz* can in principle be altered by a simple parliamentary majority. The Bundesbank, therefore, must keep at least one eye on the political balance in the Bundestag. Many aspects of law and public policy, particularly concerning federalism, must also pass the Bundesrat, the upper chamber of the German government, in which the representatives of the Länder are seated. Significantly, the *Bundesbankgesetz* is not such a law. The Bundesbank leadership has attempted to assert that its independence has attained constitutional status, but this has not been sanctioned by the constitutional court.[29]

The second, and more important, constraint on the Bundesbank's independence is the legal primacy of the government concerning the conduct of foreign monetary relations. While the Bundesbank is authorized to intervene on international currency markets on its own initiative, the legal responsibility for international currency agreements (whether it be Bretton Woods, the EMS, or the EMU) rests with the federal government. Bonn has always regarded its international authority as its most potent strategy for restraining the Bundesbank's domestic autonomy, and, much as the Bundesbank itself, has regarded the maintenance of the German currency within stable exchange rates to be of paramount importance for German exports and also for peaceful relations with its neighbors. German governments have always feared that without strict adherence to exchange rates, beggar-thy-neighbor currency dumping could occur, as it did in the 1930s. But even from a strictly legal standpoint, a fixed exchange rate for the DM from 1948 to 1973 greatly curtailed the Bundesbank's autonomy.

This primacy of the federal government in foreign monetary relations also creates a legal and political gray zone that circumscribes the Bundesbank even when fixed exchange rates are suspended. When fixed exchange rates no longer work—as, historically, they sometimes do not—they are often suspended, to be reestablished later at a new parity. In such circumstances (as was the case in 1971 and 1973–1976), it is far from clear that the Bundesbank has the authority to chart its own course.[30] Similarly, certain exchange rate agreements may be more than economically desirable. German voters have been very pro-European, and Germany's central bankers have recognized that they stand in front of the European steamroller at their own risk. This has lent a certain quality of "Europe, yes, but . . . " to the Bundesbank's pronouncements and its dealings with Bonn on European monetary cooperation and integration. And it has been established by the German Constitutional Court that the articles of the Treaty of Rome as amended, which constitute the legal basis of the European Union, take legal precedence over ordinary German law and therefore over the *Bundesbankgesetz*.[31]

Internal Structure of the Bundesbank: Procedural Corporate Culture

In the 1970s, the superior capacity of the Bundesbank to debate its mission and goals internally was a result not so much of its formal independence from government as of its internal personnel structure and its relations with constituencies in the policy environment. For the Bundesbank, this meant not only tenure for the men and women who run it, but procedures which ensured that expertise, an intellectual division of labor, and a high level of engagement with problems of policy management would be brought to bear on delicate questions. The foundation for the Bundesbank's superior mobilization of expertise is the internal organization specified in the *Bundesbankgesetz*.

Although strictly speaking the Bundesbank is not organized according to normal German corporate law, the principles of collective management which structure the leadership of German publicly owned companies have analogues in the central bank. In particular, the Directorate is based on a model of collective responsibility, and the power of the president as chief executive officer is diluted. The relationship of the directorate to the staff and to the presidents of the Land central banks is also based on collective management. These features combine to foster more decentralization than in the Federal Reserve, more autonomous centers of professional authority, and, ultimately, more intellectual balance and collegiality. This "structure as culture" can more effectively reflect interests and theories outside the independent institution itself.

The highest decision-making body of the Bundesbank, the Central Bank Council (CBC), originally comprised the eleven presidents of the Land central banks (LCBs) and the directorate of the Bundesbank's head office in Frankfurt. This council meets regularly every two weeks and decides the principal direction of monetary policy for the bank. The day-to-day management of the Bundesbank is conducted by the Directorate in Frankfurt, which is composed of the Bundesbank president, the vice president, and up to eight other individuals. Members of the Central Bank Council are normally appointed for an eight-year term (little more than half the term of a Federal Reserve governor) and can only be removed when they reach the statutory retirement age or for personal malfeasance. Salaries are set by the federal government in accordance with the salaries of all its senior officials (*Beamten*); as *Beamte*, the council members and their staffs also have tenure in office and generous pensions.

The major indicator of the *Bundesbank's* collegiality is that the authority of its president is lessened, to the benefit of his colleagues. Although the president of the Bundesbank is in fact the highest paid public official in Germany, earning more than the chancellor or the President, he is simply *primus inter pares,* and—unlike his predecessor (or, often, his American counterpart)—he is not a CEO.[32] Voting records remain sealed for thirty years, yet officials of the Bundesbank indicate that the president has always lost votes in the Central Bank Council and the Directorate, far more often than the Federal Reserve chairman. Moreover, lost votes are generally understood to be less of an issue within the Bundesbank.[33] As one former insider observed, "The Bundesbank is much less respectful of its president than the Federal Reserve is of its chairman.[34] The Bundesbank president is nominated for eight years, like all other members of the CBC. The Bundesbank president always has a significant political counterweight, in the office the vice-president; by contrast, the vice chairman does not typically play such a role in the Federal Reserve.[35] In Germany, not only has the vice president been comparable to the president in intellectual and professional stature, but the unwritten rule was that he should come from the opposing political coalition.[36] This pattern dates to the founding of the Bundesbank, when the SPD's support for the original Bundesbank law was secured by promising it the vice presidency. Thus, when Karl Blessing of the CDU was appointed the first Bundesbank president, Heinrich Troeger of the SPD was promoted from president of the Land central bank in Hessen and made vice president of the Bundesbank. This pattern continued in 1970, when Karl Klasen (SPD) replaced Blessing and Otmar Emminger (CSU) was promoted to vice president. Subsequently, when Emminger became president, Pöhl, as Schmidt's protégé, became vice president; when Pöhl became president two years later, Schlesinger (CDU) was made vice president. This pattern diminishes the capacity of the president to dominate the council.

That the Bundesbank president simply wields less internal influence than his counterpart in Washington is not entirely due to the status of the person at the top. Various mechanisms contrive to enhance the powers of the other members of the council relative to the president. Chiefly, the Bundesbank's internal organization distributes power and access to staff expertise among members of the Directorate by making them line managers of the major departments within the bank. The Bundesbank's major *Dezernat* (divisions), *Abteilungen* (departments), and *Amter* (bureaus) are responsible for the major activities of the central bank: international currency, macroeconomics, credit, and banking. The director's administrative responsibilities mean that a high degree of executive and academic accomplishment is not only a legal but a functional prerequisite for appointees; this is not true in the same way at the Fed, where management and policy are separated. Each Bundesbank department or LCB represents an institutional and informational power base for a CBC member, especially important for access to the data and staff resources in line departments for waging "religious wars" over "the numbers" that often typify the way issues are debated in the Directorate and the CBC. At the Bundesbank, staff members do not even attend meetings of the CBC.[37] The structure of departments and personnel cannot be altered from within the Bundesbank except by unanimous vote of the CBC, which denies the president a weapon—reorganization—that could otherwise be used to undermine his colleagues and promote his own policies. Votes of directors and the CBC are by simple, secret majority.

The German tradition that central banking is a highly technical profession animates staffing decisions from top to bottom. In this spirit, the Bundesbank runs its own Fachhochschule (Technical Institute) to train its newly recruited staff. A Director's eight-year term is less than the fourteen years in the Federal Reserve, but in practice it has involved a much longer period in office; the central bank councilors' overall length of affiliation with the bank vastly exceeds that of members of the Federal Open Market Committee with the Federal Reserve System. Particularly during the 1970s, the average length of service of Bundesbank directors exceeded that of Federal Reserve Governors by about 162 percent. The reason for this is that membership in the Central Bank Council (usually as a director, but sometimes as president or vice president of a Land central bank) is often the culmination of long service within the Bundesbank. However difficult scaling the heights of the Bundesbank may be for an ambitious young official, the appointment of directors from within the ranks of the senior staff is not unusual. The careers of the two most critical monetarists in the Bundesbank, Otmar Emminger and Helmut Schlesinger, illustrate an important fact about the directorate. Their attitude to the institution they would lead in the 1970s and 1980s reflected their experiences in policy battles as staffers in the 1950s and 1960s. In contrast, by the 1970s Federal Reserve governors were more likely to regard their office as a tour of duty in a career primarily outside the Fed.

Although German governments change their political orientation less frequently than American presidential administrations, the longer de facto term in office of the directors means that there has been a broad balance in the number of directors appointed by coalition governments led by the SPD and the CDU. Just as directors have greater independence than Fed governors, the presidents of the Land central banks have greater autonomy than their counterparts in the Fed. In both Germany and the United States, the regional bank presidents are more likely sources of rebellion and more conservative, if perhaps having fewer resources than members of the Directorate.[38] But in comparison with their American colleagues, Bundesbank regional presidents are privileged. First, unlike the presidents of the Federal Reserve Banks, they outnumber and thus theoretically can outvote their Directorate. Second, the federal component of the Bundesbank system strengthens the political power bases of the regional presidents. Presidents of the Land central banks are nominated by the Bundesrat (federal upper house) on the advice of the appropriate Land government. The contribution of federalism in this appointment procedure mimics the effect of the Bundesrat itself in reflecting the nationwide balance of power between the CDU-CSU and the SPD within what Manfred Schmidt has aptly termed a "Grand Coalition state." Although they are formally independent of the Land governments (unlike the delegates of the Bundesrat) the fact that they owe their nomination to Land politics is significant: they know they can rely on political backing from their Land governments, and this legitimacy not only "stiffens their backs" but wards off attacks from those who might otherwise accuse the council of being undemocratic.[39] For their part, LCB presidents have resisted the arguments of some members of the directorate that more subtle instruments of policy, such as open-market operations, replace changes in administered prices. They worry that this would shift too much power from the council to the directorate. And, regardless of political stripe, this appointment procedure ensures that a majority of CBC members understand that the Bundesbank acts in a political environment reaching beyond Bonn.

In sum, voting and patterns of debate within the Bundesbank are pushed toward collegiality by the division of labor and the different sources of nomination and legitimacy of members of the Central Bank Council. It is neither expected nor possible that the policies or attitudes of one individual should dominate the entire institution. Moreover, this procedure provides multiple points of access for different intellectual viewpoints, so long as they are sufficiently qualified. Leading intellectual figures recruited from the cream of the staff or from outside expert bodies sponsored by Germany's universal interests exploit their departmental or LCB resources to become poles around which the Bundesbank's policy debates are organized. Indeed, these strong analytic perspectives themselves may be the ultimate sanction for council members' autonomy.

Internal Cleavages and Substantive Culture

In the early years of the Bundesbank, the primacy of international currency commitments meant that (as with the Bank Deutscher Länder) defending the currency meant defending its international parities. This was no mere nominal commitment but a deeply internalized value derived from a perception of the central bank's weakness in the face of economic uncertainty. The Bundesbank believed that only international support could ensure Germany's stability and prosperity. Karl Blessing, who became the first president of the Bundesbank, believed, like his predecessor at the Bank Deutscher Länder (Wilhelm Vocke), that a fixed exchange rate was a matter of *noli me tangere*—it was untouchable.[40] For Germany to formulate its currency problems in terms of the Keynesian-monetarist choice between "full employment" and "price stability" would have been nonsensical: Germany would shortly have both. By 1955, the massive postwar unemployment had been dealt with, and the Bank Deutscher Länder was reporting that full employment was in sight (registered unemployed workers in 1961 would be below 1 percent) and inflation seldom exceeded 2 percent a year.[41]

Rather, German currency debates were originally framed in terms of *external* choices. Within a decade, Germany went from a country with an acute shortage of currency to one whose exports were earning an excess of reserves. Consequently, policy debates turned on how exchange rate adjustments could best preserve macroeconomic stability. The majority of the new Bundesbank's directors, most of whom were carried over from its predecessor, wanted to maintain DM parities and defend existing exchange rates as long as possible. According to the original concept of the Bretton Woods system, at least some inflation in surplus countries was expected as a normal mechanism for restoring international equilibrium among trading partners. When arguments in favor of revaluing the currency carried the day, the crucial point was less that revaluation would guarantee price stability than that it would restore the equilibrium in international trade that Germany's IMF membership obligated it to maintain. Operating by these precepts, the Bundesbank championed Keynesianism in Germany. The monthly report of November 1959, for example, urged the government to prevent disequlibrium by engaging in deficit spending.[42] Otmar Emminger, who would lead a monetarist coup within the Bundesbank in 1973, remembers himself as a minority faction of one ("completely isolated") among Bundesbank directors in seeking timely revaluations in the late 1950s and early 1960s, for the sake of disinflation alone.

By the late 1970s, the Bundesbank's debate over revaluations merged with a debate about how the bank could best exercise its power in the economy. Generally speaking, a central bank's power has two aspects: general influence over economic conditions as a whole and selective (dirigiste) control over the decisions of individual agents. Here there is an echo of the old Reichsbank and the Bank Deutscher Länder. The "influence" view holds that monetary developments exogenously influence conflict between interest groups over the division of the economic pie and that this social conflict represents the greatest danger to social stability and the autonomy of a central bank. The bank should therefore prefer indirect methods of economic control (stabilize the business cycle) and avoid dirigism. This is the lesson of the Bank Deutscher Länder. Conversely, however, others assert that interest-group conflict is endogenous—spontaneously determined within society itself. This is especially true when one considers the power of national governments to tax, spend, and coerce. The central bank's influence is constrained by the support or acquiescence its actions receive from the government and powerful social interests. Above all, the central bank manages a banking system whose nature is to make specific and often substantial loan commitments to clients. The central bank's obligations as lender of last resort for these banks mean that it cannot be indifferent to the nature of such commitments. At a minimum, some degree of direct regulatory control is necessary to define money and ensure the integrity of the financial system through which the central bank's monetary policy will flow. This was the lesson of the Reichsbank. Chapter 3 will demonstrate in more detail that as the Bundesbank's commitment to fixed exchange rates grew ever more difficult to meet, the logic of ever more dirigiste measures of controlling the economy became more compelling.

Thus, if monetarism is defined as the primacy of a stable currency achieved through a free float and the control of monetary aggregates, the presumed monetarist immaculate conception of the Bundesbank was scarcely in evidence. Rather, monetarism was at best the unformulated answer to a still-unasked question: did Germany really need fixed exchange rates? Only years of internal and external debate would propel the "early revaluation" proponents into a monetarist alliance. By that time, the "fixed exchange rate" perspective would have merged with the dirigiste perspective. The proponents of monetarism would have to challenge both these perspectives.

In sum, the Bundesbank enjoyed a corporate decision-making culture which was from the outset more suited to collegiality and openness than the corporate culture of the Fed. The Bundesbank's division of managerial authority and its federal construction created multiple points of entry for outside perspectives. But this internal bifurcation of perspectives reflected, ultimately, a universalistic bifurcation of interests within the Bundesbank's policy environment. The universal banking system with its rivalry between commercial banks and Sparkassen—and the rivalries between employers' federations and industrial unions—were all to some extent a legacy of Germany's postwar defeat of American attempts to graft pluralism onto the German body politic. In this rejection were born those powerful domestic social actors that would help reeducate and discipline an otherwise independent central bank toward the necessity of domestically oriented monetary policy in a democratic society. The universal bank system would also provide a robust instrument for this tough stabilization policy when it finally came in the 1970s. These factors, as I shall argue in Chapter 3, were the crucial preconditions for the defeat of the growing internationalist and dirigiste program within the Bundesbank and its early replacement by a moderate, consensual form of a monetary targeting in the mid-1970s.

Chapter Three

The Bundesbank's Monetarist Regime Change, 1970–1985

In the tumultuous years of the early 1970s, the German Bundesbank embarked on an experiment that was unprecedented in economic history. Through a combination of skill, incentives, and opportunity, the Bundesbank broke free from the international system of fixed exchange rates and steered its wholly fiat currency into a position of international strength with no further guarantee of its financial soundness than the capacities of its central bank directors and the monetary theories which guided them. Most prominent among these theories was the monetarist doctrine that central banks should aim the money supply at a publicly announced target. Guided by this doctrine, Germany's currency, the deutsche mark (DM), completed its transformation from a "child of the military occupation" to a major international reserve currency, a "world star" on the international economic stage.[1] The Bundesbank's decades-long "experiment" with monetarism demonstrated concretely what had previously been only a controversial theory: that a major currency could be managed so as to combine the soundness expected of international commitments with the social sensitivities of a domestically oriented monetary policy.

The ultimate adoption of this experiment, however, was by no means foreordained. In 1970, the Bundesbank's council was profoundly divided. From interest and conviction, Germany had long been a party to international agreements which fixed its currency to those of its principal trading partners. Now these parities, rather than securing stability and prosperity, were importing inflation, which Germany experienced as an economically and socially damaging price-wage spiral. Inevitably, in addressing this problem, the Bundesbank had to choose between two quite distinct theories. Contrary to some subsequent portrayals, the first approach to win a majority of votes from the council was the authoritarian or dirigiste solution advocated by the Bundesbank's president, Klasen. This approach sought to preserve the fixed exchange rate and harmonize European central banking by giving the Bundesbank greatly enhanced regulatory power over commercial banks' creation of credit. This dirigiste approach would have included, for the first time since 1945, mandatory credit ceilings, selective controls, and an activist minimum-reserve policy. Had this option been implemented, the political pressure to transform the Bundesbank into a more typically dependent European central bank would have been enormous.

Nonetheless, much sooner than was the case in the United States, the German authoritarian solution was vigorously challenged from within the central bank by a monetarist free-market option, championed most effectively by Otmar Emminger, who was then the Bundesbank's vice president. This option included a free float of the deutsche mark against the dollar and the use of monetary targets both inside and outside the central bank. During the late Brandt years and the early Schmidt years, both options were vigorously debated within the Central Bank Council (CBC) and with the government, in what one Bundesbank official described as a *Glaubenskrieg* (religious war) of Wagnerian proportions.[2] Even so, the first adoption of monetary targeting in 1973 required not just an internal victory by the Emminger faction but also luck—several of Emminger's strongest opponents fell ill. And as a concession to the dirigiste faction, the Bundesbank treated its new program as an experiment and implemented it with concomitant moderation.

This chapter will show how the early and moderate nature of monetarism's supplanting of the dirigiste alternative in Germany originated in the interaction of the Bundesbank's collegial corporate culture with socially embedded expertise and the universalistic economic institutions in its policy environment. Of particular importance were the Sparkassen, the unions, and the economists in the official research institutes. This chapter will also show how the Bundesbank's moderate implementation of the market approach affected German politics over the long run: the early, moderate adoption of monetarism helped preserve the scale and scope of the German welfare state well into the 1980s (even if the cost would prove to be a much higher rate of unemployment). Accommodations to Keynesian fiscalism by German monetary targeting recognized that fiscal policy had a crucial constituency. With monetary policy shouldering the burden of macroeconomic management after 1973, a newly expansive fiscal policy shored up political support for the government. A simultaneous stabilization of wage costs and an expansion of the "public corridor" helped preserve the balance of power between business and labor and reduced political pressure for a rollback of taxes and regulations. Early monetary targeting meant that the policies of Helmut Kohl would not be those of Ronald Reagan. Perhaps the most interesting aspect of this reconciliation was the politics of German economists themselves. Over the course of the 1970s and 1980s, monetarist and Keynesian economists who might otherwise have become partisan activists for radical change moved to the heart of German policymaking. Some of the most prominent of these economists advanced from embedded research centers like the Council of Experts to the Central Bank Council itself. There they became loyal negotiators of the Bundesbank's "monetary corporatism."

Effective Corporate Culture and Early Monetarism, 1969–1974

The story of Germany's choice between dirigism and monetarism begins in the spring of 1969. For the first time since 1961, Germany confronted international trade imbalances creating pressure for an upward revaluation of the DM. In 1968 and 1969 political unrest in France triggered a currency crisis which was only partially resolved by a German "ersatz" revaluation. Combined with a booming American economy absorbing more and more German exports, the German trade surplus looked increasingly unsustainable without either tighter foreign monetary policy, a higher rate for the DM, or capital controls. When the issue came to a head in May 1969, CDU Chancellor Kurt-Georg Kiesinger, an "economic dilettante," was torn between two conflicting sets of advisers.[3] Karl Blessing of the Bundesbank, under pressure from the "group of ten" central bank governors, advised a revaluation, while the finance minister, Franz Josef Strauss, close to the interests of the exporters, declared that any "manipulation" of the exchange rate would happen "over his dead body;" the economics minister, Schiller, wavered.[4] Kiesinger, partly bowing to business pressure, partly thinking of the recent recession, and partly fearing the effect of a downturn on the electorate, rejected revaluation.

Forgoing revaluation would prove disastrous for Kiesinger's chancellorship and the country. Pressures in the currency market continued to build. In the summer of 1969, the federal election campaign seemed preoccupied with the currency question. Ordinary Germans had come to see how intimately their economy was linked to the exchange value of the DM. The election campaign became, to the horror of some in the Bundesbank, "plebiscitary" in nature.[5] In contrast to the CDU's opposition to a revaluation, Karl Schiller eventually persuaded the rest of his SPD colleagues that a revaluation would help restore the long-term health of the exchange rate system. This position enabled the SPD to make common cause with the FDP, which was less beholden than the CDU to big business. Thus in October 1969 a new coalition was formed, with the SPD's Willy Brandt as chancellor, and the FDP as junior partner. On October 24th the DM was revalued 9.3 percent against the dollar.

Unfortunately, the revaluation was too little and too late. Currency problems began to spread disorder to the very roots of German society. There was no more vivid demonstration of this than the increased militancy of German workers that erupted in September 1969. The additional six months of low export prices had reaped for German business a bonanza of unanticipated profits, aggravating the continuing effects of the "wage pause" of the 1967 recession. In response to that crisis, unions had not only negotiated quite modest pay increases but also allowed these contracts to run for eighteen months, a full 50 percent longer than normal. Now the undervalued currency and strong demand from the United States meant that German exports were offered at a discount in a buyers' market. While workers' take-home pay had barely changed since the recession, the profits of German metal firms were soaring in late 1969 at a rate of up to 100 percent per annum. Unemployment was practically zero, and labor shortages were doubling the number of guest workers from abroad. In September 1969, complacency about these conditions on the part of unions' and employers' negotiators led rank-and-file workers to down tools and launch an unprecedented series of wildcat strikes in defiance of German labor law and their own leaders.

These strikes stabbed at the heart of the postwar German order. Germany had seemed immune to the inflation, strikes, and ungovernability afflicting its neighbors. Germany had lost but one-hundredth was many working days as Britain to strikes. But in the current strikes, shop floor radicals were egging workers on to greater demands, and for the first time red flags and anarchist leaflets joined workers' placards and pickets. As the German minister of labor observed, it was "the first time—outside the universities—that [the Federal Republic] had been confronted by the well-organized disruptive efforts of left wing extremists."[6] The reaction by employers was immediate capitulation. The strike in the Ruhr was settled at a rate much higher than the workers' original demands. German industry, fearing lost foreign sales as a result of copycat strikes, quickly responded with payouts of additional bonuses. Wage contracts that still had months to run were ripped up and renegotiated with 11–14 percent wage increases, the highest the Federal Republic had seen to that point.

The revaluation crisis of 1969 transformed the climate of labor relations, which the Bundesbank characterized as a "price-wage spiral." From this point on, union leaders would have to bargain more aggressively to maintain the loyalty of their mass membership. In June 1971, a major strike in one of Germany's leading exporters, the chemical industry, was followed by a major stoppage in the automobile industry, Germany's first since 1963. In both strikes, the rank and file's chief complaint was that previously negotiated contracts were not keeping pace with the rising cost of living. As in 1969, shop floor radicals exploited workers' anxiety about inflation to undermine the authority of the union leadership. The response by IG Metall helped make the automobile strike the bitterest dispute yet seen in the metalworking industry. Furthermore, this stoppage in the auto sector in North Baden–North Württemberg demonstrated that increased rationalization and interdependence in the metalworking sector meant that a strike at even a single key node could rapidly paralyze the entire industry, and, if not resolved in time, could cripple the entire economy. From boardrooms and union halls to editorial pages, talk was of Germany's "English disease," the new militancy, and the threat to German social peace.[7]

Intellectual Mobilization and Internal Bundesbank Conflict, 1971–1973

The next episode of external disequilibrium, which followed in 1971, was, for the first time, a result not of trade flows but of speculation. The year 1971 saw the floating of the DM from May through December, when the Smithsonian Agreement was initialed, punctuated by the closing of the "gold window" by the Americans in August. Following hard on the events of 1969–1971, these currency crises brought into sharp relief the profound differences among leading central bank figures about appropriate remedial action. In the negotiations and disagreements that ensued over the next two years, those in the Bundesbank who favored the monetarist approach of free floating and monetary targeting would find themselves in a distinct minority.

As described in Chapter 2, the Bundesbank shared a widespread belief—held in virtually all corners of German life—that the fixed exchange rate system was sacrosanct. Politically, the Bundesbank's prejudice could be traced to its legal obligation to support the federal government's international agreements as well as its commitment to economic integration in Europe and the West, which was thought to imply fixed exchange rates. Germans had believed since the 1920s that changes in the exchange rate heralded escalating hyperinflation at home, and they could remember the collapse in international trade in the 1930s, when one country after another abandoned gold. While the Bundesbank's hawks were more prepared than most to contemplate revaluation, they did so with the intention of restoring the system to a new equilibrium of fixed parities. Thus, the majority position of the Bundesbank in the early 1970s was more hostile to monetarism than has been recognized, at least insofar as a floating exchange rate was the *sine qua non* of monetarism. Other central banks, including the U.S. Federal Reserve, had been publishing data on monetary aggregates for several decades, but the Bundesbank did not deem it necessary to publish figures on M1 until 1971.[8]

The balance of power among the Bundesbank's leading personnel also reinforced this disposition. Especially significant was the arrival in 1970 of its new president, Karl Klasen, a steadfast opponent of revaluation. By contrast, its new vice president, Otmar Emminger, was a self-described pragmatic monetarist who had always preferred timely revaluations to prevent currency crises. Interestingly, Emminger's doctoral thesis had applauded the British for unfettering sterling from the gold standard in the 1930s. Under the leadership of these two men, the Bundesbank's highest policy bodies split into two distinct viewpoints. While it was theoretical conviction that led Emminger to be the first to publicly oppose Klasen and promote the idea of a float against the dollar in 1970, it was Emminger's secure perch at the head of the Bundesbank's "foreign ministry" that allowed him to take the initiative and persuade the government to disengage the mark from the dollar and launch the Bundesbank's experiment with monetarism in 1973.

Nonetheless, despite Emminger's patronage, monetarist thinking made only slow headway at first. The Bretton Woods taboo demonstrated its ability to block monetarism in the debates concerning the currency crisis of 1971. Speculation in the dollar came to a head May 5th of that year. On that day the Bundesbank's council was asked to advise the cabinet on the choice between floating the mark and imposing capital controls as envisioned in article 23 of the foreign trade law. Klasen spoke vigorously in favor of capital controls while Emminger advocated a float. Klasen carried the council 11 votes to 7.[9] In the event, however, the economics minister, Karl Schiller, persuaded his cabinet colleagues to ignore the Bundesbank's recommendation and temporarily suspend dollar convertibility. Schiller, a Keynesian with a pronounced sympathy for the free market, saw this not as a permanent solution to the currency crisis but rather as a heuristic device. A float could also allow the mark to ride out the market turmoil until the parity system could be rejoined.[10] Schiller felt that any more permanent float would threaten both the power of the government and international economic stability. Paradoxically, for the time being at least, Schiller's inclinations postponed the Bundesbank's flirtation with dirigisme.

While it did not yet translate into policy, the vote delineated the Bundesbank's internal cleavages in no uncertain terms and signalled a significant erosion of its traditional commitment to international liberalization. An official of the U.S. Treasury, Robert Solomon, would recall being "deeply impressed then by a comment of a German friend who said to me that if his country started down the road of using foreign exchange controls, German 'thoroughness' would assert itself. Those aging Germans who had carried out Schachtian policies in the 1930s would 'come out of the woodwork,' and the result might be an excessive and highly undesirable shift in Germany's basic stance away from freedom of international transactions."[11] Thus Klasen's ability to secure a majority for this reversal requires some explanation. Part of the explanation has to do with personal leadership. Klasen, although formerly with the Land central bank in Hamburg, had more recently been with the Deutsche Bank, and this implied a strong commitment to fixed exchange rates. Moreover, he was a lawyer by training, with a lawyer's predisposition toward legalistic solutions to public policy problems. Klasen put great stock in Germany's legal obligations under Bretton Woods and in the efficacy of government regulation. He also feared that a float would probably lead to revaluation, with unfortunate consequences for output and employment that he was not prepared to accept.

On the other side of the issue, many of the Bundesbank's anti-inflation hawks were not yet full-fledged monetarists and did not have the commitment to free markets that monetarism implies. Many of these hawks were most fundamentally predisposed toward *Herrschaft,* or control.[12] In the early 1970s, some of them still believed that regulatory mechanisms were acceptable in the war against inflation. One of Emminger's staunchest allies at the time dismissed monetarist analysis as "archaic quantity thinking," an attitude that pushed some of Germany's rising young monetarists to leave the Bundesbank's research staff and to take up university positions; at least one of them would later join the monetarist Shadow European Economic Policy Committee.[13] In other words, alienated and subsequently politicized monetarists were a real possibility in Germany—as was later also true in the United States. Third, there was the question of European integration. The European Community had recently decided to bring its members' currencies into closer alignment, and the Bundesbank's council, overwhelmingly integrationist, feared German isolation.

The relative success of this first floating experience did little to promote the Friedmanite position advanced by Emminger. With the resumption of fixed parities after the Washington agreement of December, the float of 1971 revealed that the independence of the Bundesbank existed in a kind of legal limbo, which influenced politics within its council. As noted in Chapter 2, the *duration* of floating raised the question of who controlled monetary policy if it was the government's intention to reestablish a fixed exchange rate in the future. Here again, the principal line of cleavage was between the majority faction, which deferred to the finance ministry, and the minority, which saw even a transitory float as falling completely under the purview of the central bank. Thus if 1971 established a precedent for the post-1973 period, it was an ambiguous one. Floating, if anything, might secure the Bundesbank's independence from Washington only to subordinate it to Bonn.

Another explanation for the susceptibility of the Bundesbank to the dirigiste approach was the fact that monetarist theory in its modern guise was a late arrival in Germany. In part, this was a reflection of what German monetarists considered traditionalism and a lack of sophistication on the part of the country's economists. Although certain individuals within the Bundesbank had taken an interest in monetarist debates for some time, the first concrete interest in the practicalities of monetary targeting in Germany came when Karl Brunner initiated the Konstanzer Seminar on Monetary Policy in June 1970. In attendance were two of Emminger's allies, Helmut Schlesigner and Heinrich Irmler.[14] This seminar, funded in part by the Deutsche Girozentrale–Deutsche Kommunalbank, and later the Sparkassen Verband, was intended to introduce the latest American monetarist theorizing into European academic and policy discussions. These conferences were kept relatively small, with some fifty participants on average. Unlike the American or European Shadow Open Market Committees, which Brunner would later help organize, the Konstanzer Seminar was not intended to become a public interest group. The organizers hoped that running the proceedings on nondeferential ("American") norms and inviting younger scholars would challenge the complacent assumption that fixed exchange rates and interest-rate targeting were the *ultimo ratio* of monetary policy. Although the participants were not guaranteed publication, in fact the results of these initial meetings appeared in the German journal *Kredit und Kapital.* This set off a debate over monetary policy, much of which took place in that publication.

The early support for the Konstanzer Seminar from the Sparkassen and the credit cooperatives was not the typical response of German finance and industry to monetarism. Far sooner than Germany's big commercial banks, the savings institutions discovered they had a vested interest in the anti-inflationary prescriptions of the monetarists. The savings institutions worried that increased inflation would erode the German public's propensity to save, and thus their critical deposit base. While other sectors of finance or industry would later advocate a return to controlling interest rates, or more tolerance for growth and jobs, the Sparkassen under the leadership of Helmut Geiger became the staunchest advocates of a strict monetarist course for the Bundesbank during the 1970s. Yet at the same time, the Sparkassen knew of the Bundesbank's traditional preference for fixed exchange rates. They did not want to put themselves on the wrong side of the Bundesbank, toward which they felt very vulnerable. The fact that savings accounts were subject to smaller reserve requirements than transactions accounts made them wary of a politically motivated administrative standardization of reserves for all types of account balances. By the same logic, the Sparkassen became the arms-length financial backer of the Sparschutz Gemeinschaft (Association for the Protection of German Savers).[15]

The support of the Sparkassen as a constituency for Bundesbank monetarism can be seen by considering the case of German industry as represented by the Bundesverband Deutschen Industrie (BDI), the federal association of German industrialists. By 1971 it was clear to some of the staff of the BDI that fixed exchange rates needed to be reexamined. Thus in 1970 they began to study the ideas of Friedman—quite independently, according to former senior officials, of the Konstanzer Seminar. The principal conclusion of this internal investigation was that while it remained the case that industry made substantial profits from fixed exchange rates, industrialists were drawing a false conclusion from the premise—that they would do worse under an alternative arrangement. As a result of this study, the research staff of the BDI favored a complete free float combined with monetary targeting by the Bundesbank. But this view was never made public. Given the traditional commitment of the BDI to the stability of the Bretton Woods system, a wholesale repudiation of fixed exchange rates was difficult to swallow. The special working group on Friedman's ideas within the BDI was only able to persuade senior officials to adopt an official position favoring a "crawling peg." This episode thus revealed how much German monetarism would have to rely upon other, more domestically oriented interests to make headway in the German policy community.[16]

1972–1973: The Dirigiste Temptation

The resignation of Karl Schiller in June 1972 was the next watershed in the crisis leading to German monetary targeting. Schiller's policies as economics minister (and later as "superminister") largely dovetailed with those of officials in the Bundesbank who preferred both financial liberalization and the preservation of fixed exchange rates. Although fearful of the depressive effect of revaluations, Schiller was prepared to endorse them when necessary. His departure would pave the way for a more intense flirtation by both government and central bank with the dirigiste approach he had so staunchly opposed. This clash of perspectives produced a political crisis in the late spring of 1972, when the sudden weakness of the pound sterling triggered strong speculation in the deutsche mark. A cabinet meeting in June 1972 reprised the showdown in 1971 between Schiller and Bundesbank president Klasen. Klasen, supported by a majority vote of the Bundesbank council, advocated a 100 percent reserve requirement for foreign currency in German bank accounts *(Bardepot)* and invoking the controversial (because dirigiste) paragraph 23 of the foreign trade law. By contrast, Schiller wanted another temporary float against the dollar, ideally in conjunction with the French, but by Germany alone if necessary. During the cabinet discussions, both men bolstered their proposals by threatening to resign. By the end of the meeting, the dirigiste measures had won overwhelmingly, and within a week Schiller's resignation had been accepted. It was a stunning and unexpected blow to one of the most powerful politicians in Bonn—a man who, since his handling of the recession of 1966–1967, had been the veritable czar of economic policy in Germany. It is also highly unusual in the annals of national politics in any country that a senior politician should be forced to resign over a policy disagreement with a central bank. The myth of the Bundesbank's political omnipotence may fairly be said to begin with this victory.[17]

Nonetheless, Schiller's resignation was by no means a straightforward victory of a monetarist central bank over a free-spending Keynesian politician. Nor was it testimony to any high regard for the Bundesbank in the public eye. While it was certainly true that the cabinet would not have enjoyed going to the voters in that election year with a public fight with the Bundesbank on its hands, the real significance of Schiller's defeat lay elsewhere. Schiller's dispute with Klasen was in reality not the cause but the opportunity for his departure. Schiller was perhaps Germany's last true Keynesian. He followed the Cambridge school's original doctrines, which prescribed running deficits only during recession and at all other times a balanced budget or even a surplus. But the rest of his government and the SPD's rank and file were growing impatient with this hardheaded approach. Schiller's refusal for reasons of financial orthodoxy to fund their pet projects, as well as his haughty and imperious manner, earned him more and more hostility among his colleagues.[18]

Perhaps most important was the question of the coming federal elections. Schiller's replacement as finance minister was Helmut Schmidt. Klasen and Schmidt were both from Hamburg, and they were old allies and close friends who addressed each other with the intimate *du*. Schmidt was known for the slogan "5 percent inflation is better than 5 percent unemployment," pronounced while he was defense minister. In settling upon Schmidt to replace Schiller, Brandt chose a politician who understood full well that the effect of floating on unemployment could hurt the government's standing with the voters. Schmidt's memoirs suggest clearly that almost immediately after he took over the finance ministry in July, the approaching federal elections were decisive in his preference for shirking a float that might produce undesirable results:

> In July 1972 I flew back to Bonn [from Washington] knowing only too clearly that we too were facing national elections in the fall. Until then there was little we could do about the massive rush of speculative dollars from the whole world on the German mark . . . other than to use government control of foreign currencies to expand the money market supply with marks and consequently defend ourselves against a worsening of our inflation rate as best we could.[19]

Indeed, with Brandt's subsequent campaign on a platform of growth and full employment, it quickly became apparent that Schiller's defeat marked a sea change in German fiscal policy, with profound implications for overall economic policy. Germany's public authorities had successfully balanced their budgets for most of the years since the founding of the Federal Republic. After Schiller's defeat, the government's books would be continually in the red. Ironically, Schiller's ouster represented a defeat for cabinet control over countercyclical policy. Klasen's proposals, having successfully shifted the responsibility for countercyclical policy to the Bundesbank, unchained fiscal policy from its last remaining anchor. Schiller, now banished to the political wilderness, was bitter in his opposition to his former party's fiscal laxity—indeed, in the subsequent federal elections it almost seemed that he was campaigning on behalf of the opposition. Ironically, ten years later, when the Bundesbank rediscovered the virtues of fiscal responsibility, its target would be none other than Helmut Schmidt.

Nonetheless, Klasen's recommendation to Bonn had won majority backing within the Bundesbank's council. The implementation of the dirigiste measures of June 1972 was another major setback for the bank's long-standing policy of financial liberalization. Foreign trade was instantly made more burdensome, creating serious complications for German industry. The Bundesbank even became embroiled in a major court case involving German exporters. Three factors explain this reversal on the part of the wider leadership of the Bundesbank. First, there was a desire to defend the new parities of the Smithsonian Agreement, which German negotiators had taken great pains to achieve. Second, it was not clear that the crisis in sterling warranted a more drastic response. Third, in May 1972, the EEC's Council of Ministers had decided to advance European monetary union. This meeting, in which Bundesbank directors had been leaders, envisioned both an eventual block float of the member currencies and a harmonization—not to say standardization—of the legal powers of the central banks. As Germany's major partner central banks were more dirigiste than the Bundesbank, there seemed a certain logic to making Germany conform to European practice. There was thus a consensus against a go-it-alone approach on the part of Germany. When France indicated that it was not ready to float, the Bundesbank again recommended capital controls, *faute de mieux*.

Yet as international and domestic turmoil continued, the dirigiste approach took on a life of its own. Both the consensus concerning European monetary integration and the defeat of Schiller became part of a new power alignment which linked Klasen's wing within the Bundesbank to Schmidt's finance ministry. This constellation of forces began to draw the Bundesbank into the orbit of the government. In almost perfect fulfillment of Robert Solomon's prophecy, the centerpiece of this alliance was a proposed new Bundesbank law which would give the central bank sweeping dirigiste powers that no German central bank had possessed since the abolition of the Reichsbank. In September 1972, Schmidt's finance ministry organized a high-level governmental meeting to which representatives of the chancellor's office, the foreign ministry, the Bundesbank, and the economics ministry were invited. The principal purpose was to consider a major legislative renovation of the Bundesbank's powers and responsibilities. With a future European currency union in mind, the conferees imagined that some weak member currencies would trigger into the mark the kind of speculative deluge that had recently been stimulated by the dollar. Thus, it was felt on all sides that the Bundesbank needed to be better equipped to deal with disruptive currency movements, especially as it was quite likely that the dollar itself would continue to prove troublesome for the foreseeable future. In the autumn of 1972, the finance ministry asked for and received from the Bundesbank a draft revision of the Bundesbank law.

The Bundesbank's proposed amendments had two key provisions: general administrative credit ceilings *(Kreditplafondierung)* and an activist minimum-reserve policy *(Aktivzuwachsreserve)*, which would have imposed higher reserve requirements on increases in credit for particular purposes. In addition to erecting barriers against disruptive currency speculation, it was thought that these measures would enhance the domestic steering capacity (or as commentators like to put it, "shorten the braking path,") of the Bundesbank, so that anticyclical policy would work more efficiently. These new provisions were to be softened by allowing the Bundesbank to grant selective exemptions. In addition, the reach of all Bundesbank measures was to be greatly extended. The new legislation contemplated requiring reserves not only from banks but also from a wide range of nonbank institutions including insurance companies and construction firms; even such quasi-public agencies as the Employment Office were to be subjected to the Bundesbank's new powers.

When Helmut Schmidt announced his ministry's intention to enhance the Bundesbank law at the beginning of 1973, private opposition among bankers and industry officials was intense. However, the commercial banks' desire to defend the exchange rate system and the specific deference of the Sparkassen to the Bundesbank muted public criticism.[20] Initially, the main objection was to the extraordinary degree of intervention in the economy these new measures represented. The most energetic and efficient banks and firms—perhaps most especially the Sparkassen—were those most likely to be hurt by the new regulations. The cost of credit in general would go up, and international trade, the lifeblood of the German economy, would suffer. The banks also feared continuing growth in the "gray market" for credit, which was colloquially referred to as the "Industrie Clearing" phenomenon. Ever since the regulations of 1972 were imposed, it had become apparent that industry was looking for easier and cheaper credit outside the banking system. Firms such as Metallgesellschaft and Degussa were thought to be using their vast monetary resources (which were not subject to reserve requirements) to make loans to other firms. The banks believed that more regulation by the Bundesbank would accelerate this trend. More alarming still was the provision for selective exemptions. Bankers and industrialists quickly discerned that this threatened the kind of "structural policy" practiced by the statist Banque de France. Given that the Bundesbank was formally unaccountable to the government, industrialists asked, who would determine the exemptions, and by what criteria? The risk of bureaucratization and politicization seemed enormous. As *Wirtschaftswoche* editorialized ruefully in February 1973, "More power for the Bundesbank is by no means the same as more price stability."[21] But from the point of view of the banks, the Bundesbank's departure from the path of free-market economics was not as bad as it was to get. As the inflation crisis worsened over 1973 and 1974, the bank's apostasy risked becoming a full Schachtian conversion.

Corporate Culture to the Rescue: The Bundesbank "Palace Revolt" of 1973

In the first quarter of 1973, the fixed exchange rate system lurched into its final crisis. American dollars subject to price controls at home began seeking a safe haven abroad. At the same time as the power alignment between Bundesbank president Klasen and finance minister Schmidt pursued the dirigiste option, rebellion was fermenting within the upper reaches of the Bundesbank. Speculation in the currency markets brought German decision makers—divided with regard to monetary philosophy—to their own final crisis. In the end, what mattered was that the intervening months of inflation's impact on currency markets, unsettled labor relations, and (very important, in Emminger's mind) the erosion of the savings climate, helped tip the balance of power within the Bundesbank council toward Emminger's perspective. Strengthened in particular by support from the presidents of the Land central banks, Emminger was able to seize the initiative and impress on chancellor Brandt the option of floating the mark.

The precise timing of the switch to floating was decided partly by growing turmoil in the international markets and partly by unanticipated developments in the Bundesbank's power alignments. The worsening American trade balance had led to increasing speculation that the strong European currencies would be revalued. When weakness in the Italian lira led the Swiss to block all speculation in the franc, the DM became the principal target of speculation against the dollar. With the new Bundesbank law not yet in place, Bonn's existing measures to stem the inflow proved ineffectual. Thus in February of 1973 alone, the Smithsonian Agreement required the Bundesbank to create an additional 24 billion DM.

In the first of weeks of February, a series of heated discussions erupted again within the Bundesbank and with the federal cabinet about how best to proceed. The Bundesbank, however, was represented not by Klasen, who was being operated on in the hospital, but rather by his vice president, Emminger. Emminger argued energetically for a temporary suspension of dollar purchases. He was opposed once again by the finance minister, Schmidt. Quite apart from his concerns about the now successfully won elections, Schmidt opposed any kind of floating on philosophical grounds.[22] As Emminger points out in his memoirs, Schmidt had given a "sensational" interview to the London *Times* only two weeks earlier, in which he suggested that inflation was more tolerable than the uncertainty of floating. The first, inconclusive meeting of the Bundesbank and the cabinet was followed by another on February 8th, during which the ailing Klasen's views were invoked *in absentia*. In response to Emminger's recommendations, Schmidt apparently asked, "But is your president of the same opinion as you?" to which Emminger replied that his president was in the hospital and he hadn't inquired; besides, Emminger indicated that he now had the clear majority of the Bundesbank council on his side. Schmidt's rejoinder was that he had asked Klasen for his views, (subsequently confirmed by Emminger's own inquiries) and he reported Klasen's opinion that Germany should continue to support the dollar and disregard the inflationary consequences.[23]

When the February 8th meeting again provided no effective remedy against speculation in the mark, Emminger and his key supporters decided to take matters into their own hands. Aided by his ally Helmut Schlesinger, who had been appointed to the Bundesbank council only the year before, Emminger prepared a lengthy statement analyzing the problems with the current monetary situation, which was signed by Emminger and Schlesinger on behalf of the directorate. The statement concluded by saying that the Bundesbank could no longer "accept responsibility" for the inflationary consequences of the government's refusal to float the mark against the dollar. Although an unexpected "Volcker devaluation" on February 12 preempted the release of this statement to the public, the evident implication is that the Bundesbank's directorate was prepared to resign *en masse*.[24]

The parities established by Volcker's February shuttle diplomacy proved even less resilient than those they replaced. The immediate trigger of their collapse was not so much economic data as rumors of political developments. Specifically, a visit to Bonn by prime minister Heath of

Great Britain raised speculation that a joint European float was imminent. On March 1, the most turbulent day yet of speculation against the dollar, the Bundesbank's defense of the dollar forced it to purchase an unprecedented $2.75 billion, equivalent to a one-day infusion of 8 billion DM into the German economy.[25] The likelihood that this onslaught of dollars would give another violent twist to Germany's domestic price-wage spiral led Emminger, still in temporary command of the Bundesbank, to request that government close the currency markets. Although German inflation as measured by consumer prices was still relatively low, at least one measure of the money stock was increasing at an unprecedented 28 percent (annualized rate) in the first quarter of 1973.[26] Industry and banks swam in money. Germany was experiencing an "escape into concrete money." Perhaps most important for Emminger and his allies in the Land central banks was that this monetary "escape" (including growing speculation in the real estate and housing markets) threatened to destroy the German public's famous postwar propensity to save, which Emminger for one regarded as the foundation of the Federal Republic's prosperity and stability. For the presidents of the Land central banks who knew all too well what this meant for the Land-owned Sparkassen, this was inevitably a compelling concern. Moreover, shortages were developing in commodities of all kinds, and industry was bidding up wages to limit a repetition of the wildcat strikes of 1969.[27]

Once again Emminger made the pilgrimage to Bonn to request that the Bundesbank be released from its obligation to defend the exchange rate. Now, however, fortune helped Emminger win the argument in the chancellor's villa. By sheer coincidence, not only was Klasen in his sickbed, but Schmidt had been hospitalized also. Moreover, Schmidt's *Staatssekretär* in the finance ministry, Karl-Otto Pöhl, was on a skiing trip and could not be summoned in time. In fact, the only senior cabinet minister in attendance was Hans Friderichs, head of the traditionally more free-market economics ministry, and who as a member of the FDP was very sympathetic to the positions taken by Emminger. With neither of the two leading proponents of fixed exchange rates in attendance, Emminger had little trouble persuading Brandt that Germany should no longer try to defend them. In giving the Bundesbank a green light to suspend purchases of dollars, Brandt apparently remarked, "If the Economics Ministry and the Bundesbank are of the same opinion, then it is probably right."[28]

With this fait accompli, all that remained was to determine the details of the float against the dollar. Schmidt returned from the hospital and acquiesced in the decision that had been made. He pressed the French to join the Germans in a common float but threatened to lead Germany in an independent float if necessary. Nonetheless, he was prepared to let the

French ride out elections scheduled for March 18th. Thus on March 19th, the markets reopened; a new system of European parities, the so-called "snake," went into effect; and the Bundesbank was freed from its obligation to intervene in the dollar market. With its most vulnerable international flank protected for the forseeable future, the Bundesbank could now move immediately against the growing forces of domestic inflation.

THE BEGINNINGS OF THE MONETARIST "EXPERIMENT"

From March 1973 to the end of 1974 the Bundesbank fought a nip-and-tuck battle to bring the German money supply back into line with its internal targets. In so doing, it discovered that controlling money was not merely a matter of controlling unwanted international influences; now there were domestic obstacles to confront, powerful interests that wanted more money, not less. Thus, the Bundesbank's experiment with monetarism proceeded in two distinct stages, each shaped by its need to stabilize one of the major social interests in its policy environment. The first stage stabilized Germany's banks; the second stage stabilized the unions. The interaction of the central bank with these two crucial actors in its policy environment produced a version of monetarism that not only reflected the ideas of academic monetarists but also contained a distinct legacy of Keynesianism. So constructed, Bundesbank monetarism became an instrument for the academically negotiated stabilization of two profoundly different social interests.

The First Phase of the Monetarist Experiment: Stabilizing the Banks

Even before the reopening of the currency markets on March 19, 1973, the Bundesbank began to institute what it called the postwar era's "most determined attempt at stabilization" through the implementation of "highly restrictive" monetary policy that began the moment the markets closed.[29] Despite a speculative first-quarter surge in money creation, bank lending would prove to be 10 percent less for 1973 than for 1972. By putting a "total stop" to the creation of new money for the rest of the year, the Bundesbank's main measure of the money supply (CBM) increased only 8 percent compared with 14 percent in 1972; M2 grew by 14 percent (versus 17 percent); and M1 grew by 2 percent (versus 14 percent). But this relative success was not apparent at first. And although the universal banks became the chief instruments in the Bundesbank's struggle against inflation, they were its first opponents, and their resistance gave shape to the Bundesbank's monetarism.

Prior to March 1973, the traditional relationship between the central bank and the universal banks had been based on so-called free liquid reserves. Free liquid reserves were the sum of banks' excess reserves, un-used rediscount quotas, and money market paper. Under this system the commercial banks had often held a strong hand in the money-creation process, even when the system was working as the Bundesbank desired. In normal circumstances, the universal banks liked to keep a fixed propor-tion of these reserves unutilized as a safety margin in their transactions with the central bank. By manipulating its side of the ledger, the Bundes-bank could signal the direction of its desired policies to the banks, which would expand or contract their lending to restore their preferred ratio. The Bundesbank primarily used regulatory mechanisms such as changes in minimum reserve requirements or changes to the discount and Lom-bard rates to influence the free liquid reserves. Open-market policy was used only lightly, and then in conjunction with changes in one or the other of the administered prices. This regulatory character of the Bundesbank's policy instruments made them cumbersome to use. Some measures entailed excessive announcement effects, while other required full meetings of the council for their authorization. Consequently, changes in free liquid reserves would sometimes arrive too late, or they would oversteer the market. In periods of expansion or contraction, this unwieldiness became an endogenous procyclical variable. Manfred Willms and other monetarists argued that at least in the short run, the dominant impulse in the creation of free liquid reserves lay with commer-cial banks' lending, not Bundesbank policies.

By 1972, this unwieldy though crudely effective control procedure no longer worked. The rapid development of the Eurodollar markets awak-ened a new, more aggressive approach among German banks. Access to the vast reserves of dollars in international currency markets meant that they no longer needed to rely exclusively on their free liquid reserves in making loan decisions. This new relationship was not really discovered until the Bundesbank attempted to reduce free liquid reserves in 1972. Contrary to the wishes of the monetary authorities, bank lending actually increased.[30] Yet this response was not simply a matter of choice for Ger-many's banks. Unregulated bank deposit rates left them exposed to de-positors' declining confidence as inflation accelerated. Tightening spreads on interest rates pushed the banks to compete harder for assets. In such circumstances, banks with access to the London money markets could no longer afford to let free liquid reserves sit idle. The Bundes-bank's studies showed that all of the increase in the German money sup-ply (such as the 14.5 percent increase in M1 in 1972) were due *entirely* to the importation of foreign currency.[31]

The events of March 1973 allowed the Bundesbank to change not only the content but also the form of its relations with the universal banks. With dollars no longer automatic D-Marks, the Bundesbank would once again call the tune for the banks—but now with even greater effectiveness. Free liquid reserves were virtually eliminated, and with them the excessive reliance on the unwieldy administrative price measures. The Bundesbank raised reserve ratios and reduced rediscount quotas, and it let the banks' desperate scramble for reserve balances push interest rates to unprecedented heights. There were painful moments for the banks as interest rates on the newly important market for overnight money *(Tagesgeld)* reached as high as 40 percent after the Lombard rate was suspended in May but before the Bundesbank introduced a cap of 13 percent (a so-called special Lombard rate which the Bundesbank could vary on a daily basis).

The intellectual foundations of the new strategy of monetary control elicited considerable controversy among policy analysts outside the central bank. Replacing free liquid reserves as the central concept of the Bundesbank's new policy was a home-made aggregate called *Zentralbankgeldmenge* (variously translated into English as central bank money and central bank money stock—hereafter, CBM). The Bundesbank defined CBM as currency in circulation plus the reserve requirements of banks' domestic liabilities adjusted at constant reserve ratios as of February 1973 (subsequently January 1974), weighted to reflect the degree of "moneyness" of the different categories of deposits.[32] In fact, although many alternative aggregates had been analyzed in the scholarly literature up to that point, the Bundesbank's choice of CBM came out of the blue. Quite apart from CBM's lack of an intellectual pedigree, monetarists objected that it fulfilled neither of the two functions required of a proper monetary aggregate. First, CBM was not an intermediate (target) aggregate comparable to Friedman's various M aggregates. Second, and much more important for a pure monetarist procedure, CBM was not a control variable like the monetary base in the Brunner-Meltzer theorem, though it was often confused with the monetary base. The crucial difference was that CBM was constructed from the member banks' balance sheets, not the Bundesbank's. Monetarists argued that had the Bundesbank controlled the monetary base instead of CBM, the Bundesbank would have achieved much more precise control of the money supply and less inflation.

Bundesbank officials conceded that such control was not a characteristic of CBM but noted that there were good reasons for this. First, the Bundesbank claimed that CBM had an advantage over the monetary base because CBM paralleled the development of nominal GNP on a one-to-one basis. In this respect, it was similar to the broad indicator M3. The Bundesbank also felt that CBM underlined the Bundesbank's unique responsibility for monetary policy. Second, CBM changed "mark by mark" according to the central bank's foreign exchange transactions, and it was directly influenced by open-market operations and the size of the central bank's transactions with banks. CBM was more rapidly and more easily measured, with statistics available to the Bundesbank daily (for currency) or weekly (for reserves). Third, since all public authorities are required to keep their balances with the central bank, CBM increases as these decrease, providing a direct statistical link with government fiscal policy, which Bundesbank officials considered to be highly important. Formulated in this way, CBM acted as a bridge from nominal GNP to government fiscal policy. The Bundesbank was thereby allowed to monitor fiscal policy through a device that dovetailed with the government's own financial practices, and it offered the Bundesbank an avenue for future arm's-length influence on fiscal policy.[33]

In the final analysis, however, the Bundesbank's failure to control the monetary base lay with the legal and political foundations of its tutelage of the universal banking system. Under existing legislation, the Bundesbank's power over lending by private banks rested on the legal obligation of banks to fulfill reserve requirements, which the central bank manipulates by way of liquidity squeezes. By legal definition, and as a practical matter, this occurs post facto, not ex ante. Moreover, the banks are collectively, not individually, in debt to the monetary authorities, a fact reflected in the existence of the interbank market for reserve balances. Squeezing liquidity by the central bank's restrictive policy catches some banks short (for the monthly reserve settlements) in a process that is not unlike a game of musical chairs:

> Just who it is [that fails to meet reserve obligations] may have little to do with the business policies of the banks concerned. Under such conditions the sanctions for non-compliance with reserve requirements can hardly be applied with an easy conscience. But whether they are applied or not, the minimum reserve regulations rapidly lose their binding character if such situations become the rule. . . . The money monopoly of the central bank is not a monopoly to initiate money creation processes, nor does it empower the central bank to impose sanctions with which it could tolerate or nullify money creation that is already in progress.[34]

Formally, the ultimate sanction for banks that fail to meet their reserve requirements (i.e., are in default to the central bank) is bankruptcy. But this was a sanction that the Bundesbank simply could not contemplate for banks as enormous as Germany's universal banks. What the central bank could do, however, was honor the banks' money-creation process at penalty rates that would discourage them from deviating from the Bundesbank's desired growth path for money. Thus under the new procedures, as under the old, the central bank was still very dependent on the banks for cooperation even as it was bringing them to heel.

A further important consequence of the banking system's universal character was that it confined the costs of the Bundesbank's tightening predominantly within the banking sector itself, with less collateral damage to the nonfinancial sector. The lower level of regulatory differentiation among banking sectors meant that the Bundesbank could tighten the reins more sharply without the risk of prematurely illiquid banks. Although the streets of Frankfurt were rife with rumors of impending failures, the absence of American-style portfolio regulations allowed all affected banking sectors to make whatever adjustments they deemed necessary to cope with the stringency of the Bundesbank's tight-money policy. Only a few small specialist banks were ever jeopardized.[35]

In similar fashion, Germany's universal banking system limited overexposure of individual banks to weak sectors of industry. Even the savings bank sector was only partially implicated in the overheated real estate market and the construction industry. Nonetheless, one notable example of a bank that was put at risk—Hessische Landesbank—illustrates the problem which the Bundesbank sought to forestall. Hessische Landesbank (Helaba) was a regional savings bank whose conduct seemed to herald an erosion of the traditional orientation of the Sparkassen toward domestic stability. Helaba was managed in the early 1970s by the recently appointed Wilhelm Hankel, one of West Germany's leading neo-Keynesian economists and a former advisor to the SPD government on monetary policy affairs. In the Bundesbank's eyes, Helaba's management represented a dangerous new trend, operating according to explicit Keynesian assumptions that the Bundesbank could not or would not control inflation or the money supply. Hankel, rejecting warnings that his bank's aggressive use of state debt to finance construction development was fueling inflation, revealed his intellectual orientation when he characterized such arguments as a "relapse into naive quantity theory."[36] Despite the warnings and higher interest rates, Hankel ignored the Bundesbank's restrictive policy throughout most of 1973 until Helaba began to slide toward bankruptcy in December. The denouement of this affair illustrates the close political links between the savings institutions and the Bundesbank's Land central banks. Though technically insolvent, Helaba was simply too politically important to be forced into receivership, and so the Bundesbank engineered sweeping changes in its senior management, including the ouster of Hankel and his replacement by Leopold Broeker, who had been president of the Bundesbank's Land central bank in Hesse.[37] By contrast, Herstatt, a commercial bank in Frankfurt that was too heavily involved in foreign exchange transactions for the Bundesbank's liking was allowed to go under.

But in the spring of 1973, the certainty that the Bundesbank would control the banks' money-creation process lay far in the future. Bankers could not gauge the Bundesbank's credibility because they did not know whether or when this float, like its predecessors, would eventually be replaced by new fixed parities. In fact, the formal changes to the IMF treaty legalizing the float against the dollar were not signed for several more years. In addition, governmental authorities continued to conduct fiscal policy as if nothing had changed. Thus, the Bundesbank's restrictions were at first anything but a tour de force. In April and May, the unions went public with their warnings that inflation was exacerbating the militancy of their members. Not until May did the federal government belatedly bring its fiscal policy into alignment with the Bundesbank's restrictive stance. A federal "stability loan" of 2.5 billion DM was deposited with the Bundesbank to be neutralized. Bonn also imposed a 10 percent stability surtax, reduced its outlays by 700 million DM, and together with other restrictive measures absorbed something on the order of 9 billion DM in excess liquidity.[38] But even these measures seemed insufficient to stop inflation's upward climb. As inflation increased, IG Metall once again found itself with wildcat strikes on its hands. Scholars and editorialists began writing of the "powerlessness" of the Bundesbank.[39] Bundesbankers themselves judged this phase of the monetarist experiment inconclusive at best.

Against this backdrop of the Bundesbank's apparent helplessness the finance ministry disclosed its final draft of revisions to the Bundesbank law in August, 1973. The contents caused widespread shock in financial circles, not least among Bundesbank officialdom. In addition to the Bundesbank's original proposals for dirigiste control over bank lending, the finance ministry had unexpectedly added a "two-key" control provision. As the bill envisioned the new measures, the Bundesbank would be able to use them only with prior approval from the finance minister. While the finance ministry downplayed the amendment as innocuous, bankers feared that the second key would be only the thin edge of the wedge leading to a loss of independence for the Bundesbank and increased state control over the commercial banks themselves. They feared that over time, the initiative for these measures and perhaps even ordinary policy moves would pass into the hands of the finance ministry. While proposals to end the Bundesbank's autonomy are not infrequently heard from special interests, this proposal was the first of its kind by a government of the Federal Republic. As such, it was the most direct assault ever seen on the legal basis of the Bundesbank's autonomy, and it came at a time when the Bundesbank was most vulnerable. As one commentator observed, by trying to win more power for itself, the Bundesbank had laid a "cuckoo's egg" in its own nest.

Perhaps even more astonishing was that political momentum for these changes continued to build. Klasen and his supporters on the council remained undeterred, even as others in the governing party proposed that the stability mandate of the Bundesbank be watered down. Klasen was quoted in a prounion newspaper as saying that the "primary responsibility" of the Bundesbank was to support government policy. Germany's economics minister, Hans Friderichs of the FDP, traveled to Frankfurt to dissuade the Bundesbank majority from its official support, but without success. At last, the private commercial banks had a compelling reason to acquiesce in the Bundesbank's monetarist programme: if it failed, legislative victory for the finance ministry's reforms would be assured. In the summer and fall of 1973, all the banking associations stridently professed their support for the high money market rates that were driving their members ever closer to the financial cliff. Only when Friderichs declared his party's opposition to the measure, threatening a split in the governing coalition, was some of the wind taken out of the dirigistes' sails.

Monetarism, Phase Two: Stabilizing Labor

Economic developments in 1974 moved the Bundesbank's struggle to regain control of the money supply onto a new battlefield. In that year, the Bundesbank discovered that it is one thing to reassert control over the banks but quite another to extend that control to the nonfinancial economy. In this latter effort, the central bank ran afoul of another powerful social actor—the union movement—with altogether different priorities. This was to some degree inevitable. As noted in Chapter 2, wage costs are the largest single component of the general price level. If the Bundesbank could stabilize these, it would win a significant battle in the war against inflation. But doing so would entail the widest assault yet on the pecuniary aspirations of ordinary Germans—not to mention that the unions valued their constitutionally guaranteed right to autonomous wage bargaining perhaps even more than the Bundesbank valued its own independence. Therefore the trick for the Bundesbank was to find a means of influencing wage settlements without appearing to do so. Once again, the Bundesbank would tailor its monetarist procedures to this purpose.

Two major events in late 1973 aroused exaggerated expectations of inflation among the general public, which significantly complicated the Bundesbank's stabilization efforts the following year. The first of these was OPEC's quadrupling of oil prices. With wide but mistaken agreement the Council of Experts, the five leading economics institutes, and the OECD conveyed to the public the view that, given Germany's dependence on oil, the Bundesbank would be helpless to stop further price increases, and that inflation would excede 10 percent. This message was passed on by banks to their clients, who continued to raise their own prices and relax their stance with respect to wage bargaining.[40]

Unions were particularly receptive to predictions of continuing expansion. It is true, as Scharpf has argued, that unions, like everyone else, were skeptical about the Bundesbank's powers.[41] But more than that, unions' focus on fiscal policy made the Bundesbank a "blind spot."[42] Unions believed that not monetary policy but the government's taxing and spending programs determined the business cycle and especially the demand for labor. Thus for the unions, expectations raised by OPEC were reinforced by the next major development of the year. To cope with the anticipated recessionary effects of OPEC's price shock the Bonn government immediately relaxed the strict stabilization program it had imposed in May. It increased spending, granted tax concessions, and sped construction orders to help relieve the sudden collapse in the construction industry which the Bundesbank's policy of high interest rates had caused. Despite the rising DM, Germany's exports remained strong, and unemployment averaged only 1.3 percent. Unit labor costs increased 9 percent in the fourth quarter of 1973, compared with only 6 percent in the third quarter. Together, these two major developments—the general underestimation of the Bundesbank's anti-inflation policy and the switch to expansionary policies by the government—inflamed the redistributive struggle in wage negotiations in 1974. In this struggle, the Bundesbank found itself caught in a political no-man's-land.

The conflicting interpretations of the economy became especially significant in 1974, when IG Metall, burned twice by unauthorized strikes by its own members, passed the leadership of the collective bargaining round to ÖTV, the public services union. In 1972 chancellor Brandt had led the SPD to its biggest election victory by promising to safeguard full employment. This meant that government, the nation's largest employer, was now bargaining with ÖTV with its hands tied politically. Nor was the government's backbone stiffened by ÖTV's strikes in garbage collection and other municipal services. These reminded more than a few older Germans of the debilitating strikes by public employees in the twilight of the Weimar Republic. Politics thus led the government to misread the peculiar dynamics of that year's wage negotiations. Earlier, the DGB had taken the unusual step of declaring publicly that an 8 percent settlement was a nonnegotiable demand for the federation as a whole. This action put the ÖTV in a difficult position, because it had already committed itself to a six percent catch-up relative to other unions. Given its lead in the wage round, ÖTV was now bargaining for a previously unheard-of framework settlement: 14 percent. If this were generalized to the entire economy, it would represent an extraordinary increase in unit labor costs, another turn in the price-wage spiral, and enormous redistributive gains against employers. The final step toward a mismatch between wages and monetary policy came when the government accepted ÖTV's demands outright, rather than recognizing, as other employers normally would do, that a first position is never to be taken as a final settlement.[43]

As the federal government took the lead in conceding aggressive wage increases, the Bundesbank and the trade unions increasingly focused their displeasure on each other. Early in 1974, the Bundesbank warned that these wage settlements were "out of tune with the efforts to achieve more domestic stability."[44] In a year in which output was to grow by only half a percentage point, the average increase in workers' earnings reached almost 13 percent. Business earning declined substantially, and bankruptcies increased by over 50 percent. In the Bundesbank's view these factors were combining with higher costs of raw materials to sharply reduce enterprises' willingness to invest. Only continuing demand from abroad for German capital goods was preventing a serious crisis. For their part, the unions rejected both the Bundesbank's policy and its justification. In 1973, many officials in the DGB had recognized the need for some kind of anticyclical policy to cool off a few overheated sectors of the economy, such as the construction industry.[45] But 1974 proved a different matter. Unions now felt that the Bundesbank's tight-money cure was worse than the disease. Focusing too narrowly on price stability, the Bundesbank was maintaining its restrictive policy far too long, so that unemployment climbed significantly, reaching 4.7 percent at year's end, a total of 1 million unemployed workers for the first time since the 1950s. The unions argued that the Bundesbank was deliberately engineering a "reprivitization of employment risk"[46] in violation of government full employment policy. The DGB and IG Metall accused the Bundesbank of "having no social sensitivity," of being "irresponsible," and of "playing with jobs."[47] They objected vehemently to the Bundesbank's apparent meddling in wage bargaining. Reacting to the Bundesbank's characterization of that year's pay-round as a "wage-rate mistake," Hans Mayr of IG Metall would later speak for a broad constituency when he called this a "shocking faux pas on the part of the guardian of the currency."[48] For the unions, the Bundesbank was coming dangerously close to compromising their constitutionally guaranteed right to autonomous wage negotiations.

To avoid future misunderstandings and confrontations the Bundesbank now inaugurated the external component of its monetarist experiment. There were two aspects to this initiative. First, the Bundesbank moved in the latter part of 1974 to lower interest rates—the first time it had done so in almost two years.[49] Second, in December it publicly announced the first in a series of annual targets for monetary growth based on CBM. After extensive consultation and ultimate agreement with the federal government, the Bundesbank's president, Klasen, announced a target of 8 percent for 1975 to help clarify the central bank's intended monetary policy. The Bundesbank's year-end on year-end target of 8 percent was a reprise of the growth achieved in 1973 but was noticeably more expansionary than the 6 percent of 1974. The Bundesbank's strategy was, in Klasen's words, to "gradually ratchet down inflation."[50] Together, these actions heralded a move to head off the looming recession while keeping inflation in check.

The lowering of interest rates and the announcement of targets for monetary growth resulted from extensive and hotly contested negotiations, both between the Bundesbank and the federal government and among the various wings of central bankers themselves. This was first apparent in the decision to lower interest rates. In April 1974, Klasen had publicly suggested that the Bundesbank's task of fighting inflation might be made easier if an official representative of the labor unions sat on the Central Bank Council.[51] While no union official was ever appointed, in the balance of power between anti-inflationary hawks and pro-stimulus doves the doves gained significant reinforcements. In April 1974, Schmidt orchestrated the nomination of a former *Staatssekretär* in the finance ministry, Hans Hermsdorf, for the presidency of the Land central bank in Hamburg. In May 1974, he did the same for the Social Democrat Alfred Härtl, who was appointed LCB president in Hessen. Finally, Schmidt named the prominent Keynesian monetary economist Claus Köhler, formerly of the Council of Experts, to the Bundesbank directorate in October. This shift in factional alignments helped prepare the ground for the negotiations that followed. Klasen, Schmidt, finance minister Apel, Bundesbank directors, and LCB presidents caucused among themselves from mid-September until late October in search of a majority for loosening. Apel was in attendance at the key meeting on the last Thursday in October. After the usual detailed presentations by various directors outlining the current economic situation, he made a plea that, while deferring to the independence of the Bundesbank councilors, framed their pending decision in terms of Germany's constitutional stability. Arguing that recession threatened the "greatest test of democracy since 1930," he asserted that "right-wing and left-wing radicals [were] ready to step in with their own solutions," and that "even the Bundesbank must keep this background in mind when it makes its decisions."[52] When the vote was tallied on three moves to lower interest rates, only a minority of the council was opposed. Simultaneously, Bonn began to implement 14 billion DM in tax credits. The Bundesbank's easing of interest rates beginning in October lowered the Lombard rate from 9 percent to 6.5 percent in the new year, and the discount rate from 7 percent to 5 percent.

This pattern of arm's-length influence and compromise was reflected in the intent and content of the monetary target announced a month

later. In the broadcast sense, the CBM target was self-consciously conceived to "influence the inflationary expectations of the public."[53] Privately, monetary targeting was described by senior Bundesbank officials as
a kind of "disguised incomes policy."[54] The form of this communication—the publicizing of the targets—reflected the Bundesbank's bitter
lessons about its imprudent candor concerning wage settlements. The
year 1974 taught the Bundesbank to exercise its influence more circumspectly. The central bank thus deployed the public target as an "intellectual device with which to pursue consensus with the unions."[55]

Apart from attempting to influence inflationary expectations a priori,
the main avenue by which the Bundesbank sought to articulate a "consensual" variant of monetary targeting was the concept of "unavoidable
inflation." After background consultation with the key Bonn ministries,
the Bundesbank ascertained that in the coming year it could reasonably
expect a 3 percent increase in production potential, an increase of 2 percentage points in the rate of utilization of existing production, a 4 percent "unavoidable" price increase, and a drop of 1 percent due to increased velocity of money circulation. This formula summed to the
announced 8 percent increase in CBM targeted for 1975. Germany's
dyed-in-the-wool monetarists were quick to point out that from their
point of view, "unavoidable inflation" was a misnomer. They argued that
what the Bundesbank was doing was, in fact, *tolerating* that amount of inflation.[56] This was an explicit pragmatic adjustment in the very heart of
the monetarist prescription. It signaled to the unions that the Bundesbank intended to fight inflation while respecting the adjustment capacities of the social partners. By tolerating somewhat less "unavoidable" inflation each year, the Bundesbank hoped to bleed out price increases
over the medium term, rather than all at once. The Bundesbank claimed
that if wage settlements heeded this "monetary cloak"—a big "if," under
the circumstances—inflation could be reduced without sacrificing employment. The Bundesbank officials were saying to the unions, in effect:
In your wage negotiations you can set the wage rate or the unemployment rate; the inflation rate we determine ourselves.

In the event, the Bundesbank's announcement received general endorsement. The main reason for this was that first of all, the target was
part of an antirecessionary package. On the left, Rudiger Pohl of the
union-affiliated WSI research institute endorsed the combination of liquidity expansion and lower interest rates, but he expressed doubts about
targeting.[57] Heinz Rapp, spokesman for the SPD, praised the target, but
he was careful to stress that the process was to be gradual.[58] On the right,
a strongly monetarist report by the Savers' Association endorsed the
adoption of CBM as a target but urged that interest and exchange rates
be left to market forces. All the major research institutes were generally

supportive also. It fit the logic of transparency of concerted action, and something like it had been suggested by the Council of Experts. So well-liked was targeting, in fact, that within the year chancellor Schmidt would try to claim it as his own invention.[59]

The Consolidation of Monetary Corporatism, 1975–1979

The public announcement of monetary targets was the last important plank in what at least some of the Bundesbank's directors were prepared to call a "regime change" in German macroeconomic policy.[60] As of March 1973, the mark was floating freely against the dollar and the Bundesbank had tightened its grip on the creation of CBM. Within two years, the "astonishing" effectiveness of this monetarist experiment had greatly enhanced its stature within the Bundesbank and the public at large. The Bundesbank's president Klasen himself had never thought it possible that the inflation problem would be mastered so quickly.[61] In the winter of 1974 the dirigiste Bundesbank bill was quietly removed from the government's parliamentary order papers.[62] But precisely because this experiment proved a success, the question needs to be asked: in what specific ways did these changes represent a durable or significant transformation in macroeconomic policy in Germany? What lessons had been learned, and by whom? Was the Bundesbank now a monetarist monolith? Were other economic actors monetarists? And what were the consequences of this new monetary targeting regime?

The official Bundesbank interpretation was that its new procedures fulfilled two purposes, one internal, the other external. Internally, CBM was held to be a necessary compass for the bank's independence and for incorporating domestic price stability into its stabilization mandate. Externally, the Bundesbank's targeting was offered as a guideline for other economic decision makers whose deference to this monetary cloak would ensure stable, noninflationary growth over the long term. This interpretation is superficially correct: to a considerable extent, monetary targeting did become a meaningful part of the economic decision-making process, both for the Bundesbank and for the important social actors in its policy environment. This did not operate in the magisterial fashion described by the Bundesbank however, and its fans in the conservative press. Instead, as the following sections will show, monetary targeting represented a transfer to the Bundesbank's council of those elements of negotiation and compromise toward which the universalistic construction of the German political economy had already been moving. These forces turned to the social-scientific proxies of economists and economic data to replace the genuine corporatist consultation of the collapsing Concerted Action. If corporatism typically involves policy negotiations among representatives of government, labor, and capital, then the consequence of the Bundesbank's successful experiment with monetarism was to create a de facto monetary corporatism in which monetarists and neo-Keynesians, internationalist doves and domestic hawks hammered out the contours of medium-term economic strategy for Germany.

Although monetary corporatism might suggest an equal balance among the economic theories represented in the council, it should not be taken too far. Monetarists held the dominant position in this dialogue simply because recent political events had demonstrated that money alone—not memories of hyperinflation or norms of social solidarity—influenced the decisions of economic agents, and that this in turn mattered for social and political conflict. In the diagnosis of Wilhelm Gaddum, an economist who would later by appointed to the Bundesbank's council, "It is characteristic that an increase in social conflict parallels an increase in inflation. Only in organized [interest] groups may the individual protect himself from permanent inflation policies. The consequences of sharpened [social] competition are dangers for the economic system and the democratic state."[63] The Bundesbank became the central arena for negotiating macroeconomic policy because monetarists had proved their political point; although Keynesian would help negotiate the terms of monetary discipline exercised by the Bundesbank, the events of the early 1970s seemed to demonstrate that monetary control brought not just an economic balance but a new balance of social power. For this very reason external agents—whether banks, unions, or governments—sought to have their ideas heard in the Bundesbank's boardroom. Over the next few pages we will examine this construction of monetary corporatism. Within the Bundesbank, we will focus on the direct and indirect negotiations over targeting, the recurrent overshooting of targets, and the unique transformation of representation within the Central Bank Council. Outside the bank, the effects of monetary corporatism can be detected in adaptations made by both working-class and propertied interests. Adaptations made by the SPD and the unions on the one hand and banks, business, and conservative economists on the other helped demobilize support for the kind of radical overhaul of the economic machinery that the delayed application of monetarism would bring in the United States.

Internal Monetary Corporatism: Monetarism in the Bundesbank

Two avenues for social scientific negotiation now became part of the targeting formula. The first was a process of informal bidding for each new year's target. In anticipation of the announcement of the second target figure, for 1976, interested parties began proposing their own. For example, the SVR wanted somewhat less than 8 percent; the Savers' Association wanted 7 percent; some of the conservative institutes suggested numbers as low as 5 percent and 6 percent; the influential *Franfurter Allgemeine Zeitung* advocated 7 percent.[64] That the Bundesbank's eventual target of 8 percent in 1976 was higher than any except the one proposed by the WSI (which eventually wanted the target amended to embrace specific employment goals) suggests how little the Bundesbank was using either monetary targeting or its institutional independence to impose a forced march to disinflation. While it is uncertain how much direct influence these proposals had, there is no question that this process became a useful way for the Bundesbank to gauge public opinion regarding the future course of monetary policy. And indeed, the Bundesbank overshot all of its announced single-point targets until it switched to a target corridor in 1979.

The second and more important avenue is the indirect consultation between the Bundesbank and the economics and finance ministries with regard to the so-called *Eckdaten* (roughly, data cornerstones). These are the key economic variables made available to the members of the Bundesbank's council as they consider the annual targets. Many of these numbers derive from policies undertaken or planned by the federal and state authorities: anticipated tax receipts, net borrowing requirements, planned revenue transfers and outlays, and decisions regarding the management of short-term cash-flows.[65] These bear directly on key factors of the monetary target, such as expected changes in capacity utilization and changes in the velocity of money circulation. By far the most significant relationship is that between government expenditure on personnel and "unavoidable inflation." As 1974 demonstrated, the government's intended expenditures for public-sector wages and salaries are a major influence on the overall climate of wage negotiations. Negotiations with the government about these data give the Bundesbank an opportunity to exercise its influence discreetly. While the Bundesbank may not always get its way, it is better prepared for the eventual result. So, even though the specification of the annual monetary targets is exclusively in the hands of the Bundesbank council, the government will have already had an extremely high level of input into shaping the economic data which influence the directors. As one official at the economics ministry observed, "Once you knew what the *Eckdaten* were, the monetary target was fairly automatic."[66] This cooperation was indicated most concretely by the attendance of German cabinet ministers at the Central Bank Council meeting at which the yearly target is formulated, and the government's public endorsement of each target became *de rigeur.*

With the growing recognition that the Bundesbank was now the locus of macroeconomic steering, the locus of coordination shifted as well. Concerted Action, the semicorporatist body originated by Schiller, now fell into disarray. Its primary role in steering macroeconomic management was usurped by the superior effectiveness of monetary policy, at whose heart monetary targeting lay. While the reasons for Concerted Action's demise were complex, the most important reason was its inability to make enforceable decisions. Its consultations raised unfulfillable expectations, and dashed hopes provoked unpunished defections. As one long-time participant remarked, "In good times it wasn't necessary, and in bad times it didn't work."[67] As the years wore on, governments, experts, central bankers, and employers increasingly found themselves arrayed against the unions, who refused to allow Concerted Action to infringe on their sovereign bargaining rights. The unions, resenting this isolation, and provoked by a lawsuit by the employers' federation against new code-termination laws, withdrew from the meetings altogether in 1976.

Nonetheless, Germany's social partners—unions especially—were too important and too powerful to remain wholly unrepresented in macroeconomic policy. Inevitably, a surrogate evolved. At the same time as Concerted Action waned, the power of economists within the Bundesbank's council waxed. The new importance of economists on the council first came to light in a sudden politicization of the appointment process after March 1973. The appointment of new directors and LCB presidents, on which the council always takes a nonbinding vote, had proceeded without incident since 1959. But between 1973 and 1976, no less than six new appointments were seriously opposed by the council on the grounds that the nominees lacked appropriate expert qualification; two of these nominees were rejected outright in secret balloting. Since many of the new appointees were political favorites of the government appointing them, the Christian Union opposition in Bonn at first tried to portray this trend as simply a partisan threat to the independence of the Bundesbank.[68] But in fact, controversy dogged appointments by governments of all party stripes, as was shown in 1976 with regard to two appointments of LCB presidents in the conservative-controlled Länder of Lower Saxony and Bavaria. Some commentators in the press then suggested that all governments were nominating party friends, thereby subjecting the Bundesbank to proportional political patronage akin to Austria's corporatist "Proporz."[69]

Upon closer examination, however, one finds that this politicization actually reflected an important controversy about the professional qualifications appropriate for council members. Prior to 1970, the overwhelming majority on the council, both directors and LCB presidents, had been bankers by training or experience. A few council members had even been trained in-house by the old Reichsbank, which had taken in two retiring council members (Fessler and Rahmsdorf) as teenage bankers' apprentices. But now the Bundesbank's president, Klasen (himself an alumnus of the Deutsche Bank), complained that as bankers on the council retired or died, they were increasingly replaced by individuals with quite different professional qualifications. "Prominent representatives of economic theory and successful [finance ministry] administrators have become more numerous," Klasen complained, "while experienced bankers are now less frequently appointed to the Central Bank Council."[70] In other words, the wave of negative votes against new appointees showed that an old guard of bankers on the council were defending their traditional interpretation of the Bundesbank law stipulating appointees' "special expert qualifications." But as other commentators pointed out at the time, the Bundesbank law does not specify the content of this requirement.[71] Only the traditional involvement of the Bundesbank with bank activities and the previous subordination of monetary policy to the system of fixed exchange rates had made the council a bankers' preserve. But as the Bundesbank had redefined its powers and mission, so too it would have to redefine its concepts of expertise and representation. As it thrust itself into a new and more powerful role with wide impact on every corner of German economy and society, outside interests clamored to influence it. It became harder to make the case that prominent professors of economics with long careers as policy advisers were unqualified to sit on the council. Economics minister Friderichs declared that a new national strategy for coordinating appointments was required, to ensure that the most urgently needed specialists from whatever profession would be seated in the council.[72] Ultimately, this issue was resolved with the passage of time, when the new generation of central bankers acclimated themselves to a broader definition of the economic expertise necessary to lead the central bank.

External Monetary Corporatism

This process of widening the range and nature of representation of perspectives within the Bundesbank—perhaps the most direct manifestation of an enhanced monetary corporatism—clearly helped defend the institution from political and economic forces that might otherwise have proved troublesome. This process of demobilization occurred primarily by removing other groups' economic incentives to alter existing institutional relationships. We will examine this process by looking at the diminished opportunities for political mobilization found on both the left and the right of the political spectrum.

Bundesbank Monetarism: Demobilizing the Political Left

It is clear that the Bundesbank's monetary targeting was successfully institutionalized in part because the redistributive conflict with unions abated, leading to more moderate wage increases. The point to be investigated, however, was the precise nature of monetarism's effect and labor's response to it. There are two major interpretations of this question. The first is that the Bundesbank's monetarism represented a de facto "peace treaty," which appealed to the much vaunted moderation of German unions.[73] And indeed, many in the trade union federation came to recognize that the Bundesbank was attempting to be flexible in implementing its strategy. Thus one of the senior officials of the DGB could say that the union federation lived in *"weitgehend Übereinstimmung"* (far-reaching agreement) with the Bundesbank's monetarism, even if this did not mean that it had itself become monetarist.[74] The second, more skeptical interpretation, was that Bundesbank monetarism succeeded not because of the unions' cooperation, but rather because of the not-so-subtle *force majeure* inherent in a tight-money policy.

In many ways, this question of unions' response to monetarism goes to the heart of the historical mythology surrounding Germany's experience with money, Weimar, and hyperinflation. Bundesbank officials believed that monetarism appealed over the heads of the union leaders to the members' traditional fear of hyperinflation.[75] The Bundesbank believed that its numbers "structured other people's numbers,"[76] forcing the unions to engage in public debates about the inflationary implications of wage demands, and to limit those demands to what the German public's angst about inflation would tolerate. Here the Bundesbank officials believed that the centralization and universality of Germany's unions played directly into their hands: to a very considerable extent, they felt that they could treat German unions' mass membership and the German public as largely identical. And union leaders certainly recognized that their members' attitudes affected how aggressive they could be in wage negotiations, and that these attitudes were not as militant in the latter half of the 1970s as they had been earlier in the decade.[77] Thus in the mid-1970s, the DGB hired its first monetary economist, and this put it in a position, for the first time, to consider an anticipatory wage policy that conformed to the Bundesbank's monetary cloak. In fact, some union leaders were persuaded that at least in principle, it would be reasonable for them to conform.

However, officials of the member unions who actually participated in wage bargaining reject the suggestion that Bundesbank targets played any role in wage negotiations, either directly or indirectly.[78] Their alternative interpretation stresses not reciprocal understanding based on the myth of hyperinflation, but the threat of unemployment latent in monetary targeting. In essence, unions believed (as some Bundesbank officials conceded privately) that the Bundesbank and the unions were caught in a game of "Schwarze Peter" (the German version of the game "Old Maid") and that the Bundesbank's monetary targeting and its invocation of the shades of 1923 were merely a stratagem to avoid being stuck with the "booby card" of blame for unemployment.[79] In this view, the decisive influence on the membership's *Streikbereitschaft* (militancy) was actual labor market conditions. If unemployment was minimal, union members knew that strikes and higher wage demands posed little risk to jobs. Conversely, if unemployment was high, moderation was more or less automatic, because members saw their grasp on their jobs as more tenuous. Union negotiators discovered that they simply could not sell an anticipatory bargaining stance based on targets to their membership.[80] In this interpretation, the crucial fact about monetarism was that tight money produced a chastening dose of joblessness, in Emminger's sardonic phrase, a downturn *"nach Mass"* (custom-made). Even though union membership is concerned about inflation, it worries as much or more about unemployment. Mass unemployment, after all, was a specter from the Weimar years just as hyperinflation was, and it had the added force of being a more present reality for workers. Since the 1970s, polls have indicated that unemployment is a more salient political issue among the German public than inflation.[81] This has been confirmed by the Bundesbank's own confidential polling.[82] Thus on balance the memory of hyperinflation, nurtured so assiduously by the Bundesbank to account for the success of its monetarist experiment, serves to deflect attention away from the strong link between monetary policy and lost jobs. While memories of 1923 live on in Frankfurt press releases, memories of 1929 haunt union assembly halls.

In fact, the unions throughout this period never abandoned their essentially neo-Keynesian focus on fiscal policy. German unions continued to believe that the primary problem confronting the German worker was lack of demand. Unions continued to pressure the government to spend more, and unions such as the construction workers believe that the SPD's post-1973 accommodation of these demands with its unprecedented spending policy went a long way toward compensating politically for the new restrictive monetary policy. Fiscal policy responded to the challenge of recession with an aggressive increase of 13–14 percent in expenditures, causing the deficit to climb to 66 billion, a remarkable 7 percent of GNP. The Bundesbank, perhaps surprisingly, said that this was "in keeping" with cyclical economic necessity. However, when Bonn's "Future Investments Program" threatened to leave the core structural deficit (costs that do not vary with the business cycle) a larger proportion of Germany's GNP than before, the Bundesbank began to sound the alarm bells.

Bundesbank Monetarism: Demobilizing the Political Right

The Bundesbank's monetarism influenced forces on the political right mostly by what it prevented them from doing. Primarily, the early adoption by the Bundesbank of the theoretical innovations of the monetarists left conservative groups and economists with little incentive to undertake further political initiatives. In this, the experiences of Germany would differ from the United States in several key respects.

Bundesbank monetarism had different effects on the financial and business community, particularly on different sectors of the universal banks, but overall the effect was to lessen interest in a neoconservative revolution. The Bundesbank's monetary policy created a strong appreciation of the DM against the dollar, which initially had a quite negative impact on exporters and their sponsors in the big commercial banks. The DM appreciated 15 percent against all other currencies from 1972 to 1975, and in 1976 it increased another 15 percent. This corresponded to an average 30 percent increase in the value of the deutsche mark relative to the currencies of Germany's thirteen biggest trading partners. Of all the commercial banks, Dresdner was most unrepentant in its adherence to the old premonetarist mind-set. A year after the introduction of monetary targeting, it spoke of the new regime's "all too mechanical" rules, based on "dubious premises" and causing "more harm than good." Dresdner rejected the idea that money and monetary targets should steer the economy, arguing that "the danger of an overestimation of old and new instruments of monetary policy seems to us to lie in that the real causes of inflation and recession will be missed and its perpetrators relieved of responsibility."[83] A year later, Dresdner summed up its feelings about monetarism with the sarcastic phrase, "Operation monetary targeting successful: economy dead."[84]

Yet Germany's exports, so crucial to its economic well-being, did not suffer as they might have. First, since so many of its imports, particularly of raw materials and energy, were invoiced in dollars, an appreciating DM progressively lowered these import costs and further moderated the pace of price increases, which reached 4.5 percent for the year 1976, compared with 6 percent in 1975 and 7 percent in 1974. Second, whether owing to rising unemployment or the appeals of the public authorities, labor relations improved, contributing to an advantage in export markets. By taming the inflationary price-wage spiral, the Bundesbank found that it had effectively put a damper on Germany's strike rate. Many of Germany's leading competitors, such as Great Britain, continued to experience difficulties exporting because of the labor unrest associated with their high-growth policies. The German strike rate dropped from over 1 million days lost in 1974 to a mere 68,000 in 1975 and only 23,000 by 1977. With its own labor relations on an even keel, Germany's exporters were able to step into the breach, a fact which the Bundesbank did not hesitate to note in its reports. And, as long as the markets believed that the Bundesbank's monetarism made the DM a perpetual candidate for appreciation, the Bundesbank had greater freedom to lower interest rates. While the rate of price increases declined to 3.9 percent in 1978, long-term rates of 5 percent and 6 percent were lower than they had been at any time since 1959. This allowed the Bundesbank to tell workers and employers alike that it was doing its utmost to promote the recovery without endangering the gains made in the battle against inflation.

In these circumstances, Germany's monetarists had little incentive to seek a radical revolution in German macroeconomic policy. After the Konstanzer Seminar was founded, American monetarists in attendance were astonished to hear their German colleagues criticizing the Bundesbank's performance.[85] In comparison with the Federal Reserve, the Bundesbank in the mid-1970s seemed a paragon of virtue to many monetarists. Consequently, nowhere in German monetarists' analyses was there anything like the political economists' critique of the central bank's independence that was increasingly expounded in the American Shadow Open Market Committee. Otmar Issing, a conservative economist who would later be appointed to the Bundesbank, assailed American monetarists for their dogmatism, arguing in the early 1980s that Germany's experience with an independent central bank belied the political economists' theory that independence promoted bureaucratic obstructionism and inflation. In the years after 1973, German monetarists increasingly became the Bundesbank's defenders, especially against those who wanted the Bundesbank to artificially manipulate the exchange rate. In conjunction with some American and European colleagues, German monetarists helped form the Shadow European Economic Policy Committee (SEEPC), the counterpart of America's Shadow Open Market Committee. Significantly, however, the SEEPC's chief target was not the Bundesbank but rather the Keynesian-influenced OECD in Paris, whose publications lent intellectual weight to American government pressures to reflate the German economy.[86] Even in 1979, with Volcker and Thatcher launching their own programs of monetarism, German monetarists continued to defend the German central bank's moderate course. Counseling the Bundesbank to avoid the bottom of its target corridor that year, the European Shadow Open Market Committee wrote, "Policy should avoid too sharp a deceleration in monetary growth, so as to maintain the recovery in real growth into 1980."[87]

Perhaps the most striking difference between the German monetarists and their American colleagues was the Germans' attitude toward fiscal policy and budget deficits. They were far less sanguine about tolerating deficits, and they continued to see a link between deficits and inflation. They argued that what was required was "a reduction in the nominal growth of government expenditure so that the government's share in nominal GNP does not increase above its current 47 percent . . . in order to contribute to fighting the new round of inflation." The priorities of the Shadow European Economic Policy Committee were clear: eliminate the deficit in the early 1980s, and lower tax rates only "thereafter."[88] This dovetailed perfectly with the Bundesbank's own preferences, which would seek to make those views known in ever more public—and political—fashion in the years ahead. But the cost of this success with targeting, as one monetarist was later to observe, was that "with inflation under control, we could not convince the German public that even more fundamental economic reforms were needed."[89]

MONETARISM AND THE FAILURE OF GERMAN REAGANOMICS, 1979–1985

The years 1979–1985 represent the final episode in the rise to hegemony of Germany's monetary targeting regime. Several features of this era are especially noteworthy: the swift reassertion of Bundesbank monetarism after a brief departure from monetary virtue in 1979; the role of the Bundesbank in bringing fiscal policy under control, with important implications for the switch from Schmidt's government to Kohl's government in 1982; and the realization of zero inflation in 1985. All this was accomplished without any significant changes in the contours of Germany's economic institutions. In short, this era demonstrates the fruits of Germany's early adoption of monetary targeting: any potential neoconservative revolution died on the vine, its place taken by a moderate center-right coalition. In the elections of 1983, this coalition campaigned by mimicking some of the radical monetarist and supply-side rhetoric of Reagan and Thatcher; but once in office, it left the German economy and social structure essentially as it found them, with the major exception of raising taxes to trim the deficit. If Reaganomics may be defined as the alliance of monetarism with deficits and deregulation, this alliance was scarcely in evidence in Germany. The remainder of this chapter will show how the Germans' logic of early but moderate adoption of monetarism fostered this development.

In 1982, an economic policy debate, which had been raging in Germany ever since the second OPEC price shock of 1979, erupted into coalition politics. The background to this debate was not only the restoking of inflation (as had happened after the first oil crisis), but also, (unlike the earlier experience) the unexpected weakening of the DM and German exports. With both Thatcher's Britain and Volcker's United States now implementing their own monetarist-inspired policies, Germany's gradualistic monetarism proved not to afford as much shelter in the international marketplace as many in Germany had expected. Thus, a question arose about how best to restore Germany's competitiveness in a world where monetarist virtues (to say nothing of high interest rates) were increasingly commonplace. In the resulting debate, Germany's early conversion to monetarism would continue to have its effects. On one side stood Germany's monetarists along with the Council of Experts, the Bundesbank, the FDP, and the centrist wing of the SPD, who held that Germany's production and employment problems derived from a shortage of productive investment. They argued that this shortage was in itself caused by excessive fiscal stimulus—in other words, the crowding out of private by public capital.[90] These so-called supply-siders—not to be confused with American supply-siders—were opposed by the "demand-siders" (chiefly the union movement, some left-wing economists, and the left wing within the SPD), who continued to argue that Germany's problems of employment and growth were due to insufficient demand. This controversy became the wedge that split the SPD and drove the FDP into the arms of the CDU, bringing a new government to power under Helmut Kohl.

In this debate, the Bundesbank threw the full weight of its powerful public relations department behind the supply-siders, albeit in a technically nonpartisan way. It did so primarily by seeking to link high fiscal deficits, the current account deficit, and the pressures on the DM together in the public mind.[91] While the Bundesbank welcomed the fact that speculation was no longer exaggerating the value of the mark, it did not welcome the idea of a depreciating currency. At a time when the German authorities might have accepted a declining DM as a way of reducing the external trade imbalances that were now in the offing, the Bundesbank vigorously rejected that possibility. It argued that Germany must rectify its current account deficit with increased productivity, conservation of energy, and higher interest rates to restore the confidence of international investors. At first, the Bundesbank's arguments enjoyed the nominal support of the Schmidt government, which now looked for a reduction in governmental shortfalls beginning in 1980.[92] Planned reductions in the deficits failed to meet their targets, however, with high interest rates contributing to unexpectedly low growth, tax revenues declining and social security outlays increasing. Nonetheless, political pressure continued to build. In 1982, the SPD government felt compelled to undertake the most un-Keynesian task of raising taxes to reduce the deficit during a recession. With this "Operation '82," as it called its fiscal consolidation, the Schmidt government brought its policies into much closer alignment with the recommendations of both the Bundesbank and German monetarists.

There was, however, clearly more to this fiscal retreat than any putative SPD conversion to monetarism. First, the extraordinarily high level of interest rates, when combined with the record deficits, meant that the government was having to pay out an unprecedented share of the national income in interest payments on its bonds. Second, public criticism of the SPD was having politically important side effects on its junior coalition partner, the FDP. The FDP's polls were finding that it was beginning to lose its political identity with its core constituency of liberal, free-market voters, who were becoming disenchanted with its continued support of the social democrats.[93] In the circumstances, the FDP had to distance itself from the SPD in order to maintain its position in the Bundestag. In 1982, Otto Graf Lambsdorff, the FDP's spokesman on economic policy, delivered a speech which rejected much of traditional SDP policy and was intended, in part, to resonate with ideas expressed by the Bundesbank.[94] This widening rift between the senior and junior coalition partners ultimately led to the defeat of the SPD chancellor in the Bundestag, and the naming of CDU leader Helmut Kohl as his successor. In the election which followed in 1983, the CDU's supply-side rhetoric was able to rally voters who had been disappointed by the SPD's failure to cut taxes as promised—a retreat which, of course, the SPD had made primarily in an effort to accommodate its coalition partner.

Nonetheless, it is important to recognize that the German supply-side agenda proved to be the antithesis of supply-side economics as practiced in the United States under Reagan. This can be seen most clearly in the actual policies pursued—or not pursued—by the Kohl government. The most substantial change of the new regime was, as might be expected, the success of fiscal consolidation. The deficit declined to 56 billion DM in 1983 and was followed by a deficit of 49 billion DM in 1984. In 1985, government borrowing continued to be reduced to the point where government deficit as a proportion of GNP was 2.5 percent, half its level in 1980. Yet this balance was achieved by some cutting of costs and much raising of taxes. Thus, average personal tax rates—which stood at 44.9 percent in 1982 under the Schmidt government—were raised to 46.6 percent by 1987 under Kohl. Similarly, a family of four earning DM 72,000 per year (approximately $45,000) faced a marginal tax rate of 59.8 percent in 1982 but one of 62.8 percent in 1987.[95] Consolidation of expenditures was especially marked in compensation of public employees (salaries and pensions), which declined at a somewhat faster rate, a fact that may have contributed to further moderation in overall wage increases. Significantly, stable prices helped to preserve and enhance the position of German labor unions, as the rate of unionization in the German economy—which had been declining before the implementation of monetarism, from about 38 percent in the early 1960s to 36 percent in 1970—climbed to 39 percent in 1975 and to 41 percent in 1985. The cloud behind this silver lining for labor was the almost total inability of the German economy to make any inroads against unemployment. In 1985, two full years into the recovery, the jobless rate stood at an astronomical (by postwar German

standards) 9.2 percent. Yet the continuing strength of the union movement and the unwillingness of the Kohl government to seriously attack the
German social safety net left labor in far better shape than Kohl's original
supply-side rhetoric might have led it to expect.

As the Kohl government pared down Germany's deficit, monetary policy resumed its triumphal march to price stability, aided by falling oil
prices at the end of 1985 and the beginning of 1986. The increase in
West German price levels fell to zero. The Bundesbank hit the CBM target of 3 to 5 percent with a year's growth rate of 4.5 percent and permanently discarded the component of "unavoidable inflation" that had figured in the target's construction since its birth.

In fact, one of the remarkable features of German monetary policy was
that it continued to use monetary targeting at all. In the United States,
the heyday of monetary targeting lasted only from 1979 to 1982. Thereafter, the Federal Reserve deemphasized targeting not least because financial deregulation had transformed the empirical behavior of the aggregates. By contrast, Germany's lack of innovation in the financial sector
meant that the Bundesbank was never suddenly confronted with the Federal Reserve's question, "What is money?" In a lengthy retrospective
analysis which the Bundesbank published on the tenth anniversary of its
targets, the bank argued that lack of financial innovation was itself primarily accounted for by the light hand of regulation affecting Germany's
universal banks. After the last controls on imported capital were lifted,
German bankers and their customers had no further incentive to develop
new financial products.[96] In a survey of eighteen sectors of the German
economy, German banking was virtually the only sector less subsidized
and less regulated in the mid-1980s than at the beginning of the 1970s.

Nonetheless, the OECD argued that a "gentleman's agreement" between the Bundesbank and the universal banks maintained a "negative
list" of disallowed financial instruments. Thus, for example, securities
with maturity of less than one year were not permitted because the
Bundesbank considered them too close a substitute for short-term bank
deposits, and they were not subject to reserve requirements; likewise, the
Bundesbank prohibited securities with variable interest rates, as it prohibited all forms of price indexation.[97]

In other areas of economic policy dear to neoconservative economists,
the Kohl government effected no significant change whatsoever; certainly
nothing on the order of the transformation seen among Germany's
Anglo-Saxon partners. Monetarists now found themselves in the peculiar
position of making common cause with the OECD in worrying about German unemployment. Their common diagnosis focused on rigidities in
the labor market caused by unreformed prounion legislation. These
rigidities (as the monetarists argued) prevented the downward pressure

on wages that would have allowed employers to shift from a policy of "capital deepening" (installing laborsaving capital equipment) to "capital widening" (installing additional capital). A lack of reforms in wage bargaining, the continued strength of the labor unions, the requirement of substantial "social plan" provisions by employers, and continued government subsidies to lame-duck industries were all identified as root causes of Germany's persistently high unemployment during the recovery from the recession of 1982. Yet the Kohl government, having fought under the banner of balancing the budget, lacked the political will to embark on substantial reforms in any of these areas. As two of Germany's leading monetarists observed with chagrin, "It seems fair to conclude that, apart from the successful [budgetary] consolidation policy, preservation of inherited structures rather than fundamental reform has been and still is the dominant principle of economic policy in Germany. In this respect, the Kohl government has proved to be as conservative as the preceding Schmidt government."[98]

In summary, there were two ways in which the universalistic organization of the Bundesbank's policy environment (described in Chapter 2) conditioned the timing and implementation of monetary targeting, as described in the present chapter. The first influence was on the nature of the Bundesbank's intellectual infrastructure itself. Both the polarity and the cooperation in the policy environment between universal banks and labor, monetarists and Keynesians, conservatives and social democrats were mirrored in the Bundesbank's council itself. This nurtured a corporate culture uniquely positioned to recognize and respond to the challenges of instability that confronted the central bank. No more dramatic demonstration can be seen than the protracted contest between the Klasen and Emminger wings of the Bundesbank over appropriate remedial responses to imported inflation. The eventual implementation, success, and institutionalization of the Bundesbank's monetarist approach—to which even many of its original opponents became reconciled—would certainly not have happened as it did in a central bank with a more hierarchic, less embedded culture.

Second, the greater universalistic organization of the German economy created powerful challenges for the Bundesbank but also made those challenges more susceptible to indirect management. It also affected the Bundesbank's sense of its time constraints. Given the power of unions and banks in Germany, it was almost inevitable that the Bundesbank would prefer to prevent recession or inflation than to let it get out hand. The Bundesbank was therefore encouraged to respond earlier, rather than later, not only to inflation-driven dislocations in 1973 but also the threat of recession in 1974. Incentives and corporate culture together contributed to the Bundesbank's self-consciously gradualist monetary targeting, which attempted to give room to both governments and the social partners to adjust to policies of stabilization. In a remarkable institutional transformation, economists and government experts of all persuasions joined bankers on the Bundesbank's council to institutionalize the arm's-length politics I have called monetarist corporatism. Monetarist corporatism contributed to labor peace, declining inflation, and a strategic advantage in the international marketplace. And even though German unemployment soared to unprecedented and stubbornly high levels, unions in 1985 mobilized a larger proportion of the workforce than they did in 1970, and the welfare state remained largely intact. In short, the early and sustained victory for monetary targeting preempted a more radical populist monetarism and rendered superfluous any serious assault on the powers and rights of the labor movement. Thus, those who managed monetarist corporatism had good reason to rediscover, if not actually invent, the lessons of Weimar: to stabilize money is to stabilize politics.

CHAPTER FOUR

The Origins of the Federal Reserve's Corporate Culture

The later and more contentious adoption of monetarism in the United States grew out of the Federal Reserve's hierarchic and chairman-centered corporate culture. As Chapter 5 will describe in more detail, the Federal Reserve in 1970 seemed poised on the brink of an easy transition to monetarism and monetary targeting. Yet the Federal Reserve, one of the most stability-minded central banks of the postwar era, did not take that step as, or when, expected. That individual policymakers, including Fed chairmen in the 1970s, could make theoretically questionable or politically opportunistic policy is neither surprising nor the heart of the problem this book seeks to explore. Rather, what is surprising and problematic is the failure of an ostensibly collegial decision-making body such as the Federal Reserve, with its twelve-member Federal Open Market Committee, to compensate for or resist such policies for so many years. The delayed recognition of monetarism was the most important consequence of this problem, and it is the puzzle of the Fed's corporate culture.

   In this chapter I describe the historical relationships between the Federal Reserve, its banking system, and its wider policy environment that account for this chairman-dominant policy culture and the ultimate crisis of monetarist targeting. I will present evidence that the weaknesses in the Fed's policy culture which delayed the adoption of monetarism originated in its fragmented policy environment, particularly the specialized structure of the U.S. banking system. Unlike German financial institutions—which in the postwar years enjoyed a virtually unrestricted right, as so-called universal banks, to act as intermediaries across regions, assets, and sectors of the economy, and were held accountable by an equally universalistic central bank—America's banking system by the late 1960s had been fragmented by populist-inspired legal firewalls which circumscribed its members' activities within narrow geographic and economic limits. While many of these populist restrictions were legacies of the nineteenth-century, the most important ones were more recent coinages. A major wave of regulation during the New Deal reduced America's commercial banks to utilities in all but name, and further regulation of interest rates in the 1960s imperiled the thrift industry during periods of monetary restraint. The growing fragility of the financial system led to a climate of hesitation and defensiveness within the Fed, while lack of a universal savings-oriented banking sector, such as the Bundesbank acquired with the Sparkassen, meant that there was no powerful constituency for stability within the Fed's monetary system. The Fed discovered that a regulatory institution is no stronger than the industry it supervises. Consequently the embattled Fed circled its wagons, and the chairman grew ever more able to assert unchallenged authority. As the Fed's corporate culture became more and more closed and deferential, it dramatically reduced the opportunities for monetarism, or any other new policy doctrine, to gain a meaningful hearing within the Fed.

The present chapter consists of three parts. The first will place the history of American banking and central banking in the centuries-long context of populism to help explain the absence of a unified financial system. I also describe the origins and the Depression-era crisis of the Federal Reserve system. The second section will describe the particulars of the New Deal reforms of the 1930s and sketch how they affected the Fed over the ensuring decades under Martin's chairmanship. Finally, in the third section, I describe the Fed's corporate culture as it stood at the threshold of the monetarist controversy, especially the (growing) imbalance between the chairman's authority and that of his fellow policymakers. This section will foreshadow how the Fed's chairman-centered culture set the stage for the institution's resistance to monetarism during the tenure of chairmen of very different attitudes and talents in the 1970s.

AMERICAN CENTRAL BANKING: THE POPULIST LEGACY

To understand why the Federal Reserve came to be situated in a highly specialized and constraining banking system, it is important to recognize how venerable democratic sentiment and recurring episodes of populist agitation have leveraged government policies toward banks in ways that may be peculiarly American. As a result, intertwined financial panics and regulatory reactions have shadowed American central banking from the founding of the Republic to the most recent movements of the Dow Jones index. Inflation, depressions, and populist backlash have washed across the American economic landscape for some 200 years. Major panics and their attendant political reactions occurred in 1837, 1858, 1873, 1896, 1907, 1921, and 1929–1933. For American monetary policy the link is clear: panics beget populism, and populism's natural response is to regulate the financial system. Since its founding in 1913, the Federal Reserve has been caught at the hinge of these forces. Indeed, for the first century of the American republic, it appeared that the forces of populism would prevent the country from having a central bank at all. Almost from the very beginning, grassroots democrats, southern and western farmers, advocates of states' rights, and small businessmen reviled eastern banks and overbearing federal power in Washington. These two aversions underlay the populists' veto of both commercial and central banking, which long denied them a legitimate place in national life.

The Nineteenth-Century Veto of Central Banking

In Germany, central banking was born as a self-confident instrument of national power under an authoritarian regime. In the United States, by contrast, central banking first had to establish itself as such an instrument by overcoming localist and democratic sentiment. Among the earliest obstacles to modern banking in America was the doctrine of states' rights. The Constitution grants to the federal government the right to coin money but reserves to the states the right to regulate banking. Such was the hostility to banking in general in the nineteenth century that many states, particularly on the southern and western frontier, either banned banks outright or confined them within very strict geographical limits—a single county, perhaps, or even a single branch in a single town. Indeed, to this day some states, such as Illinois, still prohibit branch banking. Accordingly, early Supreme Court decisions construed the constitutional division of responsibility narrowly in favor of the states. In the view of the Court, central banking, including the issuing of banknotes and paper money, involved not monetary policy but bank business and regulation and so was withheld from Washington.

The notion of states' rights proved central to the demise of the Federal Reserve's most important predecessor, the Second Bank of the United States. The Second Bank of the United States was created to help the national government finance the War of 1812. Though not originally intended to conduct an active monetary policy, the bank began doing so in the 1820s, when Nicholas Biddle assumed its presidency. Biddle sought to contain fluctuations in local credit by actively redeeming the notes of state banks he considered unsound. Although Biddle was generally conceded to be a man of probity, his interventions imposed real burdens on some banks while favoring others. Biddle's policy was seen as unconstitutional interference with states' rights and local interests, especially in the South. Andrew Jackson made his opposition to Biddle's bank one of the chief issues of the presidential campaign of 1832; his Whig opponent, Henry Clay, was equally staunch in Biddle's defense. Upon his reelection, Jackson vetoed the bill reauthorizing the Second Bank and directed the Treasury's deposits to state banks. For almost the next three decades, this successful coalition of small-town bankers and farmers exploited the language of localism, states' rights, and democracy to abet other southerners—chiefly the slaveholding agrarians—in resisting northerners' efforts to outfit the economy with a modern, centralized banking system.

The defeat of the Second Bank of the United States meant that until the outbreak of the World War I, America would be the only major western nation without a formal central bank. Monetary conditions remained hostage to the probity of local bankers and the energy of state regulators. Merchants engaged in interstate commerce had to keep catalogues at their desks updating the current value of thousands of different state banknotes. Time and again, events as happenstance as a gold rush or a railroad scandal made the banking system lurch from boom to bust, or vice versa. The first major panic occurred in 1837, a mere year after the abolition of Biddle's bank. This released the grip of the southern populists long enough to allow the passage of the Independent Treasury Act of 1846, which gave the federal Treasury greater independence to act as a quasi-central bank and relieved Federal finance from some of its dependence on state banks.

With the Union victory in the Civil War the industrial North at last overcame southern agrarian opposition to federal banking legislation. The year 1865 saw the chartering of the first banks by the Federal government, creating a parallel, second tier of commercial banks. The legislation of 1865 established a federal bureau, the Comptroller of the Currency, to supervise these new national banks more closely than their state competitors; the national banks' presumed greater soundness was meant to afford them a competitive advantage in attracting business from state banks. National banks were required to accept the banknotes of all other national banks at par, and the federal government accepted these notes as legal tender for its own transactions and taxes. This coast-to-coast system of federal banks laid the foundation for a uniform national money much more suited to the needs of northern industrial interests engaged in interstate commerce than the welter of dubious state banknotes that continued to exist alongside it.

Having failed to prevent national banking, the forces of localism and popular sovereignty turned their attention to a question which would also figure prominently in the monetarist debate: what would ultimately determine the quantity of (paper) money in the economy. As nineteenth-century politics would show, America has never known a firm consensus on this issue. Many powerful forces questioned whether dollars should be backed by specie and, if so, by which metals and in what proportion. Gold enjoyed only brief, and never unchallenged, supremacy; its propensity to provoke bank runs and recessions was too widely recognized. Prior to the Civil War, for example, America often practiced bimetallism, with the ratio set at 16.5 ounces of silver to 1 ounce of gold. Many people believed that bimetallism provided a more elastic currency than one backed by gold alone. Then, during the Civil War itself, both belligerents suspended convertibility, and in the North, unconvertible "greenbacks" won favor with the Populist Party. After the war, the great question for northern monetary affairs became "resumption." After considerable delay, the federal government returned to a metallic standard in 1873, when it legislated that national banknotes would henceforth be redeemable, but only in gold. The long period of disinflation that now settled like a drought on America's agrarian hinterland was said to be the fault of the "crime of 1873"—a myth of European bondholders who had descended on Washington that year and bribed congressmen to vote for gold.

There is no evidence that any such crime had been perpetrated, of course. But the popular reaction suggested that money policy and what— or perhaps who—should govern it had become a question of increasing national significance. The bank crises and depressions associated with gold hurt agrarian and small-town interests and struggling families who saw clearly that inflation would lighten their burdens. They hoped to better their lot with silver's cheap credit, and the proprietors of western mines were only too eager to endorse their cause. Together, suffering and avarice raised up a growing cry to monetize silver. William Jennings Bryan's failed campaign for the presidency in 1896 is often represented as a populist tragedy, the small man crucified on a "cross of gold." But as historians have shown, the real damage to the cause of silver had come from the tight-money policy of the eastern Democrat Grover Cleveland in 1893. That the Democrats nominated a free-silver, populist candidate, Bryan, was more than anything else an effort to ward off the looming electoral disaster brought on by Cleveland's depression of 1896. With the resounding Republican triumph at the polls, the Democrats became the first American party to be held accountable in a presidential election for the performance of the national economy.

Despite Bryan's defeat, populism continued to deform the growth of central banking and inhibit the emergence of universal banking. The big national banks invested heavily in the consolidation of America's growing industrial prowess. The biggest bankers—particularly J. P. Morgan of New York—assembled vast industrial trusts like U.S. Steel, America's first billion-dollar corporation. Like his German counterparts, Morgan provided the trusts with loans, leadership, and equity, to the point where "at the height of his power, J. P. Morgan dominated the American business community to a greater extent than any individual previously or subsequently."[1] But in an era bracketed by such populist measures at the Sherman Antitrust Act and the breakup of Rockefeller's Standard Oil Trust, these universalist ambitions could not last. Before long, a congressional committee on the "money trust" was gathering evidence that Morgan controlled assets worth three times the value of all real and personal property in New England.[2]

Heavy exposure of a limited number of banks to such enormous financial undertakings heightened their interest in a proper central bank that could be a proper lender of last resort. So powerful was Morgan's bank, in fact, that Morgan attempted at times to exercise this function himself. His was but one of several turn-of-the-century experiments with surrogates for a central bank, experiments that sometimes seemed to work at cross purposes. For example, commercial banks in different regions banded together to form not quite legal clearinghouse associations, which during panics surreptitiously issued emergency money to stop the drain on their members' reserves. Meanwhile the "independent Treasury" under its secretary Shaw pursued an activist policy of redeeming banknotes. But these makeshifts always operated in the twilight of public approval and legality, and always lagged one or two crucial steps behind the needs of the real economy. Shaw's activism triggered a bank crisis in 1906–1907, which Morgan barely prevented from becoming a widespread financial collapse. Such experiences helped persuade the banking community that the exposure of individual banks to systemic risk was now so great, and federal involvement in the economy now so extensive, that a greater degree of financial coherence was imperative.

The Origins and Crisis of the Federal Reserve System

The founding of the U.S. Federal Reserve in 1913 has always proved an easy target for those who—now as then—would portray the Fed as simply another "trust" organized by the big banks—this time on their own behalf. Murray Rothbard called it a "government-sponsored and enforced cartel promoting the income of banks."[3] Authors with perspectives as divergent as Kolko, Livingston, and Timberlake agree, to a remarkable extent, when they point out how creating a Federal Reserve system benefited the banks and the business class. Livingston and Kolko note a broad, newly emerging class of national "corporate capitalists" with interests opposed to those of small proprietors and workers, who believed—anachronistically—in the blessings of a truly competitive marketplace. As Kolko wrote, "It was generally appreciated that the Aldrich plan would increase the power of the big national banks to compete with the rapidly growing state banks, help bring the state banks under control, and strengthen the position of the national banks in foreign banking activities."[4] According to these interpretations, any appearance of genuine popular control over the Fed was merely that—just an appearance. The Fed was to be a banker's bank with the merest political camouflage.

Yet efforts to organize a proper central bank in the broad daylight of politics encountered genuine opposition from populists and proponents of state banking. It took a Democrat who had learned the lessons of Cleveland's defeat to become president in 1912 before the Federal Reserve's enabling legislation could overcome congressional resistance. The committee work of Carter Glass transformed Nelson Aldrich's "blatantly cartelist"[5] original plan into a bill which, by having the president name the members of the board, presented Woodrow Wilson with a measure he could approve, and the result was the Federal Reserve Act of 1913.[6]

Thus the Federal Reserve was born—a curious public-private hybrid. Nowhere was its hybrid nature more visible than in its dual leadership structure. On the one hand, the twelve newly created Federal Reserve district banks (successors, in some ways, of the old clearinghouse associations) were privately owned by the member banks in their districts, which elected their boards of directors, who in turn elected the presidents of the Federal Reserve Bank. Yet these banks were charged with exercising public functions. For example, all national banks now transferred to the Federal Reserve banks their previously hard-won monopoly of issuing banknotes. Moreover, the district banks were under the nominal control of the Federal Reserve Board in Washington, a board which included both the secretary of the Treasury and the comptroller of the currency ex-officio. The Federal Reserve Board's vague mandate, to provide for an "elastic currency" and for the "rediscounting of commercial paper," reflected this uncertain compromise about whose interests the institution was intended to serve. The reference to elasticity acknowledged the seasonal monetary demands of the harvest in an economy that was still significantly agricultural, while the reference to rediscounting commercial paper indicated the interest of business in access to credit and the need of member banks for a lender of last resort. These mandates provided little day-to-day operational guidance. Economists hoped that science would fill the breach. J. Laurence Laughlin believed that the central bank should be "wholly free from politics, or outside influence—as much respected for character and integrity, as the Supreme Court."[7] The Fed's designers, in true progressive-era fashion, eschewed any form of overt partisan or federal involvement, and so, in classic pluralist fashion, made the Federal Reserve accountable to interest groups. The legislation directed the president to make appointments to the board with due regard for regional representation and the various interests of agriculture, commerce, industry, and banking. From its political constituency, the Fed imported the gold standard; from its banking constituency it adopted a doctrine of "high-quality commercial paper" or so-called "real bills," whereby Federal Reserve banks would accept for rediscounting only those "real bills" created in the course of ordinary commerce.[8]

Between the wars it became clear that the Federal Reserve's original design was severely flawed. The tendency of the various Federal Reserve presidents to pull in different directions vitiated its capacity to make coherent policy. Each Federal Reserve bank set its own discount rate, but there was no national body like the later Federal Open Market Committee (FOMC) to reconcile their policies. Given the concentration of the largest banks in New York City, some presidents of the New York Fed, such as Benjamin Strong, could become de facto leaders of the system. But with the death of Strong in the early 1920s, neither the Treasury secretary (who was ex-officio chairman of the board) nor the governor (the de facto chairman) assumed the mantle of leadership envisioned in the founding statute. Between 1914 and 1934, no fewer than six men held the post of governor (chairman), an average of little more than three years each. (Compare this with subsequent tenures of Eccles—fourteen years—and Martin, nineteen years.) Harold Reed observed that the board had become:

> subject to all the unwieldiness of committee organization. It is composed of men who have been trained in different industrial activities. . . . It is confronted by problems that lie at the very heart of much that is controversial in scientific circles, and whenever wide differences of opinion exist, it is inevitable that slow and tedious diplomacy must be exercised.[9]

Above all, perhaps, the board was never able to transcend its initial self-concept as a mere patron of banking interests rather than a national economic authority. Roy A. Young, governor of the Federal Reserve Board in 1928, said that the primary aim of the system should be to preserve "a healthy banking situation. . . . It would be unfortunate if the Federal Reserve system were to be charged with still further responsibilities which are not directly related to banking, such as responsibility for the stability of the general price level or for moderation of ups and downs in business conditions."[10] Given the Federal Reserve's structural incoherence and intellectual parochialism, it seems almost inevitable in retrospect that the Fed should be widely blamed for the Wall Street crash of 1929, the Great Depression, and the nearly total failure of the banking system in 1933, when some 4,000 depository institutions failed—by far the largest run on banks in American history.

THE FED'S POLICY ENVIRONMENT: LEGACIES AND RECONSTRUCTIONS

Franklin Delano Roosevelt took office in 1933, and his new administration introduced more deep-seated reforms, affecting more areas of publicly policy, than any administration before or since. In no area of public policy was this more true—or perhaps, more necessary—than the devastated banking system, at whose head stood a much discredited Federal Reserve. Before considering the structural changes in the Federal Reserve itself, it is important to understand how the New Deal and the legacies of American government itself combined to define the Fed's policy environment in the postwar years. These transformations of the New Deal—in banking, labor, the international environment, economic advice, and the federal government—were all intended to defend the national polity from the recently demonstrated excesses of capitalism. Structurally, they created a more unified, more independent Federal Reserve that was much more capable of imposing its will on the banking system it was charged with running. But these reforms tended not only to sustain the pluralist fragmentation of the Fed's policy environment but to exacerbate it, and this tendency eventually deformed the Fed's policy culture in such a way that it never fully acquired the capacity to mobilize or respond to the more scientific or universalistic norms pressed on it by scholars from the outside.

Reconstruction of Banking

The stock market crash of 1929 and the collapse of the banking system over the next four years sealed the fate of a more universalistic banking system in the United States and of the Fed's incentive to see itself as steward of the national economy. Of the various types of fragmentation, it is this which most clearly originated in the New Deal and most sharply differentiated U.S. banking from its German counterpart. After the collapse of Wall Street, the intimacy between the Fed, the commercial banks, and the owners of industry provoked a debate about the Fed's involvement in the market's failure. There were two broad interpretations of about the precise nature of this responsibility. According to the dominant, populist interpretation—which swept through Congress in the 1930s and shaped the reformist legislation of 1933 to 1935—the Fed, in thrall to the greed of commercial bankers, indulged stock market speculators with inflationary finance, creating a classic "bubble," and the ultimate victim was the small investor and saver.

The second, minority, view would later become one of the major theoretical planks in the monetarist campaign against the Fed and in favor of bank deregulation. Irving Fischer of Yale University, the academic grandfather of monetarism, argued that the Fed's chief problem was not so much institutional as intellectual. In this analysis, the Fed's "real bills" doctrine was dangerously procyclical. It interpreted credit conditions exclusively from the viewpoint of banks, without considering the context of the wider economy. Thus, according to the "real bills" doctrine, almost all firms appear solid during conditions of prosperity, and their bills will be accepted for rediscounting, thereby increasing an already buoyant money supply. But during periods of contraction, the situation is reversed, and the Fed will reject what few bills come its way because their issuers appear risky if not insolvent, thus reducing the money supply and business activity still further. Charting its course by this flawed map, the Fed failed to discern the difference between individual bank failures due to bad management and a systemic liquidity crisis. In this view (subsequently confirmed in monetarists' eyes by the even worse crash of 1987) there need not have been any necessary link between the stock market crash of 1929 and the banking armageddon of 1932–1933.

Nonetheless, the populist view prevailed and inspired sweeping pluralist legislation. Congress passed the Banking Act of 1935 to distance the Fed from the banks and sever the links between banks and industry. The president of the New York Federal Reserve bank was stripped of his power to autonomously determine the discount rate, and this power was transferred to a reformulated (and renamed) board of governors in Washington. The secretary of the Treasury was removed from his ex-officio membership on the board, as was the comptroller of the currency. The new board of governors had seven appointed members, each with a tenure of up to fourteen years—a tenure exceeded in Washington only by the fifteen-year appointment of the director of the General Accounting Office and the lifetime appointments of Supreme Court justices.

Henceforth, banks were required by the Glass-Steagall Act (1934) to specialize in either investment banking (underwriting shares) or commercial banking (taking deposits and granting loans). The Federal Deposit Insurance Corporation was created to restore the solvency of the banking system, and the public's confidence in it, by insuring deposits in commercial banks, thereby reducing the likelihood of bank runs. In exchange, however, commercial banks were subject to strict regulations, which limited their competitiveness. Of these, the most important was "regulation Q," which by imposing a ceiling on interest rates severely inhibited the growth of savings accounts within the commercial banking system.

Another populist response to the discrediting of the commercial banking system was the creation of policies to promote the thrift industry as its financial rival. The savings and loan industry benefited from the New Deal in three ways. First, the federal government granted federal charters and created the Federal Home Loan Bank system and the Federal Home Loan Bank Board to perform for the thrift industry the same functions performed for commercial banks by the comptroller of the currency and the Federal Reserve Board. Second, the Roosevelt administration extended to the thrift industry a range of direct and indirect subsidies, including deposit insurance, guaranteed deductible mortgages, public housing programs, and urban renewal schemes. Finally, the federal government exempted the thrift industry from regulation Q, which gave it a near-monopoly of the vast pool of consumer savings which Americans proceeded to amass to finance home purchases. Accordingly, the thrift industry grew from an underdeveloped $6-billion marginal player in the 1940s to a $200-billion giant by the late 1960s. By the late 1960s, the thrift industry numbered 489 mutual savings banks in New York and New England and 5,544 savings and loan associations which predominated in such fast-growing states as California, Florida, and Texas. By 1971, the mortgage sector controlled by the thrifts represented $499 billion, of which $374 billion was residential housing, some 15 percent of all assets in the credit market. It would eventually be the largest component in the U.S. capital market, dwarfing even the market for U.S. government debt. The development of this "popular" financial sector linked the aspirations of a wide segment of the American population to a financial sector that was untouched by the Federal Reserve, if not diametrically opposed to it.

As a result of the New Deal reforms, the single most relevant fact about the U.S. financial system for the Federal Reserve was its volatile juxtaposition of overwhelming size and pronounced fragmentation. During the 1950s and 1960s, the credit market comprised approximately 50,000 financial institutions, including 14,000 banks; 35,000 noncommercial depository institutions (the so-called thrifts); thousands of investment bankers, securities dealers, and brokers; and numerous government agencies. Within each of these there was often a bewildering diversity: the banking sector alone was markedly segmented by size, type of business, geography, type of assets, ownership, and regulatory supervision.

Above all, only one-third of America's financial institutions were members of the official monetary system over which the Federal Reserve presided. Unlike the situation in postwar Germany, where all financial institutions were subject to control by the Bundesbank, the great majority of American institutions were not directly subject to the Fed's reserve requirements, did not have access to its discount window, and were only indirectly affected by its open-market policies. The thrift institutions had their own agencies, and nonmember banks relied primarily on their own management skills for survival. These banks, registered with state authorities, had still lower reserve requirements (indeed, Illinois had no reserve requirements), and twenty-five states allowed their bank regulators considerable latitude in varying reserve requirements according to the per-ceived soundness of the banks. But many of these banks expected in ef-fect to free-ride on the Fed's obligations as a lender of last resort. Even the monetary system itself was structurally fragmented. It included both national banks (whose membership was required and accounted for 80 percent of the Fed's membership) and state banks that chose voluntarily to affiliate with the Fed. Member banks accounted for 80 percent of de-posits within the commercial bank sector. However, of the 5,700 Federal Reserve members, only 178 were the major "reserve city banks," while the remainder, the vast bulk of the Fed's membership, were so-called "coun-try banks" that used the reserve city banks as quasi-central banks and were subject to more relaxed reserve regulations, including both lower reserve requirements and longer delays in meeting those rates.

These patterns of financial specialization made American banks much more vulnerable than German banks to the economic fate of a region or a single set of industries, because German banks had freedom to diversify their risks more widely. Except for the postwar period, when Europe and Japan were rebuilding, American banks have not been truly dominant players either in the world economy or at home. The largest American banks were not large relative to the rest of the financial sector, nor were they large relative to American industry. In the late 1960s, 75 percent of American banks had less than $50 million in assets. The top ten banks in the United States in the late 1960s had only 25 percent of the total assets of the commercial banking sector. In West Germany fewer than a dozen universal banks controlled over 60 percent of the nation's banking assets; in the United States, a similar degree of domination required counting 417 banks. For firms with access to banks in large money centers, there was a high degree of choice. American corporations had more freedom to minimize banks' control over their activities by splitting their accounts among different financial institutions. For banks, however, this meant less capacity to supervise the firms to which they were lending, and a greater degree of exposure and risk.

One principal consequence of such regulatory division and depen-dency was a weakening of American financial institutions' political capac-ity to formulate preferences about monetary policy and press them on the Fed. Because of the high degree of regulatory restrictions on the U.S. banking sector, bankers' relations with the Fed revolved almost exclu-sively around regulatory issues and not at all around monetary issues. As one senior staff member of the American Bankers Association (ABA) put it, "If we were to divide all the times the banks discussed regulation with the Fed by all the times we discussed monetary policy, we would run into the problem of division by zero."[11] In fact, relative to banking sectors in other countries, the American banking sector as a whole had remarkably little sense of its collective interests regarding monetary policy. Thus, in the banking sector there are deep political splits among the ABA (representing the large commercial banks), the Independent Bankers Association (small rural banks) the Mortgage Bankers Association, the Investment Bankers Association, and still other groups representing other financial intermediaries.

While the ABA has often found a sympathetic ear on regulatory issues at the Fed, on Capitol Hill the smaller banks were traditionally able to mobilize localist sentiment to resist repeal of those Glass-Steagall regulations which protected them from competition from commercial banking. Even small changes in regulatory practices, such as changing minimum balances or time periods for certain types of accounts, can shift market share among products and financial sectors far more immediately than can alterations in monetary policy. A reading of the ABA's briefing book, *Compendium of Banking Issues,* reveals that the banking sector's priorities are overwhelmingly legislative and regulatory. For years the ABA has stressed such issues such as structure (for example, the repeal of the McFadden Act), "new service opportunities" (repeal of Glass-Steagall, access to the insurance market, etc.), supervisory issues (capital adequacy, etc.) and consumer issues; only last and superficially do the ABA briefing documents turn to economic and monetary policy. There one finds— after high-minded support for the guaranteed student loan program— pro forma calls for balanced budgets, price stability, free trade, and lower taxes.[12] When we add that Fed governors are "allergic" to discussing monetary policy with outsiders, the resulting picture is clear. There is simply no easily mobilized constituency for monetary policy of any type among the banking community. And in Washington, constituencies are everything.

The political weakness of American financial institutions would leave them vulnerable to further regulation, and this could only further weaken the powers and culture of the Fed. It is important to recognize the absolute limits to Fed policy imposed by the populist regulatory burden of the monetary system. Even as early as the 1960s, competitive pressures were leading financial institutions to search for new ways to profit and survive outside the Fed's regulatory straightjacket. This led to declining bank membership in the Federal Reserve system itself, as ever more banks in the 1960s found state charters, with their lighter regulatory hand, more attractive from the point of view of competitiveness. Another consequence of regulation was the dramatic growth of both the Fed funds market and the money market beyond the confines of the commercial banking system. The Fed funds market is the market for reserve balance among commercial banks which the Fed controls through open-market purchases and sales of paper in the money market. As such, it is a subset of the money market, that segment of the credit market comprising credit claims maturing within a year. During the 1960s, the money market represented the largest component of the total credit market measured by trading volume, and one-seventh of the outstanding claims measured by value. In this highly liquid and volatile wholesale market, the principal players were originally the Federal Reserve and the large commercial banks. However, because of restrictions on interest rates elsewhere in the financial system, the money market attracted many new participants. For example, the U.S. government's short-term paper came to dominate the money market (60 percent of the total) at least in part because Congress prohibited long-term bond-issues at rates of interest above 4 percent. By 1970, $180 billion of the federal government's debt was in long-term bonds, while some $160 billion was issued by the government and its agencies at maturities of 1 to 3 months. Similarly, corporations had also come to prefer the money market to placing their money with banks. Thus, whereas in 1960 significantly more than half of corporate short-term cash flow was held in non–interest-bearing demand deposits, by 1970 fully two-thirds were invested in the money-market.

The Fed's concerns about the health of the banks and its own monetary control led it to put increased emphasis on the sustained orderliness and efficiency of the banks' money market. While the Fed can never be certain about its influence on long-term interest rates, it has always known that it can exercise relatively close control over the level of very short-term interest rates. The Fed's increasing preoccupation with the stability of interest rates in the money market and on regulation was identified as a problem as early as the recession of 1960–1961. Traditionally, the Fed expressed its policy decisions as a "tightening" or a "loosening" of credit conditions in the interbank money market. The Fed assumed that higher interest rates for the banks meant tightening, whereas lowering necessarily meant loosening. But as the recession of 1960–1961 demonstrated (with echoes of 1929), this overlooked the *demand* for credit. During periods of low demand, even low interest rates could actually be restrictive. This was the conclusion of a special investigation conducted by Allan Meltzer and Karl Brunner for the chairman of the House Banking Commitee, Wright Patman. They concluded that the Fed's "traditional banking outlook" was proving to be a conceptual and operational barrier distracting it from smoothly and effectively stabilizing the wider economy.

The growth of the money market in turn had a destabilizing effect on the precarious balance among the various financial sectors. Officially, the Fed's position was that it sought to maintain "balanced competition" between the various regulatory categories of financial sectors. Unofficially, the Fed grew concerned about the possible loss of policy efficiency represented by the explosive growth of the thrift industry as a parallel banking system outside the system of monetary control. By the mid-1960s, only one third of financial institutions (measured by assets) remained in the so-called monetary system. Consequently, commercial banks sought, and the Fed approved, a series of increases in the interest rate ceilings mandated by regulation Q between 1959 and 1966. This reduced the banks' competitive disadvantage relative to the thrifts. At the same time, commercial banks had been moving into the thrifts' market by offering savings accounts to retail customers and seeking out more mortgage business. This intersectoral rivalry came to a head in 1966, when the Federal Reserve and the Home Loan Bank Board secured a series of measures and agreements whereby thrifts would now for the first time be subject to regulation Q and commercial banks would be prohibited to pay more interest on their savings deposits (in fact, they were allowed to pay slightly less) than was paid by the thrifts. This last set of regulations now created a real risk that the interaction between the Fed's restrictive monetary policy and the money market could imperil the survival of a structurally important—and politically powerful—financial sector: the thrifts.

The combination of a swollen, deregulated money market and a fragmented financial system laboring under highly restrictive regulatory constraints helps explain one mystery about the politics of monetarism. It is common knowledge that financial markets in the United States, beginning in the late 1960s, were on the whole more powerful, more entrepreneurial, and more innovative in devising new financial products than were financial markets in, for example, Germany. Yet if markets were such an active, growing force in America, why would America prove so resistant to the doctrine apparently most congenial to them, monetarism? The answer, in brief, is that the United States was really (and to some extent still is) in transition between two models of financial activity: one based on regulation, the other based on markets. In circumstances of transition, the interaction of the two may provide contradictory constraints and incentives for policymakers, which was certainly the case with the Fed in the 1960s and would remain so for some time. Growth and entrepreneurship in the money market were not merely living alongside regulation; in reality, a series of innovations were being grafted on top of, or around, a regulatory foundation.

The first problem for Fed policymakers was that the graft might kill the host before it had a chance to adapt. This was the conundrum that confronted the Fed after 1966. The regulatory inertia of interest rate ceilings, if not their mere presence, meant that when the Fed chose to combat inflation, rising interest rates on the money market siphoned off vast quantities of savings deposits, throwing the thrifts (which disproportionately controlled the mortgage market) into severe liquidity crises. Thrifts would be forced to call loans and cancel further mortgage commitments, and this loss of credit almost instantaneously suffocated the housing market, and soon thereafter construction firms, the white goods industry, and other sectors dependent on housing. Increased unemployment, when it came, would be disproportionately concentrated among home builders and construction workers. Economists called this problematic new form of stabilization a "credit crunch." The first time the Fed applied monetary restraint under the new regulatory circumstances of a credit crunch was in 1966. The impact was indeed highly selective. The housing sector suffered an immediate and unprecedented decline of 47 percent in housing starts. Thus this sector, which represented only 4 percent of the economy, bore upwards of 70 percent of the total loss of output. Conversely, other sectors of the economy, such as heavy manufacturing, commerce, and retailing, were affected hardly at all.

Few Americans whose livelihoods were gained in these unaffected sectors were even aware that there was a recession in 1966, much less that it caused the Federal Reserve and other American financial regulators great distress. For not only did this new credit-crunch method of monetary control call into immediate question the solvency of many savings and loans, but, as the Hunt Commission would later report, the new system also called into question the long-term viability of the entire thrift sector. Though the Fed was not formally responsible for the welfare of the thrift sector, it could not now escape blame for what happened to it. This fact would add to the Fed's hesitancy and defensiveness the next time it needed to cool off the economy. To be the tough regulator of one's own industry was one thing politically; to be the tough regulator of someone else's industry was quite another. This no-win political bind was thus the Fed's second problem. As the 1960s wore on, the Fed began to believe that it could not use its chief weapon, monetary restraint, without endangering the weapon itself. Yet to fail to use this weapon would provoke inflation and social discontent, particularly in those corners of the economy, such as the workforce in heavy manufacturing, that were increasingly escaping the scythe of stabilization.

The Reconstruction of Labor

Just as New Deal reforms froze in place a fragmented banking system and deprived the Fed of powerful constituencies for alternative policies, so too New Deal labor reforms severed an important link between monetary policy and America's working population. These reforms likewise removed from the Fed's policy environment a potentially important set of incentives for domestically oriented stabilization.

Prior to 1933, labor union mobilization was strongly influenced by the strength and direction of the monetary cycle. In periods of inflation, workers formed new unions and swelled the ranks of old unions, partly to exploit their increased bargaining power in periods of high demand, but even more to recoup monetary losses to inflation. Recessions and depressions had the opposite effect: increased unemployment weakened unions' bargaining power and increased defections by members. Thus, the National Trades Union was formed during the "wildcat" inflation of the mid-1830s, only to collapse under the weight of the panic of 1837 and the following depression. This cycle repeated itself with the inflation of the California gold rush of the 1840s, the panic of 1857, the greenback inflation of post–Civil War era, the long depression of the late 1800s, the war boom of 1916–1920, and the recession of 1920–1921.

However, during the 1920s, the connection between monetary conditions and the mobilization of America's workforce began to loosen. As Peterson explained:

> The chief reason for the absence of trade union growth during the 1920s was the failure to organize the expanding mass-production industries. . . . The comparatively high wages received by these workers were not diluted by rising costs of living, for the prices which workers paid for what they bought remained stable through this period. If there had been a marked increase in the cost of living, no doubt many of the un-organized workers would have sought the assistance of already established unions or formed new ones, just as they had in the past when prices were rising.[13]

Union membership, which stood at 5 million in 1920, eroded to 3.3 million in 1930.

The break in this monetary-labor cycle was completed by the legislation that swept through Congress during the Great Depression of the 1930s. Beginning with the Norris-LaGuardia Act and culminating in the National Labor Relations (Wagner) Act, legislation created regulatory bodies, such as the National Labor Relations Board, which facilitated the founding and expanded the membership of unions in the mass-production industries, primarily in the smaller urban centers in the Northeast, and in the South and West. For the first time, union membership climbed during a period of monetary slack, reaching over 8 million in 1939. This trend continued through World War II (enrollments increased to over 13 million), and neither postwar recession nor a weakening of the laws (by Taft-Hartley) stopped the unions' growth. Membership peaked at 17 million in the mid-1950's; by some measures this was close to 35 percent of the civilian workforce.

The reformation of American labor redefined its implications for American monetary policy in important ways. The major consequence was a considerable isolation of a large portion of economic activity from direct exposure to the effects of Federal Reserve monetary policy. To a much greater extent than in Germany, wage bargaining was highly fragmented, and it reflected decisions of the National Labor Relations Board more often than the central bank. American unions, for example, could win closed shops or arbitration over wage scales which German unions neither had nor desired. New Deal regulations protected but froze in place America's plethora of craft and industrial unions. In the 1960s, the AFL-CIO was a loose affiliation of 137 different unions, while 47 unions remained outside as independents. Some scholars have correctly noted that while rates of unionization may have been comparable in the United States and Germany, wage bargaining was quite different, especially with regard to units of bargaining, the length of contracts, and the rate of contract coverage (i.e., whether the same contract is automatically extended to nonunion workers). While these factors matter, they should not be exaggerated. Where union representation was heaviest—automobiles and steel, for example, were both unionized at rates of 75 percent to 100 percent—there have historically been extensive patterns of industrywide wage bargaining. During the long period of low inflation during the 1950s, the mass-production sector evolved a pattern of signing contracts lasting two years or more.

Thus, although the unions organized a relatively high proportion of the American workforce during the 1950s and 1960s—roughly comparable to the rate of unionization found in Germany at the same time—federal involvement in union organization, their organizational fragmentation, and above all, the growing weakness of the financial system in disciplining those sectors of American industry where workers were strongest made unions less influential for the policy environment of the Federal Reserve. For good or for ill, unions neither represented a nationwide constituency capable of pressing its policy ideas on the Federal Reserve nor presented themselves as a unified structural problem which the Fed could be induced to manage.

Reconstruction of the International Monetary Arena

A third potential avenue for introducing new norms and expertise into the central bank's culture and policy environment is its international relationships. Here too, the precise form of this involvement did not provide a lasting support for intellectual openness and innovation.

During the closing stages of the World War II, the U.S. Treasury helped organize the Bretton Woods system of fixed exchange rates. This system required all member countries to maintain a fixed value for their currency in terms of dollars. The United States, however, was the exception, in that it was required to maintain a fixed price ($35) for the dollar in gold. This system was meant to give international trading more liquidity and flexibility than a gold-only standard would have provided, while at the same time creating an anti-inflationary anchor. By the 1950s, the key features of the system included: fixed par values with a presumption against change; the dollar as principal reserve currency (by 1960, the dollar would overtake sterling as the most widely held currency reserve); the convertibility of major currencies, and the role of the International Monetary Fund as international central banker.[14]

The inability of the international arena to constrain the Fed was also revealed by the policy dilemma first identified by Robert Triffin. Triffin's dilemma derived from the fact that under Bretton Woods, all member currencies fixed their parities with reference to the dollar, while the dollar itself was anchored to gold. Other countries depended on America to provide liquidity to the international market by running a modest deficit in its balance of payments, resulting in a net outflow of dollars which other countries used for trade and held as reserves for their own currency. Their willingness to do so, however, rested on American policy performing a delicate balancing act to maintain the price of $35 per ounce of gold. As other countries accumulated reserves faster than the U.S. stock of gold increased, the proportion of dollars held in relation to U.S. gold reserves declined. Thus, the Triffin dilemma necessarily raised the specter of a run on dollars at some future point, *even if* the Fed pursued an anti-inflationary policy. That this was originally a mild dilemma, and not a severe one, had to do with the fact that it was more or less consciously built into the original design in 1944. That it became a crisis was primarily due to the unforeseen spectacular recovery of international trade. In the early days of Bretton Woods, the acute dollar shortage experienced by foreign governments was feared to be permanent. Only in the 1960s, when Europe's economies revived fully, did the long-term problem begin to present itself as a genuine possibility. This possibility drew closer to a reality only gradually so long as the export of dollars was accounted for primarily by military outlays, development assistance, or direct capital investment: that is to say, so long as the United States had a favorable balance of trade. International negotiators believed that they had plenty of time to fix the underlying problem by reducing the dollar's role in Bretton Woods, to make it much more a currency like any other. Measures in this direction, such as the gold pool, and above all, the invention of IMF "special drawing rights" (which conformed more closely to Keynes's original vision for Bretton Woods), appeared to have every prospect of transforming the foundations of Bretton Woods into a system whose fate did not rest on the management (or mismanagement) of a single currency. Thus the major question was whether the transformation could be effected in such a way as to help the Fed find another intellectual basis for its policies.

The Reconstruction of Government

Government shapes the policy environment of the Federal Reserve both as a legacy of the founding of the republic—particularly the separation of powers—and as a result of the expansion of Washington after 1933, which chiefly benefited the executive branch. When the founders designed a system of divided powers that offered the public multiple points of entry into the policy process, they instituted multiple opportunities for policy veto. The potential powers of the federal government vis à vis the Fed are substantial. But because these powers are in separate hands, they require a unifying force if they are to be used. Only when monetary policy crises unleash widespread discontent can Congress exploit populist sentiments to construct an anti-Fed congressional majority. Even this populism can never take effective form unless it also secures the support of the president, whose preoccupation with other matters of state often trumps his interest in domestic economic issues.

In consequence of the New Deal and World War II, the executive branch and the presidency grew enormously in size and prestige. Scholars who study the interaction of the Fed and the presidency have two alternative views about it. According to one school of thought, the central bank influences monetary policy in the short run, but in the long run, as Beck expressed it, "it seems clear that if we compare the political resources of the executive and the central bank, the executive is likely to win any fights with the central banks when the executive desires to use its resources."[15] Conversely, Kiewiet, Rose, Nordhaus, Hibbs, Cameron, and others have argued that there may be substantial short-run pressure on the Fed from the White House to support the president's electoral motives, or those of his party or political constituencies.[16] Indeed, Federal Reserve officials call the "constant drumbeat for lower interest rates" from every president, no matter what his party, "the White House disease." But the evidence from the Martin era suggests that both formulations may miss the crucial point. Although the president's long-term resources may indeed be superior to those of the Fed, a peacetime president has little concept of what he wants monetary policy to accomplish in the long-term and is less able to secure his short-run objectives without active cooperation from the Fed or Congress—which, absent those economic crises the Fed can usually prevent, will not be forthcoming.

The president's chief resources are his ability, with the advice and consent of the Senate, to appoint Federal Reserve governors and designate chairmen and vice chairmen; his authority in the realms of taxation and spending; and above all, as holder of the nation's highest elective office, his ability to propose and lobby for legislation that would significantly affect the Federal Reserve or monetary policy. That presidents usually do not have independent monetary goals to guide their most immediate tool—their power of appointment—is evident from the first twenty years of the postwar Fed. Martin was appointed by Truman; outlasted Eisenhower, Kennedy, and Johnson; and left office during the Nixon administration. During Martin's tenure, there were only eleven openings on the board of governors, which meant on average three appointments per president, usually not enough to form a solid voting bloc within the board (even assuming that board members vote the administration's interests, an assumption for which there is no evidence) and certainly not enough to form a bloc within the FOMC. Moreover, it is remarkable that Martin, having first been designated chairman for a four-year term under Truman, was redesignated chairman by Eisenhower (twice), Kennedy, and Johnson.

These reappointments, together with the unbending stabilization policy pursued by Martin, suggest strongly that under Martin the Fed, not the presidency, was in control of the politics of monetary policy. This matters because electoral cycle theory and coalition theory predict that presidents will pressure the Fed to supply them with politically self-interested monetary policy. These patterns of appointments reveal that the presidential appointment mechanism simply does not provide the leverage this theory requires. The fact that the incumbent Democrats had to run against restrictive monetary policy in 1952, when Stevenson lost, and that the Republican Richard Nixon had to run against the recession of 1960, again suggests that, in the short term, at least, patterns of influence run from the Federal Reserve to presidents and parties, and not the other way around.

This perception is reinforced by the weakness of the structures that the president can call upon to assist him with formulating economic policy. These are primarily the White House staff, the Treasury, the Bureau of the Budget (later Office of Management and Budget, OMB), and the Council of Economic Advisors (CEA). With respect to monetary policy, the Treasury is the most important. In addition to it debt issues, the Treasury is responsible for intervening in foreign exchange and monitoring developments in domestic monetary policy.[17] The chairman of the Federal Reserve and the secretary of the Treasury meet frequently. The OMB prepares the president's budget; the CEA—a panel of three economists appointed by the president—prepares the president's annual economic report, and its chairman meets with the president periodically to consult on broad issues of economic policy.[18] Their influence within most administrations is usually not great, and the economic report of the president is frequently dismissed as a partisan document.[19] The White House staff, particularly the senior advisers for domestic affairs, can be very influential but often are not well versed in issues of monetary policy. The president is normally inattentive to the Fed's actions because his energies are focused elsewhere. Budgetary policy, and especially foreign policy, are two issues that normally take precedence.

One of the clearest lessons of Fed history has to do with its mobilization into the executive branch during wartime. In both world wars, the Fed became the agent of the Treasury's war financing interests. This happened so seamlessly as to suggest that a clear national objective, combined with popular support, brought the Federal Reserve to heel. Yet absent a clear overriding national objective provided by a war effort, dissensus between the White House and Congress allows the Fed to chart its own course. Even the demands imposed by the wars fought under executive leadership—Korea, the cold war, and Vietnam—did not seriously alter the pressures on the Fed. During the Korean War, the Fed even managed to *reduce* inflation, and this low level was maintained during the cold war rearmament and well into the Vietnam War.

The case of the Vietnam War, however, is more problematic. The coincidence of creeping inflation with the escalation of the conflict in Southeast Asia is certainly highly suggestive of inflationary war finance and presidential pressure on the Fed. In March 1965, around the time of this major buildup of U.S. Ground troops in Vietnam, Johnson summoned Martin to his ranch in Texas and apparently requested that Martin keep interest rates low. Martin is reported to have listened in silence and then left. Many have attributed the pickup in the inflation rate in the late 1960s to this encounter, and of course, this cannot be dismissed. Nonetheless, the evidence suggests this was not the actual source of the problem. First, Martin returned to Washington, and at the next meeting of the FOMC the Fed voted for a significant increase in the discount rate. This suggests defiance, not compliance—and that is plausible because the majority of the governors were still appointees from the Eisenhower administration and were not likely to acquiesce in a Democratic president's request. Second, the Vietnam War was not significantly more costly than the Korean War; even in the late 1960s, the total Federal debt still consisted largely of debt from World War II and was still significantly less than that of the U.S. residential mortgage market, for example. Finally, as the previous section suggested, the sources of creeping inflation can be better explained by noting transformations in the financial sector in the late 1960s which made an effective monetary policy more difficult.

Another potential source of presidential influence is the Treasury's right to dictate the exchange rate. In theory this could have meant that the president's international commitments would override the Fed's domestic policy concerns. By the late 1960s, the U.S. trade balance started to slip into deficit. Although the United States had a positive trade balance with virtually all countries with which it traded, two others— Germany and most especially Japan—were such successful exporters into the American market that the overall U.S. trade balance became negative. This not only made the possibility of a run on gold more imminent but also raised the question of what kind of adjustment mechanism would be used. Because the system lacked symmetry (another aspect of the Triffin dilemma), disputes arose about which countries should change the value of their currencies to resolve the crisis. Was the dollar declining because the U.S. was in deficit or because Germany was in surplus? Was this a bilateral or a systemic problem? This dispute proved all the harder to resolve because of a broadly shared myth (believed by publics and governments, if not economists themselves), noted in earlier chapters, that par values should be changed only as a last resort, and because some Germans had an economic interest in maintaining their favorable export position. Thus the assumption was that international agreements would require someone's national economy to be "put through the wringer" to save Bretton Woods.

But this channel of influence had its limits. Above all, the president's international interests conflicted with his domestic political interests. This message was reinforced by monetarists, who thought that international negotiations were putting the cart—the international system—before the horse of domestic monetary policy. For them, special drawing rights and their ilk were unnecessary Rube Goldberg devices. The markets will sort things out, they argued. Expecting a system of fixed currencies to accurately reflect the world's myriad long-term growth rates and short-term business cycles was simply too much. The self-evident solution was simply to float all currencies. No complicated diplomatic summits with their acrimonious finger-pointing would be required. Domestic monetary authorities would be free to guide their policies by the best available economic wisdom and not confine their economies in any kind of international straitjacket. Increasingly, this argument found an audience in the Treasury and thus undermined the Treasury's ability to use international currency policy to control the Fed.

Conversely, Congress matters in the evolution of the Fed's corporate culture because its banking committees are lenses that gather the disruptive rays of American populism and focus them on the banking system. As the 1960s would show, Congress is susceptible to an anti-Fed populism which is easily appropriated by a variety of outside critics for their own purposes. Congressional populism has been harnessed to crusades against everything from high inflation to the high interest rates that would reduce inflation. By the 1970s, monetarist critics would be at the forefront in attempting to use Congress to bend the Fed to their will.

Normally, however, monetary policy is among those areas of public policy to which Congress pays least attention. Between the Employment Act of 1946 and the passage of House Resolution 133 in 1975—directing the Fed to target the money supply—Congress failed to enact any legislation whatsoever affecting the Federal Reserve. Not even in the 1970s could it be said that monetary policy occupied the Congressional mind to any where near the extent that for example, the budget did. Yet when aroused, as it began to be in the late 1960s, Congressional populism nevertheless showed itself a highly destabilizing force.

Congressional relations with the Fed are shaped by one overriding fact. Monetary policy is a technical issue with few, if any, tangible electoral benefits to individual members of Congress.[20] What matters to most members of Congress of any stripe is how interest rates, inflation, and unemployment affect their voters.[21] If they think about monetary policy at all, senators and representatives may indeed prefer low inflation, but they fear the electoral consequences of high interest rates, moribund house sales, bankruptcies, and layoffs—which they intuitively recognize as the price of slowing inflation. Members of Congress generally prefer questions of taxing and spending, issues which allow them to direct material benefits (patronage and pork) to their constituents.[22]

The tendency of Congress to neglect monetary policy is reinforced by its internal—party and committee—organization. Its members win office through 535 separate electoral contests that are normally of an intensely local character. Once senators and representatives are elected, their careers are only loosely connected through party membership and party discipline. Legislative success often requires great attention to the preferences of organized interest groups, especially those with influence in members' home districts. Members of Congress will therefore be affected by the geographic and sectoral distribution of the costs and benefits of monetary policy. Stable prices are a universally distributed and collective good, but as we have seen, the distribution of the costs of a disinflationary policy depends on the nature of the financial system. Those sectors which feel the brunt of disinflationary policy are not uniformly distributed throughout the country. When monetary conditions are stable, the majority of senators and representatives leave worrying about the Fed to their colleagues on the banking committees.[23] For members of Congress who are interested in economic issues, such bodies as the Senate Finance Committee and the House Ways and Means Committee, which share authority for fiscal policy, are far more powerful, prestigious, and electorally desirable than the committees (House Banking, Senate Banking, Joint Economic Committee) dealing with monetary policy.

The disjuncture between the economic importance of monetary policy and its electoral irrelevance helps explain the curious patterns of committee politics concerning monetary policy. Contrary to the theory of regulatory capture, which predicts that congressional banking committees will be populated with members sympathetic to bankers' interests, these committees have disproportionately recruited members who are either urban liberals, drawn to the committees for their involvement with housing issues, or rural or small-town opponents of commercial banking—in other words, populists.

In 1963, perhaps the most aggressive of all populists heretofore seen in the banking committees, Representative Wright Patman of East Texas, attained the chairmanship of the House Committee on Banking and Urban Affairs. For the next ten years, he would exploit the congressional seniority system to run his committee with an iron hand. Whereas previous chairmen had taken a relatively low-key approach to banks, Patman was an active interventionist, and his opposition to big banks knew few limits. Whenever he could, he championed the cause of small, independent, locally controlled banks, and especially the newly powerful thrifts. As one of his colleagues observed, "Mr. Patman hates the banks, but he loves the thrifts."[24] Patman would be the first in a line of rural representatives to press the cause of the thrifts. Although ousted from his post in the mid-1970s, he was succeeded by other populists, including Henry Reuss, Fernand St. Germain, and Henry Gonzalez. In the Senate, the Senate Banking Committee for many years was headed by the populist senator from Wisconsin, William Proxmire.

This antibank and anti-Federal Reserve tendency is normally resisted by a larger congressional consensus that respects the Fed's technical expertise and its nonpartisanship (to say nothing of this group's respect for, and support from, commercial banks). But when interest rates go up, and certain banks or industries are hurt by monetary policy, then the minority of congressmen whose districts, states, or constituencies are implicated will be induced to join the pool of Fed critics. Congressmen from districts dominated by industries dependent on credit (such as the construction industry, durable goods, automobiles, and farming) are more likely than others to feel this pressure. Only when financial distress becomes widespread will Congress as a whole take an interest in monetary policy.

The weapons Congress wields in its dealings with the Fed are few, cumbersome, and highly reactive. In any policy area, congressional powers include oversight (hearings and audits), legislation, confirmation of personnel, and budgetary authorizations (the power of the purse). However, the Federal Reserve's institutional independence blunts all these instruments. Most important, because the Federal Reserve's banking activities are enormously profitable, it is entirely self-financing. Therefore, Congress cannot seek to control the Fed by threatening to withhold or curb its funding. The Senate Banking Committee (like the House Banking and

Urban Affairs Committee) and its subcommittee on Domestic Monetary Policy have held routine oversight hearings only since 1975. Oversight hearings are limited by witnesses' complex technical arguments in defense of Fed policies, testimony which can be almost impossible for laypeople to penetrate. The Senate Banking Committee is charged with confirming the president's nominees to the board of governors and his choices for chairman and vice chairman, but it almost never fails to confirm. Turnover is rather high among members of banking committees, as they defect from these low-prestige committees to virtually any others except the post office. Given the complexity of monetary policy, this tends to inhibit the acquisition of expertise among the members, making them all the more dependent on staff.

Staff support for all members of Congress and committees grew steadily throughout the postwar era, but, resources have always been meager in the specific area of monetary policy. Arrayed against the hundreds of economists within the Federal Reserve System, the Senate Banking Committee, for example, had but one staff monetary economist, and even this position was not created until the late 1960s.[25] Additional staff support is provided by the General Accounting Office (GAO), the Congressional Research Service (CRS), and beginning in the 1970s, the Congressional Budget Office (CBO), and the Office of Technology Assessment (OTA). But, the GAO, for instance, has never had the legal authority to examine the Fed's conduct of monetary policy, and efforts by the House Banking and Urban Affairs committee to give it this authority were defeated by Federal Reserve lobbying.[26] Legislation is often similarly dependent on expertise. However, Congress can use legislation for a variety of ends: it can attempt to give the Federal Reserve a new mandate, alter its structure, subject it to audit or budgetary control, or make it part of the Treasury. As thirty years of legislative inactivity demonstrate, Congress is prevented from doing many of these things by its general lack of interest and the Federal Reserve's formidable political resources.

In sum, the Federal Reserve's proximate control over the immediate levers of financial power, together with structural divisions between the presidency and congress, help account for why the central bank was able to achieve significant victories in economic stabilization during the 1950s and 1960s and to disarm the two major political threats in its policy environment, the presidency and Congress—even though these factors failed to nurture a culture within the central bank that was as open as it might have been to new economic doctrines.

The Reconstruction of Economic Advice

One last major transformation which might have brought a wider range of expertise into the Fed's decision-making environment was the maturation of professional economics itself, and the channels by which economists' advice was carried to policymakers. The Great Depression legitimated the prescriptions of macroeconomics and increased economists' willingness and ability to enter the public domain. A full mobilization of a diversity of economists into the Federal Reserve might have widened its manifestly narrow policy horizons. But economists' penetration into the halls of power proved one-sided. The skepticism about the power of markets that the Great Depression naturally encouraged, along with the recent demoralization of the Fed itself, engendered a certain skepticism toward the power of money and promoted a rather Keynesian bias in the profession. But, as we shall see, the major reason for the partial mobilization of expertise lay with the pluralist organization of advice and the inability of American economists to transcend their own individualism.

In the immediate aftermath of the war, the economy returned rapidly to peacetime conditions. But rather than a resumption of the Depression—which many feared—the U.S. economy experienced a sharp bout of inflation during 1946–1947, the highest it had seen since the Civil War, and the strike rate increased dramatically. Memories of the Great Depression had inspired the Employment Act of 1946, which assigned responsibility for the well-being of the economy to the federal government and created the Council of Economic Advisors to assist the president in his management of the economy. The employment mandate also extended to the Federal Reserve itself. Initially, the Treasury believed that the Employment Act required the Fed to continue to fix interest rates on Treasury debt. But with the ending of hostilities and an outbreak of serious inflation, the Federal Reserve thought otherwise.

The first skirmishes in this battle were not promising for the Fed. Chairman Thomas McCabe, who had succeeded Roosevelt's confidant Marriner Eccles as chairman, resigned over the issue in 1951. The struggle between the Treasury and the Fed set off a wide-ranging economic debate in the outside community about what the proper role of the Fed should be. The analysts included the Hoover Commission, the National Planning Association, Congress's Douglas committee, and individual economists such as Milton Friedman.[27] Each of these contributions is characteristic of the way in which expertise is typically mobilized into (economic) policy debate in America. Pluralist mobilization of expertise in America employs a variety of strategies which can be ill-suited to achieving a clear national consensus: specially formed but short-lived national "commissions," a single-issue organization or interest group, a congressional inquiry, and a plenitude of offerings from individual experts. At first, however, the advisory process appeared to work well. On the key question of whether the Treasury or the Fed should make monetary policy, the verdict of these expert testimonials was nearly unanimous against the Treasury. Once again, partisans of public and private power saw the Fed as an expert agency capable of resolving disputes about policy goals and procedures that they themselves could not. That this hope was more pious than practical was evinced by the paucity of positive recommendations for the Fed: on the inevitable question—What, if anything, should replace the gold standard?—there was almost complete dissensus.[28] Every conceivable policy target was proffered—from the money supply to bank reserves, credit conditions, and the consumer inflation rate—but none found an effective constituency. Still, there was enough support behind the Fed to lead to the adoption of the so-called Treasury–Federal Reserve "accord" during the Truman administration, which freed the Fed from further obligation to support Treasury interest rates. If only by default, the Fed remained the only major central bank committed to gold.

Thus, it is wrong to suggest that the Fed's greater difficulties with anti-inflationary policy in the 1970s were due to the earlier advent of Keynesian doctrines of fiscal primacy in the United States. Neither the doctrine nor the capacity for fiscal primacy has been as great as implied. In the American system, the president shares fiscal responsibility with the congress. He proposes budgets drafted by OMB, but these are usually substantially altered by Congress. Throughout the 1950s and most of the 1960s, this lack of fiscal cooperation reduced the incentive for the central bank to respond to fiscal leadership from the executive branch. Most significantly, however, the federal budget was in balance from 1952 until 1968, and again in 1969; thus the pressures from deficit spending were greatly constrained. Walter Heller's famous tax cut of 1964, which gave such luster to the "new economics," did not prevent the Fed from raising interest rates in 1965. Moreover, the proportion of GNP accounted for by federal spending in 1965 was only 17.9 percent, approximately 5 percent lower than in 1980 and approximately 10 percent below that of Germany in the same years.

Even the particular form of the official integration of economists into national policy advice was constrained by pluralism. This can be seen most clearly in the CEA, a body composed of appointed economics professors charged with advising the executive on the direction of macroeconomic policy. But the CEA has always been viewed as a body too closely linked with the administration; rather than simply recruiting the best economists, it has drawn only those with an expressed partisan identification. It has never displayed the intellectual independence from the administration necessary to give its work authority. Indeed, one former CEA official described its work as "propaganda for the president's budget." The CEA report is only rarely very theoretical; it has limited influence even within the administration and often none with the Federal Reserve. As another former CEA official observed, "No one has ever given a damn what the CEA thinks."[29]

THE CORPORATE CULTURE OF THE POSTWAR FEDERAL RESERVE

In terms of formal powers and organization, opportunities for a collegial distribution of power and influence within the Federal Reserve system at the outset of the 1950s largely resembled those of the German Bundesbank. Within the Federal Reserve, as within the Bundesbank, all members of the principal decision-making bodies were formally equal, and decisions were subject to majority vote. All Fed governors are appointed for terms of fourteen years. Their terms are staggered to expire only every two years. Additionally, the Federal Reserve system is entirely self-financing and thus is not subject to budgetary controls by either the president or Congress, as the revenues of the board are retained from the conduct of regulatory and open-market operations of the twelve district banks.

Yet under the influence of its policy environment the Federal Reserve evolved a culture which identified its policy discussions with banking-sector issues, at the cost of more diffuse, public, or universalistic monetary policy concerns. So long as stabilizing the banking sector led to stabilization of the wider economy, and the chairman provided firm leadership, the weakness of the Fed's culture was not evident. Under Martin's chairmanship, the Fed helped the U.S. economy enjoy two decades of low inflation and strong growth. But a decade later, when the Fed's relationship to the financial system needed to be rethought, and its chairman provided weak or inconsistent leadership, the adaptability of the Fed's culture would be found wanting. This made the transition to monetarism a more prolonged and tumultuous affair.

Paying attention to the influence of the Fed's policy environment on its decision-making capacity—its culture—is important because agencies are able to redefine their statutory mission in the light of what their policy environment will sanction—what scholars of public administration call "mission creep." It is sometimes suggested, for example, that the difference in performance of the Bundesbank and the Federal Reserve lies in their founding statutes, that the Fed was charged with multiple and conflicting goals earlier than the Bundesbank, which is said to have had a clear anti-inflationary mission. In fact, though, as we have seen in 1967 the Bundesbank was charged with pursuing a "magic quadrangle" of full employment, reasonable price stability, economic growth, and international equilibrium; but the Fed was not given so explicit a catalogue until the passage of the Full Employment and Balanced Growth Act (Humphrey-Hawkins Act) of 1978. Even during the 1950s and 1960s the Fed had no trouble in reviewing anti-inflation as a consequence of its stabilization mandate. The real issue, as we shall see, was that the Fed's policy environment encouraged an excessive focus on the stability of certain banks, whereas the Bundesbank's environment allowed it to reinterpret its mission in terms of wider economic concerns and perspectives.

The primary impact of the Fed's fragmented policy environment is to be observed in the culture of the principal decision-making bodies. The Fed's decision-making powers were formally located in two administrative bodies, the board of governors (the approximate analogue of the Bundesbank's Directorate and the Federal Open Market Committee (analogous to the Bundesbank's Central Bank Council.) The board of governors comprises seven individuals nominated by the president and confirmed by the Senate. One governor is designated by the president to act as chairman, and another to serve as deputy chairman, for a renewable four-year period. The duties of the board of governors are, first, to vote on regulatory matters concerning banks within the system; second, to supervise the monetary, regulatory, and banking functions of the twelve federal Reserve Banks; and, finally, to participate as members of the Federal Open Market Committee in setting national monetary policy.

Regulatory matters, which are the exclusive province of the board, include issues with a direct bearing on monetary policy and with no direct bearing, which may therefore be considered of interest primarily to particular banks or sectors of the financial industry. Issues bearing directly on monetary policy include setting reserve requirements, approving changes in discount rates proposed by the district banks, regulating the use of credit for investment in the stock market, and raising or lowering the interest rates paid by member banks on time and savings deposits (regulation Q). Nonmonetary regulation of member banks includes such matters as conditions of membership in the system, ownership, or the types of products and services which may be offered by different sectors within the industry. The board of governors also exercises significant oversight of the district banks and their activities, including their selection of management personnel; approves nominees for district bank president; and supervises district banks' budgets, their examination of member banks, and their economic research.

The third function performed by the board—setting the overall direction of Federal Reserve monetary policy—is exercised jointly with the Federal Reserve bank presidents through the Federal Open Market Committee. The Employment Act created the FOMC in recognition of a need to coordinate the activities of the board and the district bank presidents in the interest of a consistent national monetary policy. The FOMC meets monthly and comprises twelve voting members: the seven governors and the president of the New York Federal Reserve Bank, and four of the remaining eleven district bank presidents. By convention, the remaining presidents attend and are permitted to speak at FOMC meetings; the unique status of the New York Fed derives from its residence in the nation's major financial center, and its legal status as the agent of the other district banks and the FOMC in the market. Again by convention, the chairman of the board of governors serves as chairman of the FOMC, and the president of the New York Fed serves as deputy chairman. The FOMC's principal task is to draft policy directives to the New York Fed's open-market desk. These directives set out the criteria for the Fed's sales and purchases in the Fed funds market, actions which will determine the direction of (short-term) interest rates and the growth of monetary aggregates and will ultimately influence the terms and availability of credit within the entire financial system. By examining the relationships among the chairman, the governors, the staff, and the district bank presidents, we will consider how the opportunities for a sustained balance of power and an effective mobilization of expertise were much lower in the Federal Reserve than in the Bundesbank, despite the federal Reserve's extraordinary de facto independence.

The single greatest difference between the cultures of the Bundesbank and the Fed lies in the greater authority of the Fed chairman, an authority which exceeds his formal statutory powers. By statute, the chairman is legally the active chief executive officer of the Federal Reserve. He retains exclusive responsibility for its finances and staffing. He does not, however, have the power to reorganize the fundamental management structure of the Fed; that requires legislation. Thus the principal of managerial responsibility that shapes the professionalism of the Bundesbank's council applies only to the Fed chairman. The fact that Federal Reserve chairmen have usually, though not always, been leaders in the world of finance, banking, or economics means that one of their chief sources of influence is their ability to exercise intellectual leadership. Moreover, the chairman as spokesman for and acknowledged leader of the institution is expected to articulate and defend the viewpoint of the Fed. The Fed chairman has no institutionalized counterweight. The jobs of seconds in command are divided between the vice chairman of the board of governors (a position which has come to be identified with the interests of the White House) and the deputy chairman of the FOMC.[30]

Since its inception, the Federal Reserve has striven to maintain scrupulous nonpartisanship, particularly concerning appointments of governors. But in comparison with the Bundesbank, this may undermine the governors' power. In both systems, the governors are legally guaranteed a long term of office, and their salaries are fixed by law to ensure their independence form outside political manipulation. In the selection of Fed governors the president is required to ensure a balanced representation among Federal Reserve districts and sectors of the economy. Yet in practice, by the 1950s, not only were governors without de jure party affiliation, but regional and sectoral representation had evaporated as well. Bankers from New York or other financial centers were regularly nominated to districts in the hinterland; as early as 1934, for example, Adolph Miller switched from "representing" San Francisco to representing Richmond, and the Fed managed to survive forty-four years before a governor was ever appointed to represent the Philadelphia district. Agriculture lost whatever power it ever had to secure a seat at the board table for its representatives. Instead, with the passage of time, "balanced representation" came to mean representation of the various financial sectors and banking interests, such as the securities industry, commercial banks, or country banks. Indeed, political support from the various competing banking groups helps explain why, in the highly regulatory days after the war, Martin was the longest-serving Fed chairman (nineteen years) and his chairmanship saw the lowest turnover rate in the entire history of the Fed. Governors appointed just after Martin became chairman include A. L. Mills, Jr. (thirteen years); J. L. Robertson (nineteen years); C. Canby Balderston (twelve years); and Charles N. Shepardson (twelve years).[31]

The ability of the Fed's policy environment to effectively mobilize external constituencies weakened, however, and its internal balance of power steadily degenerated as governors lost influence. Over time, the nomination of governors less frequently reflected the needs of outside groups and became increasingly influenced by, and not untypically initiated by, the chairman himself. It was the chairman who determined the Fed's "needs"—a banker, a securities expert, someone with international experience—and suggested to the White House whom it should appoint. Willy-nilly, the board gradually became "congenial to the preferences of the chairman."[32] Presidents came to appoint governors "who could work with the chairman, whoever he may be."[33] Most former governors interviewed reported that the administrations that appointed them wanted a governor to be "flexible," "pragmatic," "a team player," and, especially, "not an ideologue".[34] Unsurprisingly, as governors' authority declined, the average postwar term of office declined steadily, reaching its low point of somewhat over five years in the 1970s.[35]

Another characteristic weakness in the mobilization of expertise within the Federal Reserve is the rarely bridged chasm between the careers of staff members and governors. In the Fed, unlike the Bundesbank, only in rare circumstances have senior staff members ever been appointed to the board of governors. This removes the incentive for the highly talented staff economists to identify themselves with the governors, or to see a governor's chair as the culmination of a meritorious career. Furthermore, no Federal Reserve chairman in the modern era has been promoted from within the ranks of the board or the board staff, or—with the exception of Volcker—from the ranks of the district presidents. This means that the chairman's economic theories will not have first been tempered by experience within the central bank itself.

The weakness of Fed governors has led some observers to speculate that excessive staff power and entrenched staff procedures have been the source of the Fed's inflexible policy culture. The most likely origin of this hypothesis is the operational gulf between the governors and the senior staff appointed by the chairman. Governors frequently complain of their enforced distance from the daily workings of the institution, and makes them suspect that "we governors hear what the staff want us to hear." Certainly, governors' lack of line management responsibilities and the Federal Reserve staff's standard operating procedures (in which they privately hammer out intellectual differences before presenting forecasts and policy options in the boardroom) isolate governors from many of the issues that divide staff members themselves.[37] As one former Governor summarized his role, "A governor's job is to sit in his office, read reports, attend meetings, and vote when expected to."[36] Because close working relationships with individual governors are discouraged, staff work and staff presentations are shaped by the "collective tastes" of the governors; though individual projects may be commissioned by individual governors, this is reportedly unusual. All these factors certainly contribute to governors' individual or collective sense of disenfranchisement, yet there is virtually no solid evidence allowing the inference that the staff therefore determines monetary policy or the wider Fed culture. On the contrary, senior staff members themselves plausibly make the case that their own influence depends at least in part on the authority and professionalism of those for whom they work. Their potential for power rests on their impartiality and neutrality, their mastery of technique, and their engagement with the wider academic and policy community. But their actual influence, they believe, is dependent on the capabilities of the chairman and governors; they are "brilliant implements" which require expertise to be used properly. When the governors are less capable or demanding, the staff may be less effectively utilized.

Finally, in the United States (as in Germany), the presidents and staffs of district Federal Reserve banks are potential sources of innovation, not least because they are physically removed from the standard operating procedures in Washington. But opportunities for rebellion are more greatly circumscribed in the FOMC than in the Central Bank Council in Frankfurt. First, for district bank presidents, unlike their German counterparts, even a unified front produces only a minority of votes. Second, the "federal" component of the Fed is severely attenuated. In the Federal Reserve, the regional bank presidents owe nothing to state governors or senators; presidents are nominated by district boards of directors and vetted by the board. They are primarily "public relations" people in their home districts; the lack of an independent electoral, state, or party constituency undermines their independence.[38] An important part of the explanation for this difference is the different location of regulatory and monetary decision making in the two banks. In the Fed, all significant regulatory decisions either are taken exclusively by the board or require the board's approval. The only regulatory initiative that remains with the district banks is proposing a change in the discount rate, and even this is ultimately controlled by the FOMC. In the Bundesbank, the situation is reversed. The Central Bank Council, on which the Land central bank presidents are a numerical majority, ultimately controls the major regulatory levers, including the rediscount rate and minimum reserve ratios.

Recollections of former governors and FOMC members, combined with reports of those votes that have been made public, suggests the following picture of the relationship between chairmen, governors, and Federal Reserve district bank presidents. Federal Reserve chairmen lose some votes within the board on regulatory matters and occasionally, though quite rarely, on monetary policy; but they virtually never lose votes within the FOMC on monetary policy.[39] Members of the FOMC do not lobby each other or caucus on votes; they have traditionally come into meetings with an open mind. But as one observer said, "If you're not committed, you're swayable".[40] Indeed, it came to be understood that one of the chairman's rights—if not his duty—was to create consensus within the FOMC, and that dissenting votes were to be interpreted as "votes of no confidence" in the chairman's leadership. This perception, reinforced by the publication of FOMC minutes, has been said to give the Fed chairman an "implicit veto right" over FOMC decisions.[41] Here the contrast with the Bundesbank is most stark. Former Federal Reserve governors—both former chairmen and others—report a perception that Bundesbank presidents have found themselves on the losing side of votes on monetary policy which, had they occurred at the Fed, would have led the chairman to resign.[42]

In sum, it is evident that the Federal Reserve's policy bodies gradually lost their collegiality, whereas in the Bundesbank collegiality survived. Studies of the Fed in the 1950s revealed that the chairman had disproportionate but not excessive power. By the early 1970s, the former governor Sherman Maisel attributed a still larger influence—which he estimated at about 35 percent—on Fed policies to the chairman's influence. And in the 1990s, one of Wall Street's premier Fed watchers, David Jones, argued that the chairman had garnered "nearly absolute powers in internal administrative matters and Fed policy formulation."[43]

The Federal Reserve's parochial policymaking culture, which guided its response to the challenge of monetarism beginning in the 1970s, reflected the increasingly narrow constraints imposed upon it by America's fragmented policy environment, especially the specialized banking system. The American banking system, because of its implications for the power of the Fed itself, played a direct role in shaping the concerns, powers, and informal authority of the Fed's policymakers. While the disaggregated nature of these financial structures prevented them from wielding positive influence over monetary decision making, they exercised a wide deterrent effect that promoted closed, asymmetrical power relationships in the Fed's decision-making bodies. This chairman-centered policy culture, as we shall see in Chapter 5, would inhibit the efficient mobilization of expertise to help the Fed meet changed economic circumstances.

Yet, for all the Fed's growing cultural weaknesses at the debut of the era of monetarism, our review of the institution's history revealed another crucial reality. When it has a reasonably collegial culture and a healthy financial environment, the Fed's power and independence can be second to none. Indeed, Beck's notion that the short-run power of the central bank overrides the long-run power of the president is applicable not just to the president but to the politics of American monetary policy generally. At an extreme, the "long-run" ability of outside forces—whether political or academic—to impose their will in the Fed may never materialize, because the long run is but a series of "short runs" won by the central bank. Alas for the Federal Reserve, as we shall see in Chapter 5, its next chairman, Arthur Burns, never knew or had forgotten this lesson about the governing power of money.

CHAPTER FIVE

The Monetarist Revolution and the Fed, 1970–1985

For much of the 1970s, America's monetarists enjoyed neither power nor influence. Like their German counterparts, they found their policies resisted by a central bank that became surprisingly supportive of dirigiste economic measures to combat rising prices. In Frankfurt, that resistance was soon overcome, and another chair was set out at the central bank's conference table for monetarist doctrines. But this proved impossible in Washington. Only many years later, and after considerably more political struggle, would America's monetarists win policy measures that even approximated what their German colleagues had earlier secured. The central concern of this chapter is to describe the contrasting and unexpected American episode in the monetarist controversy. I shall show how the interaction of the Fed's chairman-centered corporate culture with growing fissures in America's cantilevered and variegated banking system produced an inefficient and contentious mobilization of monetarist expertise to deal with the problem of inflation.

Few observers of American monetary policy in 1970 would have predicted the "anguish" that awaited the Federal Reserve and American monetary policy in the 1970s.[1] As described in Chapter 4, the postwar Fed had earned a record of rectitude in monetary policy that was the equal of any of its peers. The many years of chairman Martin's leadership had shown decisively that the American central bank could use its formal guarantees of independence—its freedom from budgetary constraints, the fourteen-year term of office of its governors, and so on—to make itself an institution that even the president of the United States treated like a "foreign sovereignty." For such an institution, the step from gold to aggregates ought to have been easy. Moreover, some incipient discontent with inflation had helped Nixon win the White House in 1968.[2] Although among Nixon's inner circle only George Schultz was a self-proclaimed monetarist, many of the others called themselves "Friedmanesque," and Milton Friedman himself was one of Nixon's advisers before the election. In January 1970, at chairman Martin's last meeting, the FOMC for the first time adopted a resolution stipulating that "increased stress should be placed on the objective of achieving modest growth in the monetary aggregates." Martin was succeeded by Arthur Burns, Friedman's former mentor and an arch-opponent of wage and price controls.[3] Burns immediately institutionalized Martin's initiative into FOMC directives to the New York open-market desk. These portents led many to believe that monetarism was now firmly ensconced in Washington.

But all these portents proved misleading. Contrary to all expectations, neither monetarists nor their doctrines would quickly gain power where it mattered most—inside the Fed. The Burns and Miller eras would witness both the implementation of wage and price controls—the antithesis of monetarism—and a dramatic worsening of the inflation rate. Federal Reserve policy inadvertently led to a socioeconomic upheaval that David Hackett Fisher has aptly called a "price revolution."[4] Mounting inflation would force millions of Americans to renegotiate the most fundamental economic relationships in their lives: workers with employers, buyers with sellers, and citizens with government. In human terms, the toll of those renegotiations—in terms of lost jobs, bankrupt firms, and political cynicism—remains incalculable to this day. In terms of policy, however, one cost is evident: the New Deal itself.

Monetarists' inability to pierce the Federal Reserve's intellectual defenses eventually forced them to reexamine their assumptions about the relationship between economic expertise and governance in the American polity. These investigations eventually led them to criticize the ungovernability and bureaucratic immobilism underlying what they called the "inflationary state." Armed with this broadened and politicized concept, American monetarists called into question not just Federal Reserve policies but the central bank's "institutional integrity"—its cherished independence. Following through on the political implications of their doctrines, they founded organizations such as the Shadow Open Market Committee, made common cause with supply-siders in Congress, proselytized the Republican party, championed the populist antitax movement, and awaited their chance at power.

Although that chance appeared to have arrived when Paul Volcker opened the door to monetarism in 1979, the zenith of monetarist involvement in American policymaking came only when Ronald Reagan took office in 1981. The Reagan administration took up the radical monetarist and supply-side agenda that Friedman and his colleagues had developed and offered employment to many of its developers. The monetarists' long-professed goal was a five- to six-year reduction in the growth of the money supply. The advent of this radical agenda in Washington, however, pushed the Fed's belated experiment with monetarism to deliver most of the reduction in Reagan's first eighteen months in office. Thus, monetarists not only helped erect a macroeconomic framework for the unexpectedly rapid taming of inflation but also undermined some pillars of the New Deal and the Great Society, including deregulation of banking and a weakening of organized labor. While the monetarist counterrevolution perhaps did not quite amount to a "war" on Roosevelt's or Johnson's legacy, its aftermath tipped America's balance of power much more in favor of those with dollars and against those with only votes. This outcome differed starkly from the result of German monetarism described in Chapter 3—in Germany, the early monetarist-inspired stabilization of inflation helped preserve, not undermine, the country's postwar social contract.

FAILURE OF CORPORATE CULTURE: MONETARISM IN RETREAT, 1970–1974

The financial and political problems which in the late 1960s first spurred the Fed to delegate more and more authority to the chairman grew worse during the 1970s. Whereas chairman Martin had sought to keep these trends at bay, his successor actively encouraged them. Indeed, as will shortly be described, at least some of the threats in the Fed's policy environment, which helped Burns centralize power, were primarily of Burns's own devising. Burns was quicker than his colleagues to see financial problems, real or imagined; he was quicker than his predecessor, certainly, in dramatizing them; and he went further in entangling the Fed in the day-to-day battles of politics in Washington. Above all, Burns, despite his reputation as Friedman's mentor, waffled on inflation; and this waffling truly exposed the Fed to financial and political risks. Caught in this vortex, Burns's erstwhile peers at the Fed could do little but capitulate or resign. One way or another, Burns hastened the transformation of a formally collegial body into a less effectual rubber stamp. The consequences for the adaptability of the institution to new challenges and new ideas would prove momentous.

The Fed's Monetary Abdication, 1970–1971

Although at the time Burns took over the chairmanship in January 1970 economists agreed on very little, there was consensus about one thing: the economy no longer performed as expected. Prices climbed over 4 percent compared with the previous year, and joblessness had increased to 6 percent of the workforce. Both these numbers were worse than at any time since the immediate postwar years. This disillusioned many in Washington who thought the conjunction of inflation and unemployment had been solved by the neo-Keynesian "new economics" once and for all. For monetarists, of course, there was no disillusionment—only an expectation that reduced money creation, which they hoped the Burns Fed would soon provide, would reduce prices and allow labor markets to clear.

Although his public statements remained true to his anti-inflationary academic roots, the new chairman soon evinced a marked and growing skepticism about the applicability of monetarist lessons to America's fragmented banking system. The first hint of this began with Burns's very first meeting of the FOMC. There he intimated his fear of the financial consequences of continued monetary restraint, arguing that those who disagreed with him would have argued the same "in September 1929."[5] At the outset of his tenure, Burns discovered that fears of a banking crash would let him steer the Federal Reserve into what he believed were safer financial waters with little effective opposition. Through the FOMC decision to lower interest rates in that first January meeting produced an unusual four dissents, Burns carried the day and inaugurated a new direction for fed policy. Burns's preoccupation with the soundness of the banking system would, over the next year, help drive interest rates lower and inflation higher, and concentrate ever more power in the hands of the chairman. Burns was very concerned by the collapse of the Penn Central Railroad in June, which threatened the existence of the commercial paper market, and he took an unprecedented role in organizing Congress's financial bailout of Lockheed, a potential disaster in which several of the nation's largest financial institutions were heavily—perhaps excessively—implicated. As FOMC votes and minutes reveal, Burns's new activism elicited surprisingly little overt opposition within the FOMC. After reaching a high point of 9 percent in early 1970, the Fed lowered its crucial federal funds rate to below 4 percent in the early part of 1971, raised it again to 6 percent as the economy strengthened in the middle of the year, and then lowered it again to 4 percent during the latter part of 1971, despite what in the meantime had become a booming economy. America's monetary policy abdication was now fully under way.

Publicly, Burns explained his reasons for rejecting monetarist measures by stressing two different constraints. First, he contended that America's fragmented banking system was an ineffective and even fragile instrument of monetary restraint. In speeches in May and December of 1970, Burns explained the Fed's reluctance to deploy monetarist-type curbs on the money supply by saying that monetary policy had "highly uneven effects on different sectors of the economy." Pointing to the differential financial vulnerability occasioned by bank regulations (especially regulation Q), Burns observed "On the one hand, monetary restraint has relatively slight impact on consumer spending or on investment of large businesses. On the other hand, the home-building industry, state and local construction, real estate firms and other small businesses are likely to be seriously handicapped in their operations."[6]

Second, and even more controversially from the viewpoint of his monetarist colleagues, Burns contended that all-important wage costs were climbing virtually independently of monetary policy. Burns expressed his perspective in the very unmonetarist notion of "cost-push inflation," whereby "escalating wages lead to escalating prices in a never ending circle." And indeed, a long strike at General Motors had taken its toll on the economy. America's strike rate achieved its highest level ever. Compared with the year before, the 66.4 million working days lost to strikes represented a 50 percent increase, and this figure was more than 2 1/2 times what it had been three years prior to that (and a rate ten times that of the mid-1980s). Burns attributed some of this "cost push" to the delayed effects of multiyear wage contracts and labor arbitration. In his speeches of 1970, Burns cited third-quarter wage settlements averaging 10 percent, and wage settlements in the construction sector of 16 percent. Thus inflation was attributable not to current monetary policies but to earlier policies, which were only now showing up, in 1970, because of "lagged effects on wage rates." But even so, "a general expectation has developed on the part of both business and labor that recessions will prove brief and mild; and this expectation has influenced both the strength of wage demands and the willingness of management to accept them." This development could be attributable in part to the unevenness, noted above, of the monetary transmission process itself. More fundamentally, however, Burns argued that workers were more militant owing to a change in the social balance of power. This change he blamed on the growth of government and the social safety net. One perceives the intellectual disarray of conservatism in the early 1970s when one recognizes how plausible it was for Burns to invoke the reflexive Republican abhorrence of social disorder and an overgenerous welfare state to explain why another such reflex, "reliance on monetary restraint," would therefore be "unsound."[7] It was this heretical chain of reasoning, perhaps more than any other, that the monetarist revolution would seek to refute.

If monetary policy could not be used, the most obvious alternative, at least according to the prevailing wisdom of the new economics, would have been to curb fiscal policy. Nixon's economic advisers and the president himself had strong inclinations toward fiscal retrenchment when he entered office. For them, a reduction in outlays or even an increase in taxes was certainly consistent with traditional Republican budget-balancing preferences. It was certainly preferable to the third and more radical alternative of wage and price controls that was gaining converts at the other end of Pennsylvania Avenue.

Even though the federal budget was in balance in 1969, Nixon's administration was skeptical about what fiscal policy could achieve. First, it had only recently recognized that the federal budgetary balance of 1969 owed more to hidden tax increases provided by creeping inflation than to genuine fiscal prudence.[8] But in the early 1970s, the fiscal impact of inflationary bracket-creep was not yet well understood, even by fiscal conservatives. Nixon's advisers had to cast about for intellectual makeshifts not simply to solve this problem but even to explain it. Among their solutions was the concept of the "full employment budget," which promptly became distorted by Keynesian conceptual lenses. The media, the public, mainstream (Keynesian) economists, and even the financial markets took Nixon's budget to be pure pump-priming, when in fact the "full employment budget" was actually intended to put a ceiling on spending in the long run. (And the monetarists' concept of a "nonaccelerating inflation rate of unemployment"—NAIRU—was not yet at hand.) In the short run, however, the full employment budget appeared to send the completely wrong signal.

Ironically, the most important ground for Nixon's failure to fight inflation with restrictive fiscal policy may actually have been his administration's exposure to monetarist doctrine. Nixon's "Friedmanesque" advisers believed that the economy's real problem—inflation—could be cured only by monetary policy. But being Friedmanesque also entailed considerable ambivalence toward the Fed. While they believed that the Fed controlled the right instruments, Nixon and his key economic advisers were not completely convinced that the Fed bureaucracy could be trusted to wield them properly. Nixon himself had additional cause to fear the recession that disinflation would trigger: none other than Arthur Burns had warned Nixon that the Federal Reserve's recession of 1960 would cost him that year's presidential election.[9]

As 1970 became 1971, the halfheartedness implied in policies that were only "Friedmanesque"—whether those of Friedman's teacher at the Fed or his pupil in the Oval Office—created a political vacuum that could be filled by policies liked by neither. Nixon's "full employment budget" nearly doubled the federal deficit, to $23 billion. The brief, mild recession of 1970—the one that Burns worried might lead to another market crash—left inflation on its upward climb and the unemployment lines unaffected. The public—or at least that part of it which actively followed economic policy—was coming to believe that none of the traditional economic levers worked as advertised any longer. In their absence, wage and price controls, against which Burns had argued so strenuously in his earlier academic days, had become an *idée fixe* among banking committee populists on the Hill. Herbert Stein's memoirs of Nixon's economic policy rather gruesomely depict the Nixon administration as a "Russian family fleeing over the snow in a horse-drawn troika pursued by wolves. Every once in a while they threw a baby out to slow down the wolves, hoping thereby to gain enough time for most of the family to reach safety."[10] The White House took one step toward wage and price controls after another, hoping in vain to slow the congressional wolves. Between June 1970 and August 1971, the measures that Nixon and his advisers pushed off the troika included the national Commission on Productivity; inflation alerts; the suspension of the Davis-Bacon Act (requiring payment of the prevailing wage in federal construction projects); and the creation of the Construction Industry Stabilization Committee. As each of these measures failed to stem inflation, full wage and prices controls drew steadily nearer. Almost in desperation Nixon appointed a former Democratic governor, John Connally, as his new secretary of the Treasury. Nixon apparently hoped that Connally's glamour would improve the image, if not necessarily the content, of his economic policy. Unfortunately for monetarism, not even its admirers ever thought it glamorous.

In truth, it would have taken a more politically adroit economist than Burns to stem growing populist anger about inflation by rhetorical means alone. Gallup reported in 1970 that Americans regarded inflation as the second biggest problem facing the country, after the Vietnam War.[11] The issue simply proved too tempting for Congress to leave to the White House. The problem, in the mind of the Democratic majority led by Wright Patman, the chairman of the House Banking Committee, was how to exploit this problem on behalf of congressional Democrats while forcing Republicans in the White House to bear the costs.

The Economic Stabilization Act of May 1970 (renewed 1971) appeared to fit Patman's needs perfectly. The legislation he sponsored authorized—but did not require—the president to "issue such orders and regulations as he may deem appropriate to stabilize prices, rents, wages, and salaries" and to make whatever adjustments are necessary "to prevent gross inequities."[12] The bill's political charm, of course, was that it won public plaudits for giving the president an anti-inflationary weapon its sponsors privately assumed he would never use. The measures were simply too interventionist for a Republican president—perhaps too powerful for a president of any stripe. Critics warned that "this title would give President Nixon more power over economic decision-making than any peacetime President." But Patman was nevertheless determined to "educate the President to the fact that there is an economic crisis and that people want action."[13] Though he would have preferred to veto the controls, President Nixon ultimately signed them because they came to his desk as part of a larger defense authorization, a fait accompli. Nixon signed the renewal in 1971 in similar circumstances, but with his new Treasury secretary signaling that he himself was more favorable toward the legislation than the president. And as a harbinger of greater storms to come, Americans were now telling pollsters that inflation had displaced the Vietnam War as the gravest problem facing the nation.

The maneuvers leading up to wage and price controls suggest strongly how much Burns had become the Fed. Indeed, many observers, now as then, have even claimed that Burns was the leading proponent of wage and price controls, and that without his imprimatur these measures would never have acquired the good odor in official Washington that they ultimately enjoyed. The argument is that if Arthur Burns, the longtime opponent of incomes policies, was in favor of them, then president Nixon's opposition was intellectually unwarranted.[14] Nixon himself was said to have been outraged that Burn's speeches gave succor to the populists in Congress who were clamoring for him to impose controls. In fact, the written record reveals that Burns remained a steadfast opponent of legislated wage and price controls even if he learned to swallow a voluntary "incomes policy." Though this distinction was probably lost on the rest of America, Burns maintained it to the very end, hoping in vain to avert the greater evil by advocating the lesser.[15] Burns's Congressional testimony speaks for itself. At hearings on the revival of the acts in 1971, Burns warned, "[Congress] is giving too much power to the President under this legislation"—in fact, "giving the President virtually dictatorial power"—even if, as one suspects, Burns also doubted that the president would be so rash as to actually take up controls.[16] Whether he spoke sincerely or not, Burns, by inserting himself into the center of the debate over wage and price controls, virtually invited the sort of misinterpretation and misappropriation that his views on controls produced. In offering himself as the arbiter of economic orthodoxy in a new and unprecedented way, Burns hoped to make himself the uncontradicted defender of the rights and powers of the Federal Reserve. Whether or not such uncontradicted authority for the chairman really would preserve the Fed's rights and powers was, of course, another question altogether.

Monetarist Nadir: Wage and Price Controls, 1971–1973

The imposition of wage and price controls in August 1971 became the monetarists' Alamo, the memory of which would shape their future political calculations. As we saw in Chapter 4, the Triffin dilemma implied that at some point, either the international system should be sacrificed to save the domestic system or vice versa: either the United States would have to raise interest rates to prevent a run on the dollar by foreign central banks, or it would no longer defend a fixed price for gold, in which case it would cease to be the anchor of the international exchange rate system. But while the monetarist strategy of "closing the gold window" now had a compelling logic, since it left the Nixon administration with a greater degree of sovereignty, the domestic monetarist corollary—tighten the money supply—still found no support. The Nixon administration felt even more that if it was compelled to close the gold window, this would be perceived as a policy failure by Congress and the public. The administration felt that to recoup its political losses, it needed to make a spectacular—that is to say, nonmonetarist—move against inflation. Thus was born Nixon's curious hybrid of monetarist international policy and dirigiste domestic policy.

The evidence suggests that the decision to close the gold window and leapfrog to wage and price controls was made by Nixon and Connally sometime in the spring. The only question that remained was when their hand would be forced. The crisis in the United States' balance sheet became unavoidable in the middle of the summer of 1971. Alone in the first two weeks of August, liabilities increased an astounding $4.5 billion, or 20 percent of the total for the entire previous year, and assets declined by $1.2 billion. This drove the administration's senior economic policy officials to a secret weekend retreat at Camp David. There they hammered out the technicalities necessary to float the dollar and to institute wage and price controls. On Sunday evening, August 15th, Nixon announced a series of extraordinarily interventionist measures that included a ninety-day freeze on wages and prices (to be followed by a more flexible system in the so-called second phase); a 10 percent surcharge on dutiable imports (rescinded on December 18th); tax cuts and tax credits; an increase in the price of gold from $35 to $38 per ounce; and, of course, suspension of the convertibility of the dollar into gold. For all their "Friedmanesque" proclivities, Nixon's senior economic policy team never even discussed with Burns the option of controlling the money supply in conjunction with the dollar float.[17] Friedmanites watching from the sidelines saw all too clearly that they had been steamrollered by neo-Keynesian policies driven by fear of congressional populists, and they would never forget it. As David Stockman would grimly recall of those years, "The experience in John Connally's economics laboratory left me a born-again capitalist."[18] But Stockman and his fellow born-again capitalists would have to bide their time while wage and price controls ran their turbulent course.

Once wage and price controls were in place, they exercised an immediate dampening effect on inflation and allowed the pent-up stimulative forces of lower interest rates to work their transitory magic. The broadest measure of inflation declined to 3 percent for the six quarters after the August 1971 initiatives, compared with 4.7 percent for the previous six quarters. At the same time, real GNP growth attained 7.6 percent, and unemployment was nudged down to 5 percent from 6 percent. The Nixon administration was jubilant; the public and Congress were mollified. Wage and price controls seemed a tour de force.

But not in the eyes of monetarists, of course. Monetarist were watching the Fed's money supply numbers, and these foretold disaster in twelve to eighteen months. The Federal Reserve, characterizing its policy for 1972 as "moderately stimulative," allowed M1 to increase 8.3 percent over the course of 1972, compared with 6.6 percent in 1971, which was already expansionary. Even Keynesians should have been suspicious of the Fed's numbers for interest rates: the Federal Funds rate remained at an exceptionally low level, 3 percent, during the first quarter of 1972, and it was not until the very end of the year that this rate reached its high for the year at a more moderate range of 5 percent. Federal Reserve policies in 1972 at the very least defied chairman Martin's old dictum that at the peak of a business cycle the Fed should "take away the punch bowl."

This stimulus, coming as it did so conveniently before the presidential election, has been the subject of much scrutiny. If one assumes, as monetarists did (and has since become conventional wisdom), a time lag of anywhere from six to twelve months in the effects of monetary policy, it becomes reasonable to attribute the extraordinary figure for growth in the fourth quarter of 1972 (8 percent real GNP) to the seemingly profligate Federal Reserve policy in the latter part of 1971 and early 1972. Given another widely shared assumption—that Americans vote their pocketbooks—the conjunction of robust growth with a Republican re-election bid looked more than a little convenient. Inevitably, the question was raised: Was the Federal Reserve politically compromised in some way? Was it consciously attempting to smooth Nixon's road back to the White House?

Because other authors have discussed this issue at length, I shall only briefly summarize their tentative conclusions and draw out the implications for the struggle over monetarism. On the one hand, circumstantial evidence suggestive of Burns's complicity cannot be ignored.[19] On the other hand, it would have been quite easy for Burns to look at America's stubborn unemployment—still, in late 1971, at a postwar high—and conclude that there were legitimate economic reasons, however traditional or Keynesian, for stimulating the economy. Yet as Burns himself had predicted years earlier, one of the most insidious risks with wage and price controls was that policymakers would find it all too easy to focus on unemployment while overlooking the inflation that controls suppressed.

But the most compelling argument is that Burns had allowed himself be put into a very difficult position, bordering on an outright conflict of interest, by accepting chairmanship of the new Committee on Interest rates and Dividends (CID).[20] This committee was established by Congress as part of the overall anti-inflation program, but in the view of every reasonably orthodox economist it was incompatible with anti-inflationary policy: although without power, it was charged with preventing high interest rates as part of Congress's opposition to price increases. If the committee were given real power to impose low interest rates it would have had precisely the opposite effect to the one intended. Burns was determined that the CID should remain toothless, but this very probably tempted him to keep Fed interest rates from rising to the point where Wright Patman and the House Banking Committee would force the issue. Certainly, this was the principal argument that Burns used during a crucial FOMC meeting in August 1972.[21] The end result was that, once again, Burns used external threats to bolster his internal authority.

Yet whichever interpretation of these events one accepts, the common assumption is that all roads lead back to Burns—his analyses, his motives, his policies. Therefore, the larger significance, in terms of the battle over monetarism and inflation, is the enormous devolution of power into the hands of the Fed chairman. It should not be forgotten that the chairman was formally only one vote on the board of governors and the FOMC. This makes the growing power of the chairman also a matter of explaining the acquiescence or even subordination of the other governors and FOMC presidents. Unlike officials of the Bundesbank, the other members of the FOMC and the board of governors were not key players in the struggle against inflation. Why was that? This question matters because it goes to the very heart of how monetarists—or any other dissident group of economists—could hope to have their voices heard in the Fed's boardroom. As the contrast with the Bundesbank reveals, the culture of the Fed simply afforded far fewer opportunities for dissident ideas to gain a seat at the table.

By the mid-1970s, it was clear that the culture of the Fed had changed, and this called for an explanation. The factors cited by former insiders and observers range from the personal to the structural. From people who watched the Fed in those days come comments such as "There were very few on that Board who were going to stand up to Burns," and "Burns was just an extraordinarily persuasive and forceful individual who would naturally dominate any meeting."[22] Former CEA officials characterized boards under Burns (and subsequently, Miller) as "carefully lightweight," "increasingly hand-picked by Burns as the years went by."[23] Indeed, in the mid-1970s, turnover among Fed governors reached its highest level. What mattered for governors' terms of office proved to be not the formal fourteen-year term but the actual years served. The term served by governors on the Martin Fed averaged 9.5; the term for the entire postwar Fed (McCabe through Volcker) averaged 7.2 years; but for the Burns and Miller Fed the term dropped to 5 years.

Another structural change affecting the Fed's culture was a shift from the world of banking to the world of economics. Martin, a financier by training, had run the FOMC along very judgmental and nonquantitative lines. In their traditional (pre-Burns) policy deliberations, the governors would refer to such highly subjective concepts as the "tone" and "feel" of markets, and they expressed policy preferences simply in terms of tightening or loosening. Burns, the first Ph.D. economist to become chairman of the Federal Reserve, instituted more heavily econometric procedures that clearly disadvantaged some of the more traditional members of the FOMC.[24] During the 1970s, the background of the board members clearly changed, with a pronounced increase in the number of economists and a marked decrease in those from more traditional banking careers. Martin had discouraged the appointment of economists to the board of governors; but by the late 1970s, on average five of seven governors held Ph.Ds in economics. Ironically, the shift to a more economistic approach embraced at least some role for monetarist monetary aggregates, even if the various M's were merely part of Burn's intellectual eclecticism and scarcely represented adherence on his part to a monetary targeting procedure. The transformation of the Federal Reserve from a banker's bank to a steward of the national economy meant, at least at first, that it was increasingly up to the chairman to decide which, out of all the new numbers, the Fed would use to steer its course.

In such circumstances, opportunities to introduce controversial new procedures, such as those inspired by monetarism, were severely limited. Regular seminars for the governors were conducted by outside experts, among whom the monetarists were represented; more typically, however, exchanges between the Federal Reserve and the monetarists occurred at the staff level, where the debate was indeed multisided and vigorous but where the monetarists were not exposed to the concerns or active contributions of FOMC members. This procedure, together with the cultural prohibition against discussing the specifics of monetary policy with outsiders, heightened the isolation of the governors. It also heightened their dependence on the staff. Many governors (then as now) complained that "we heard what [the staff] wanted us to hear."[25] This was the root of monetarists' suspicions that a Keynesian bias among senior staff "barons" was the source of the Fed's hostility to monetarism.

Yet such was not the case. This hostility was actually an unintended consequence of the Fed's new corporate culture of chairman-led "consensus." The evidence was provided inadvertently, years later, by monetarist researchers who had originally set out to gather evidence for their hypothesis about staff bias. Lombra, Moran, and Meltzer analyzed the staff work that supported FOMC decision making in the early to mid-1970s and compared it with actual FOMC deliberations and decisions.[26] They found that in those years there were two quite distinct kinds of FOMC meetings, which occurred at different times throughout the year. Several times a year, the FOMC conducted major "strategy" sessions at which it would set long-term policy objectives. For these, the staff would prepare background analyses and policy options including long-term forecasts using leading and lagging indicators derived from the essentially Keynesian MIT-PENN-SSRC model of the economy. The base forecast would assume that current monetary and fiscal targets would be achieved. The staff would also produce alternative forecasts with higher and lower targets for the money supply. During the more frequent intervening "tactical" meetings, the staff would prepare Green Book analyses and forecasts, which would link different options for money market (Fed funds) policy (contained in the Blue Book) to prevailing conditions in capital markets and the real economy. As Lombra and Moran point out, of course, logic dictated that the longer-term strategic goal should, all other things being equal, determine the shorter-run tactical choices.

To their surprise, Lombra, Moran, and Meltzer found that the Fed's problems had much less to do with staff biases or econometric failings than they expected. True, the Fed staff forecasts did tend to underestimate inflation and overestimate growth in real GNP. However, these problems were not markedly worse than forecasts from other economists. The more fundamental failing proved to be the FOMC's failure to obey the logic of its own two-stage procedure. For much of the mid-1970s, the FOMC was in fact allowing short-run tactical considerations to override longer-run strategy, for reasons that appeared to have nothing to do with any school of economics whatsoever. Despite staff predictions of lengthy lags between policy moves and economic results, it was apparent to Lombra, Moran, and Meltzer that the FOMC was most reliant on current economic conditions when making its decisions. The FOMC would often arbitrarily alter staff projections to substitute what Brunner called "freewheeling FOMC judgment" for what ought to have been, no matter what the theory, a rational model-based procedure. The one recurring feature that these scholars found was the Fed's seemingly inexplicable insistence on consensus or near-unanimous decisions. Lombra and Moran cite instances of a clearly divided FOMC voting 11 to 1 for vaguely worded directives to the open market desk. Such vague directives, of course, devolved still more power onto the chairman, as the manager of the open-market desk in New York inevitably turned to him for operational guidance.

Many former Fed senior staffers concur with this assessment, at least insofar as their own working assumptions were concerned. Staff models did tend to predict that restrictive policy would have major recessionary effects on the economy while yielding only a "negligible" reduction of inflation.[27] Moreover, "many of us believed at that time that inflation was relatively harmless, especially compared to a recession." But others indicate that some senior personnel were open to alternative concepts. As early as 1972, a subcommittee of the FOMC suggested that a switch to targeting nonborrowed reserves might help "overcome" the FOMC's reluctance to adhere to long-range monetary targets.[28] This was essentially the strategy that would remain unexploited by two Fed chairmen until it was finally adopted by a third in 1979—a fact that helps locate the resistance to new ideas at the Fed.

One further illustration of the fate of new ideas in the Fed's chairman-dominant culture can be found in the unusual foothold monetarists obtained at the St. Louis Federal Reserve Bank by the early 1970s. Monetarist influence can be detected in three ways at the St. Louis Fed: in the research work of the monetarist staffers, in the publication of figures on the money supply, and in the staff's influence on a series of St. Louis Federal Reserve presidents who argued for monetarist policies in FOMC meetings. St. Louis published many important theoretical building blocks of monetarism, including Anderson and Jordan's influential "A Test of the Relative Importance of Fiscal and Monetary Policy" and the monetarist "St. Louis model" of the American macroeconomy. Not least important, it published the weekly monetary aggregate figures so lovingly scrutinized by Wall Street economists. Clearly, the St. Louis Fed was no mere monetarist outpost; in the eyes of at least one not unsympathetic former senior Fed staffer, it was the second most important source of Friedmanite influence after the University of Chicago.

Yet despite the seeming strength of the monetarists at St. Louis, the culture of the Fed denied them an internal influence commensurate with their eventual reputation. Partly, the regional staff was younger and less prestigious than the board staff in Washington. The senior staff in Washington tended to hold the St. Louis research staff in low regard in the early 1970s; the board staffers were not particularly impressed by what they considered the St. Louis staffers' presumptuous ambition to rethink monetary policy theory from the ground up. More fundamentally, however, St. Louis monetarism ran up against the disadvantage faced by all regional presidents within the FOMC. Quite apart from their numerical inferiority within the FOMC, which they shared with their colleagues, the St. Louis Fed regional presidents were suspected by their colleagues of speaking not for their region but only for themselves or a small clique of staff ideologues. The St. Louis Fed presidents were virtually alone in defying the Fed's consensus ethic; their frequent dissents left them, in effect, "ignored" at FOMC meetings. There are persistent stories—though these are difficult to confirm—that Arthur Burns was tempted to veto monetarist nominations for the post of St. Louis president on precisely these grounds. Others believe that Burns also wanted to stifle the monetarists in St. Louis by reducing their research allocations. It is even alleged that

Burns considered shutting down the publications of all the regionals in order to curtail the hostile criticism emanating from St. Louis.[29]

But the last, structural reason for Burns's growing dominance was the place of the Fed at the center of extraordinary financial volatility. We have already noted the risks to the financial system which Burns exploited in the years leading up to wage and price controls. By 1973, with the benefits of controls evaporating, financial fragility seemed to argue even more compellingly than before for deference to the man at the top of the conference table. Despite controls, inflation climbed to a distressing 9 percent in 1973. In 1974, when controls were abandoned altogether, the inflation rate shot up toward 12 percent, and the unemployment rate hovered around 7 percent—a relatively acceptable standard given what lay ahead, but quite deplorable given what had been. Burns used this opportunity to move vigorously against inflation, raising interest rates and triggering a major recession. Even so, monetarist ideas made no inroads at the Fed. Financial markets were registering a catastrophic lack of confidence in the American economy and its policymakers. To cite the two most prominent examples, the Dow Jones industrial average, which had peaked in 1973, now proceeded to wipe out 50 percent of Americans' equity over the next eighteen months, reaching, in 1975, its lowest point since the Great Depression. And more or less simultaneously came the failure of the Franklin National Bank, the biggest single bank failure in the United States since the banking disaster of 1933. As one senior Fed official from those days put it, "The markets punished us every time we appeared disunited and not in control."[30] Though the financial sector clearly hoped to open the Fed up to new policies, the Fed's fear of financial collapse served to entrench old policies even more deeply. This was the most powerful background reason for the Fed's ethic of consensus, which funneled a disproportionate share of the Fed's power into one pair of hands.

GROWTH OF MONETARY POPULISM: MONETARIST MOBILIZATION, 1974–1979

To understand the context of the extraordinary monetarist mobilization from 1974 to 1979, it is important to bear in mind the rudderless course of the U.S. economy during those years. On the heels of the quadrupling of OPEC oil prices in late 1974, America's worst postwar recession saw a 4.9 percent drop in GNP in the first quarter of 1975. Unemployment peaked in March 1975 at 11 percent, and by 1975 the dollar declined 16 percent relative to 1970. Eighteen relatively healthy months followed in 1976 and 1977, during which inflation declined, growth resumed, and the trade balance was again in surplus. By late 1977, though, signs of economic distress were again accumulating. Hourly compensation for workers, which the Fed continued to assert was the dominant influence on inflation, was increasing at 8.5 percent; America's oil bill shot up 30 percent (only one-third of this rise was attributable to higher input prices); and the slight trade surplus of 1976 became an $11 billion deficit in 1977. Once again the dollar began to tumble. In 1978, with the dollar declining 14 percent against the leading currencies, inflation worsened to 9 percent, and in 1979 it reached an extraordinary 13 percent.

These five years of abdication of monetary responsibility were all the more galling to American monetarists because this time there were no wage and price controls to blame. The Fed's stubborn resistance to monetarism and policies of inflation control eventually became a significant datum in its own right in the monetasists' economic theories. Monetarists had to rethink their simple assumptions about how experts interact with officials and replace those assumptions with something more sophisticated (and politicized) in the face of the Federal Reserve's unresponsiveness: "We [monetarists] originally thought we would only have to show the Federal Reserve what was wrong with its policies, and it would change them. But that was only until the early 1970s."[31] Resistance from the Federal Reserve pushed American monetarists to transform their narrowly economic theory into a theory of the *political* economy. American monetarists began to model not only erratic price behavior but also the bureaucratic obstructionism of institutions such as the Federal Reserve. This intellectual radicalization coincided with broad new political initiatives that culminated in government offices for some monetarist economists. And it is these two strands together, the intellectual entwined with the political, that must be understood if we are to understand the peculiarly populist element of the American monetarist mobilization. Rarely has such an elite group of scholars gone as far as the American monetarists to portray themselves and their ideas as the scourge of the establishment and the friend of the ordinary taxpayer. We will trace this intertwining of mobilization and radicalization by examining four principal developments: the work of the Shadow Open Market Committee, the adoption by Congress of monetarist legislation, the support given to the grassroots antitax movement by monetarists, and monetarists' contributions to a new monetarist-supply side "counterestablishment" in Washington.[32]

THE SHADOW OPEN MARKET COMMITTEE

The most prominent of the monetarists' political initiatives was the Shadow Open-Market Committee (SOMC), a group of monetarist economists who began to meet semi-annually in September 1973. Smaller than

Germany's Konstanzer Seminar, the SOMC was founded to turn monetarist theory into policy recommendations and to monitor and criticize national economic policies. The SOMC owed its birth, in a sense, to a simple "lack of faxes."[33] Free-market economists who wanted to put out a press release opposing wage and price controls found it easier to do so by conferring in person than by telephone. It was then a short step from press conference to regular policy forum. Throughout the 1970s, the SOMC's membership was virtually unchanged. The original participants were:

Allan Meltzer	Carnegie Mellon University
Karl Brunner	University of Rochester
Homer Jones	St. Louis Federal Reserve, retired
Thomas Mayer	University of California, Davis
A. James Meigs	Claremont Graduate School
Robert Rasche	Michigan State University
Wilson Schmidt	Virginia Polytechnic Institute
Anna Schwartz	National Bureau of Economic Research
Beryl Sprinkel	Harris Trust, Chicago
William Wolman	Senior Editor, *Business Week*

Several years later Jerry Jordan of Pittsburgh National Bank joined this monetarist honor roll. Jordan and Sprinkel would move to the Reagan administration in 1981, the former as a member of the CEA, the latter as undersecretary for monetary affairs in the Treasury Department. Allan Meltzer would also be appointed a consultant to the Treasury. The most notable absentee was of course Milton Friedman. He chose to invest his energies elsewhere in what monetarists described as mutually agreeable "division of labor."[34]

A typical meeting, lasting over a couple of days, would include the reading of background papers prepared by individual members and the adoption of a common set of policy positions. These were subsequently released to the press and were also published as part of the Carnegie-Rochester Conference series. A close reading of these documents tells a tale of opposition in two acts.

SOMC Views, 1973–1976: Philosophical Opposition

The first years of the SOMC found the lobby group in broad agreement with the recent disinflationary trend of the Fed's money supply policy after 1973, but in sharp disagreement with its handling of the technicalities of monetary control and what might be called the Fed's underlying "political philosophy." Thus in 1973 and 1974, the SOMC supported the Fed's policy of about a 5 to 6 percent growth rate for M1; and it even argued that the Fed was being too restrictive when, in 1974 and 1975, the figures for growth in M1 fell markedly below that level. The SOMC worried about the Fed's technical understanding of monetary policy, for this affected the likelihood that the Fed would make good policy over the longer term. A persistent sore point was the Fed's continuing reliance on interest rate procedures. The SOMC called upon the Fed to drop these and instead increase its technical control over member banks by targeting the monetary base, eliminating lagged reserve accounting, and simplifying reserve requirements.

But of more pressing concern was the Fed's understanding of its relationship to the financial system as a whole. As we have already seen, the credit crunches of the American financial system in 1966 and 1969 persuaded some policymakers that monetary restriction no longer worked (falsely, in the view of the monetarists). The Fed, in the SOMC's opinion, was responding inappropriately to these weaknesses. Once again, much of the problem came back to regulatory barriers between the different banking sectors, and especially the peculiar vulnerability of the thrifts.

On one side of the regulatory coin, the SOMC recognized in its report of March 1974 that the savings and loan associations (thrifts) were of course greatly imperiled when interest rates increased; and the federal government's off-budget liabilities, incurred through Freddie Mac and the Home Loan Bank Board, threatened to explode by billions of dollars during periods of restrictive interest rates. But the SOMC recommended that the Fed should not allow this problem to deter it from a disciplined monetary policy; rather, the regulatory ceiling on the thrifts' interest rates should be raised.[35]

On the other side of the regulatory coin was the greatly increased use by the general public of nonmember banks, and especially of thrifts as bank substitutes. The SOMC considered but rejected the Fed's claim that the increase in nonsystem bank deposits from 17.2 percent in 1960 to 25.4 percent in 1973 threatened the Fed's technical control over the money supply. Nor did the SOMC approve of the Fed's handling of its function as lender of last resort, as demonstrated in its rescue of Franklin National Bank. The SOMC was at pains to point out that the Fed's obligation was to preserve the banking system as a whole, not individual member banks. The SOMC pointed out that the Federal Reserve's supply of liquidity to Franklin National at below-market rates, and at terms longer than stipulated (i.e., discount rates), defied the principle, first established by Bagehot in the nineteenth century, that a central banks' rescue as lender of last resort of an illiquid bank should happen at penalty rates. The SOMC correctly observed that a failure to apply penalty rates raised the specter of moral hazard and was likely to make future restrictive monetary policy more, not less, problematic.

The SOMC's consistent theme in all of these criticisms was that the Fed should lift its eyes from the plight of individual financial sectors, individual markets, and even individual banks, and focus on its responsibilities toward the economy as a whole. In a larger sense, this meant that SOMC's quarrel with the Fed was on the ethereal plain of political philosophy and economy; the SOMC even preferred the term "monetary authority" to the more parochial "central bank." Both in its publications and in its dealings with Congress, the Fed maintained that it had little choice but to conduct a discretionary policy. In a letter to Senator William Proxmire that particularly angered the SOMC, Burns denied that the economy was inherently stable. This necessitated what he called an "eclectic approach" that responded to "special influences" as they arose. Thus it could be seen that the United States had experienced a series of unprecedented shocks which the Fed had no choice but to accommodate. In the commodities sector—not only oil, but food, metal ore, and so on—the Fed spoke in 1973 and 1974 of "shortages relative to demand." Likewise, the Fed pointed to "underlying inflationary processes" driven by workers' catch-up wage settlements—so-called "cost-push" inflation. And as James Tobin and other neo-Keynesian pointed out, the cost-push theory of inflation that was so near to Burns's heart was really a "social conflict theory" of inflation.[36] Increasingly, it seemed that in the Fed's view everything other than monetary policy was to blame for rising prices.

The SOMC countered this "eclectic," "social conflict" philosophy with a perspective that stressed the underlying stability of the economy, the ability of the monetary authorities to control inflation by controlling the money supply, and a view of social conflict as a result, not the cause, of inflation. The SOMC staked out no new ground in arguing the neoclassical case that "shocks" were in principle no different from any other price change in the economy. (SOMC members would privately disparage the Fed's philosophy as the "rising prices" theory of inflation.) But the idea that inflation drove social conflict and government intervention in the economy was a note seldom struck in Washington. The SOMC was unequivocal in its rejection of "cost-push" and other such social conflict theories: "The greatest danger of a 'social conflict theory' of inflation follows from its effect on inflation itself. It directs attention away from the crucial conditions of inflation [i.e., monetary policy] and tends to generate social policy patterns perpetuating inflation."[37] In a later report, the SOMC would describe the implications of the social conflict theory even more starkly: "An accommodating policy of persistent inflation introduces pervasive incentives into the social system [for citizens] to explore opportunities for accelerating wage and price setting as a means of competitive wealth transfers."[38]

This logic, the SOMC warned, could ultimately result in the "Latin Americanization" of American politics and economics.[39] The argument that monetary discipline promoted social order would later prove central to the monetarists' ability to forge a coalition with other types of conservatism. At the time of writing, however, such sentiments found little response in official Washington. In fact, the critical fire the SOMC directed at the Fed may have actually helped Burns politically. Even though the SOMC was actually criticizing him for moving too fast against inflation, Burns used the SOMC to portray himself as being in the middle of the policy debate, particularly when Congress became upset with him during the recession of 1975.[40]

SOMC Views, 1977–1980: From Philosophical to Political Opposition

During the Carter years, the SOMC's philosophical opposition steadily became more political and more radical. The watershed report was that of September 1977. The conventional free-market position usually favors an independent central bank. It was then, during these later years, that SOMC monetarists become most forthright in their opposition to it. The SOMC became increasingly convinced that the Fed suffered from an endemic bureaucratic resistance that only wholesale subordination of the institution itself could cure. This was especially ironic, given the success with monetary targeting achieved by the Bundesbank, which was fully as independent.

The SOMC's first objection was to the rapid increase in the money supply that began in 1977. Carter's budget projections for 1980 envisioned balancing untrimmed Federal outlays with inflation-driven tax increases.[41] Not only did the administration predict no improvement in inflation, but signals from the Fed even suggested that inflation would worsen. By 1978, increases in the money supply were 7 percent and higher—the same rate as in the disastrous years 1972 and 1973. The SOMC warned that these numbers would soon not only drive up prices again but revive the demand for wage and price controls. With the predicted high rates of inflation, there was also an increased risk that the Fed might suddenly slam on the brakes to induce a recession as an antidote. The SOMC insisted, however, that there was another course: stabilize the monetary growth rates at their current level and then reduce them by about 1 percent per year until they reached the SOMC's preferred rate of 4 to 6 percent. Three to five years of restraint would ultimately reduce inflation while minimizing the risk of serious recession.[42]

If the Fed had been hard of hearing during the Burns years, by the later Carter years it was stone-deaf. Although Carter and Blumenthal had originally talked down the dollar in 1977, by the latter part of 1978 they were recognizing that they had been too successful: the dollar was in serious trouble on the international financial markets. With the Fed ignoring its wishes, Carter's administration began to jerry-rig alternatives to help rescue the dollar. It was at this time, on October 24, 1978, that President Carter established his "national accord" with labor, hoping both to limit prices hikes to a level 0.5 percent below their 1977 rate, and to limit wages to a growth rate of 7 percent per annum. These plans were not well received by the market; shortly thereafter, on October 30th, the dollar reached a new low. According to the old Keynesian guideposts, money had apparently been made progressively tighter throughout the year, with the federal funds rate in January of 6.75 percent increasing by 2 percent and the discount rate increasing in stages from 7 to 8 percent; but this had little impact. On November 1st, the Federal Reserve and the Treasury announced a set of dramatic moves to halt the fall of the dollar. For the first time ever, the discount rate was increased a full percentage point; the federal funds rate was moved sharply upward, to 10 percent; an additional 2 percent reserve requirement was imposed; gold auctions were increased; foreign currency swap lines were augmented; and finally, as the biggest innovation, $10 billion in foreign-denominated (mostly DM) Treasury bonds were issued—the so-called Carter bonds. Gold hit a record price of $400 per ounce in September. M1 was increasing at an annual rate of 10 percent in 1979 when its target range was 1.5 to 4.5 percent. The dollar had declined 3.8 percent against the DM since June, and producer prices, one of the leading indicators of the underlying price trend, were accelerating at 17 percent per year.

The fact that all of the SOMC's most pessimistic prophecies about the Federal Reserve "drifting without a program or goal" had come true by September of 1978 inspired the SOMC to an almost biblical wrath.[43] The SOMC contended that the Federal Reserve had brought America to "an age of permanent inflation . . . previously reserved for Latin American dictatorships or disorganized democracies."[44] In the SOMC's view, the Fed's problems could "be traced to several causes: The internal procedures guiding monetary policy, the opposition to a policy of monetary control deeply entrenched among influential groups of the Federal Reserve bureaucracy, and a pervasive doubt of the role of money and monetary policy in the inflation process among major elements of our central bank bureaucracy."[45] Of course, this analysis turned the Fed's problem upside down. The real culprit was not staff bias but an excessive centralization of power in the hands of the chairman. Nonetheless, the SOMC continued to target the Fed's bureaucratic rigidity a year later, when it wrote: "The entrenched views, customs and procedures of the Federal Reserve Bureaucracy [sic] thus form a subtle but powerful barrier obstructing . . . a reliable and predictable anti-inflationary policy. . . . Any Chairman wishing to bring the Federal Reserve on a new course . . . must first start with an overhaul of the Fed's top level personnel."[46]

The next shock to monetarist assumptions came between the fall of 1979 and 1980, when the SOMC had an opportunity to watch Volcker's brand of pragmatic monetarism in action. Its first report after the switch of October 1979 was issued in February 1980. The SOMC " applauded"

Volcker's efforts to steer the money supply more directly. As Brunner put it, "No Chairman of the Board of Governors ever elaborated so explicitly and without obfuscation the crucial role monetary expansion plays with respect to our experience of inflation and high interest rates."[47] But the SOMC went on to strike a note of caution: it pointed out that the administration's own projections for inflation in the coming year wholly discounted any success Volcker might have. So the SOMC should not perhaps have been quite as disappointed as it was in the next report, in September: "We now know our hopes were ill-founded. . . . In the last year, the rate [of adjusted bank reserves] has nearly doubled. . . . The growth rate of M1-B has been reduced on average the last 11 months, but its variability was substantially higher than in the years before October 1979."[48]

With this policy failure in mind, the SOMC turned its attention to how it might secure its long-sought gradual reduction of the inflation rate more permanently. It considered the problem of "credibility" in changes in monetary policy. In its report of March 1980, the SOMC hypothesized:

> "A change in policy deemed to be essentially a short and transitory deviation from an ongoing inflationary trend hardly induces any modification of prevalent price-wage setting trends. . . . It follows that initiation of an anti-inflationary policy in a context of low credibility lengthens the lag of price-wage responses and raises the social cost of an anti-inflationary policy."[49]

Six months later, the SOMC felt that such a credible policy change would require certain institutional and political changes. As it concluded the following September, "Something is radically wrong with the Fed's policy-making, requiring at this stage some radical actions. . . . If the present staff is too incompetent or too unwilling to serve the long-run interests of this country . . . it is time to replace it with a crew who can and will."[50]

And so American monetarists laid the theoretical groundwork for a much more aggressive political treatment of the Federal Reserve. The interesting question then became whether medium-term, gradual reduction of monetary growth and a political assault on the Federal Reserve were not, at some crucial level, at cross-purposes. Clearly, the SOMC assumed not. But when key members of the SOMC moved over to the White House, events would put this assumption to the test.

Monetarists and the Changing of the Populist Guard in Congress

Monetarists, as noted earlier, became politically active in other arenas as well. In 1975 came a development which was well-nigh unique in the annals of monetarist experiments around the world. An important monetarist initiative came from a national legislature rather than (as in Germany) from the central bank. The major economic downturn of that year prompted what one observer called "one of the most remarkable aspects of the monetarist episode in America"[51]: the surprising interest in the doctrine shown by the previously indifferent—if not positively hostile—Congress.[52]

For Congress to take an interest in monetarism required two important preconditions, both of which had just been fulfilled. First, wage and price controls had collapsed into an economic shambles the year before. Second, a new, less deferential generation of post-Watergate congressmen had ousted Wright Patman from his fiefdom as chairman of the House Banking and Urban Affairs committee. He was replaced by another, but more moderate, populist, Henry Reuss. With Patman sidelined to a minor subcommittee, Robert Weintraub, a monetarist economist and senior staffer on the Joint Economics Committee, now found his way clear to harness Congress's populism to the monetarist cause. In March 1975, Congress passed House Resolution 133, stipulating that the Federal Reserve was to establish and justify growth ranges in monetary aggregates and provide quarterly testimony about its policy before the House and Senate. This resolution has been called the "strongest" and "clearest" instruction—monetarist or other—that Congress had ever given the Federal Reserve. But the underlying political significance in some ways resembled the situation in Germany: monetary targeting appealed to members of Congress because of their aversion to recession and not, as one might expect, their aversion to inflation.[53]

While this Congressional initiative (like others that were to follow) was seen as a "landmark" for the monetarist program, it was not a victory. The measure altered neither the Federal Reserve's procedures nor its policies. Burns directed his economists to write his speeches according to the letter of the resolution but otherwise evade its spirit. The Fed staff did so by targeting not one but a multiplicity of money-supply measures, which enabled the Fed to determine its own criteria for compliance. Moreover, the resolution stipulated general growth rates, not specific dollar levels for the aggregates, and most important, it permitted the Federal Reserve to roll its targets forward every quarter, creating a problem of "base drift."

But Congress persevered. HR 133 was followed in 1977 by the Federal Reserve Reform Act, sponsored by Reuss. This act now clearly specified the monetary aggregates for the Federal Reserve to target. When it was followed the next year by a title in the Full Employment and Balanced Growth Act (Humphrey-Hawkins), instructing the Federal Reserve to publicize annual (as opposed to quarterly) monetary targets, monetarism seemed to pass "from an interesting theoretical and philosophical proposition to a force immortalized in federal law."[54]

Once again, however, even these enhanced Congressional measures actually accomplished very little. The legal mandate to target the money supply did not solve the basic structural problem in congressional supervision of the Federal Reserve. Monetary targets were at best monitoring devices that entailed no sanctions. With no ability to hold the Federal Reserve's feet to the fire, Congress could not ensure compliance with much more than the rhetoric of targeting.[55] At first, monetary aggregates had appealed to Congress because they seemed to hold out the prospect of a single, easy-to-grasp variable that would open a window into the impenetrable world of monetary policy. But the Fed drew a curtain across this window by insisting upon the inclusion of multiple aggregates in both the original resolution and the final legislation. In his testimony before the banking committees Burns had successfully argued that a single target (such as that used by the Bundesbank) was inappropriate from the standpoint of economic theory; indeed, this was merely a "technical question" best left for the Fed itself to settle.[56]

Having failed to alter the relationship between members of Congress and the Fed, monetarist targets also failed to alter the basic political dynamics of monetary policy that each member faced within his or her constituency. For ordinary citizens and interest groups back in the districts, monetary aggregates were simply not "decision variables," whereas all voters with a mortgage, bank account, or credit card understood the significance of interest rates (or thought they did). Faced with demands from the folks back home to keep interest rates down, congressmen found that monetary aggregates provided no defense at all. As Senator Proxmire once remarked to a prominent monetarist, "I get letters all the time complaining about high interest rates, but no one has ever written to me about the money supply."[57] Thus neither interest in nor comprehension of the rudiments of monetarist thought or the workings of the aggregates took hold in Congress beyond the precincts of the various banking committees. "For all its monetarist weaponry," as one former House Banking Committee staffer said, "the prize of monetary policy [remained] essentially beyond Congress's grasp."[58] Congressional politics made it impossible to sell monetarism to the Federal Reserve until the Federal Reserve, in the person of the chairman, wanted to be sold on it.

Into the Political Arena: Forging the Monetarist-Supply Side Coalition

The SOMC once observed, "An explicit commitment to permanent inflation is probably motivated by the social costs associated with an anti-inflationary financial policy. These costs occur, [but] there are also social costs of permanent inflation."[59] If the Federal Reserve officials had ever thought that no social costs were entailed by inflation, monetarists set out in the middle to late 1970s to prove them wrong. Monetarists were determined to show that the Fed's inflation forced millions of Americans to renegotiate the most basic financial assumptions governing their everyday lives. Inflation, more and more Americans discovered, made one feel poorer even as the numbers on one's paycheck grew. Monetarists were determined to expose inflation as the tax that it was. Prevented from altering the Fed's policies directly, they now found it in their interest to join with other neo-conservatives to put a stop to this tax effect of inflation, even if they could not yet arrest its monetary causes. In this logic lay a political opportunity. It allowed monetarists to forge a powerful coalition with a broad array of antitax activists, many of whom later became known as supply-siders. This coalition became, as Phillips observed, a "curious mix of populism and elitism," which sought to channel populist anger "by postulating a new oppressive *public sector* economic elite—the bureaucrats and managers of the Inflationary State."[60]

The essential plank in the coalition of monetarists and supply-siders was the monetarists' belief that inflation was essentially a monetary phenomenon. This differed radically from the view of those Republican "traditionalists" who, often unknowingly subscribing to Keynesian assumptions, believed that inflation was caused by fiscal policy, wage cost-push, or—most broadly—social conflict and politics. Most especially, monetarist logic decoupled inflation's origins from budget deficits. This gave an important political opportunity to those economists who applied microeconomic analysis to the budget's selective incentives for economic activity (as opposed to Keynesians, who looked at its aggregate demand or "macro" effects). These economists became known as supply-siders. Strictly speaking, there was no theoretical difference between monetarists and supply-siders, only a difference in on the problems they focused on. (Thus perhaps the most famous supply-sider, Arthur Laffer, was originally a monetarist economist at OMB.) Both groups recognized that *total* government outlays, however funded, and not the formal budgetary deficit, represented a tax on the economy. They both regarded government expenditures as excessive. But having accepted that inflation was a monetary phenomenon, they were free to regard deficits not as a problem but as a solution. Deficit-as-solution meant seeking tax cuts first, in the expectation that shrinking the government's explicit tax revenue would restrain its total spending, "just as a limited income is the only effective restraint on any individual's or family's spending."[61]

Milton Friedman does not know exactly when he or other monetarists first came to endorse these supply-side tax rollbacks, but the evidence suggests that this position first found favor in the early to mid-1970s.[62] Friedman used this logic to support the otherwise Keynesian tax cuts proposed by Congress during the recession of 1975.[63] This logic also underlay Friedman's cofounding of the National Tax Limitation Committee

(NTLC) in 1975, which became an integral part of the grassroots antitax movement that flourished during the 1970s.

As Kevin Phillips argued, "Few movements better fit the definition of populist conservatism" than the antitax movement.[64] Friedman was unusual in throwing his considerable prestige behind the NTLC at an early date, as these movements were almost universally scorned by social and economic elites on both sides of the political aisle. Nonetheless, they flourished outside Washington and the state capitals as inflation worsened. Their most famous victory took place in June 1978, when voters in California approved Proposition 13 by a margin of 2 to 1. This plebiscite amended the state constitution to roll back and cap the rate of increase in real estate taxes. Proposition 13 set off a wave of imitators. Over the next two years, thirty-seven states would slash property taxes; twenty-eight states would cut income taxes; and thirteen states would restrict sales taxes. Naturally, the movement to restrict taxes had complex origins, owing much to such factors as growing general disenchantment with government and referendum provisions in state constitutions. Nonetheless, a persuasive case can be made that much of the antitax revolt originated in the interaction of those two forces we now recognize as central to monetarist politics: the mobilizational effects of inflation and the logic of progressive tax brackets. That the interactions of these forces provided monetarists with unique opportunities to construct and mobilize a previously unexploited coalition can be illustrated with a brief consideration of California's Proposition 13.

Monetarists were able to position themselves on the winning side of the Proposition 13 movement because they recognized sooner than virtually anyone else the underlying role of inflation in the dynamics of the housing market. Many Californians recognized that housing represented a durable investment, with mortgages deductible under federal tax law, and with a demographic shift under way creating buoyant demand. Astute Californians also recognized that housing had become a natural investment shelter against inflation. By the early 1970s, prices in the California housing market accelerated at a markedly faster rate than the increasing rate of inflation. Prices had climbed at 6.6 percent per year in 1972 (versus a statewide CPI of 3.3 percent) and by 1977 were increasing at approximately 25 percent, almost three times the local consumer price inflation rate.

But while many people saw the advantages in housing as an investment hedge, few except the monetarists at first recognized or understood the liquidity risk inflation in housing prices posed because of the interaction with real estate tax brackets. In California, as in many other localities, taxes are assessed on the current (not purchase) value of the home. In California, this meant that the tax bill was increasing in the late 1970s at

20 to 30 percent per year. By 1978, California's real property tax was 52 percent above the national average.

Particularly irritating was the way in which these rates of increase interacted with the assessment cycle. Local assessments were imposed only every two or three years by nonpartisan state agencies, which of course were not authorized to inquire about the property holder's ability to pay. These assessments were especially burdensome for owners on fixed or inflexible incomes. A tax bill on a house valued at $45,000 in 1973 came to $1160, whereas by 1976 it had almost doubled to $2070, a rate of increase with which few incomes kept up. Every Californian seemed to know pensioners who had been forced to sell their homes just to meet their tax bills. That the state was meanwhile amassing a $10 billion budgetary surplus, while state politicians of both stripes flatly refused to even debate a lower tax intake, would contribute further grist to the populists' mill, and create a growing political vacuum of unarticulated discontent.

Into this vacuum stepped the grassroots antitax organizations. These were primarily led by Howard Jarvis and Paul Gann, two political outsiders who had been campaigning against the property tax since the late 1960s. But the opportunity for monetarists to ally themselves to a popular cause can be gauged by the fact that when the Jarvis-Gann proposition was finally placed on the ballot in 1978, CEOs of major corporations, union leaders, state officials, and politicians of both major parties called for its rejection with one voice. No fewer than seven former presidents of the American Economics Association opposed the proposition, foretelling economic disaster for California if it was ratified. Only monetarists such as Arthur Laffer and Milton Friedman among professional economists endorsed it. Thus, when it passed, monetarists were uniquely placed to capitalize on what Friedman in his *Newsweek* column hailed as a "sweeping victory."[65]

It is difficult to assess the precise contributions of something as multifaceted as a tax revolt to the politics of monetarism except to relate the understanding of monetarists themselves. Clearly, however, the success of Proposition 13 and its imitators at the grassroots helped propagate innumerable state, local, and national antitax organizations, such as Friedman's own, which campaigned so enthusiastically for the Republicans in 1980. The tax revolt also confirmed what free-market economists had increasingly suspected—that the general public was no longer blinded by illusions about inflation, if it ever had been. But the most important consequence was that the success of Proposition 13 and its kin blessed the marriage of monetarism and supply-side economics as a viable political union and a potential electoral bonanza for Republicans in Washington.

Paul Craig Roberts, David Stockman, and other young Republicans in and around Congress were among the first to recognize in the alchemy of monetarists and supply-siders a new kind of "politics of joy" that might allow the Republicans to ride a wave of economic populism back into power. For what seemed like decades, Republicans had lacked a salable economic program of their own. Traditionalist Republicans' beliefs about inflation's causes had long made a balanced budget a touchstone of their politics. All too often, this reduced them to unelectable "advocates of root canal therapy" or "tax collectors for the Welfare State."[66] But now monetarists and their supply-side colleagues were teaching the Republicans that they could, with a clear economic conscience, offer the voters both lower inflation and lower taxes, a potentially unassailable combination.

The most direct impact of Proposition 13 was felt in Congressman Jack Kemp's office that very summer. In the late 1970s, Kemp's office "became a kind of post-graduate seminar on supply-side economics" with Ludwig Erhard's memoirs of Germany's postwar *Wirtschaftswunder* as its prescribed text.[67] Mere weeks after Proposition 13, Stockman helped draft the Kemp-Roth bill of 1978, which called for reduced corporate and personal income tax rates. This bill would later become the foundation of the Reagan administration's Economic Recovery Act of 1981. Kemp-Roth was based on the expectation that lower tax rates would increase incentives to work and invest. With newly rediscovered thrift and vigor, Americans would be richer and their government would receive more taxes.

But how much more taxes? Would this bill be a "free lunch" for the government? Or might there still be a deficit—perhaps even a bigger deficit? And would this matter? The claim of a free lunch seemed to play to a fear that the politics of joy had hoped to bury forever. It revealed the "hairline fracture" between those supply-siders who believed in its monetarist economic assumptions, and those who believed—whether as a result of "salesmanship" (as Stockman put it) or bad economics (as Friedman believed)—that the tax cuts would of themselves enlarge the tax base so much that lost receipts would be more than made up (the famous Laffer curve) and the budget would remain in balance. As Friedman pointed out in his *Newsweek* column, whether deficits mattered at all was the crux of the issue; genuine monetarists and supply-siders united around their belief that visible taxes could be cut now to reduce the total tax burden (i.e., spending) later, while pseudo supply-siders endorsed tax cuts only if the budget would still balance. But in 1978, it was all a matter of broadening the coalition. Laffer's curve brought in the optimists; Stockman and Gramm's proposed budget cuts (a codicil to the bill) corralled the traditionalists; and Friedman reassured everyone that deficits simply did not matter. But the coalition risked a split over the idea of the "free lunch." Congressmen Kemp and Roth, Friedman argued, "harm the cause they seek to serve by offering bad arguments for a good measure."[68] Ironically, it would be none other than Stockman who in 1981 would prove Friedman prophetic.

Before the Republican party could be revolutionized by monetarism, the insurgents first had to confront those traditionalist Republicans who detected heresy in the new doctrines.[69] This would require the creation of a new cadre of more radical Republicans for the key policy positions. Under the banner "people are policy," the New Right sought to redress the imbalance of policy expertise and personnel in Washington between themselves and the partisans of the New Deal state represented by such institutions as Brookings. Fortunately for this new wave of Republicans, the Federal Reserve's "price revolution" again furnished the money for the coming Reagan revolution in think tanks. And so American conservatism, for the first time, acquired its own intellectual vanguard. Inflation bankrolled policy institutions in Washington, which, across a whole range of issues, would recast the bluster of a populist like George Wallace into the locutions of an intellectual like George Will.

It is ironic that the policy institutions which most opposed inflation were among the sectors of the American economy which most profited from it. Of the some thousand research institutions in the United States, about two-thirds were founded during the post-1970 price revolution. Other conservative institutes, though not founded then, enjoyed a "great leap forward," thanks to an infusion of fresh cash.[70] Once again the wonderful chemistry of tax code and inflation worked its magic. The Internal Revenue Act of 1936 allowed corporations to deduct 5 percent of their net income for gifts to educational charities, but until the late 1950s, state laws made it very difficult for corporations to make any charitable contributions which were not "closely connected" with their business. (This is one reason why Ford and Carnegie money, for example, reached scholars by way of foundation grants rather than direct corporate giving.) Constrained by the New Deal tax code, these institutes derived most of their funding from two sources: donations from private foundations, and contract work from the public sector. Foundation support, although it originated in entrepreneurial wealth, was allocated by foundation heads primarily recruited from the university sector, and so it did little to deflect the institutes from their generally progovernment agendas.

Only beginning in the late 1960s did many states loosen these restraints to any appreciable degree. At the same time, the growth of inflation led firms to become increasingly interested in tax shelters. Milton Friedman nurtured this trend to some extent. Although he was philosophically opposed to corporate giving (tax-deductible or other), he felt that so long as it was established practice, it should be consistent with corporations' (presumably capitalist) principles. Friedman contended that "if businessmen are truly concerned about the threat to our free economy, they can do something about it by devoting the same care to their gifts as to their purchases."[71] Thus, in the 1970s, the higher the inflation rate, the greater the likelihood that a corporation's tax-deductible contribution to a think tank would slow the increase in its tax bill. (Parenthetically, in 1981, as if to compensate think-tanks for their impending loss of inflation revenue, Reagan's Economic Recovery Act doubled the tax-deductible amount for gifts to charities to 10 percent of net corporate income.)

The proliferation of explicitly neoconservative or free-market think tanks also grew out of Republicans' rueful knowledge that the economic catastrophe of the Nixon years had been in part of their own devising. The Nixon and Ford administrations had lacked the ideas and the personnel to chart a new course. Patrick Buchanan, a conservative populist and a senior Nixon aide, spoke of the need to create "a new 'cadre' of Republican governmental professionals who can survive [the defeat of] this Administration and be prepared to take over future ones."[72]

The change in the research institute scene was dramatic. These years saw the founding of the Business Roundtable and the Heritage Foundation in 1973, the Cato Institute in 1977, the Manhattan Institute, and the Pacific Institute. Milton Friedman joined the Hoover Institution. The American Enterprise Institute (AEI), long in the shadow of Brookings, saw its personnel and budget expand by tenfold, to a staff of 150 and a budget of $10 million during the 1970s. In 1980, AEI would send 20 of its alumni to the Reagan administration. Many of these institutes were sponsored by the conservative Olin, Pew, Smith-Richardson, and Scaife foundations. Heritage, however, perhaps the most active of the institutes, began life with a broad-based funding strategy that emphasized many small contributions—even if, in the end, its largest gifts came from corporate sources. As one senior Heritage staffer observed, "Ironically, we fed off inflation in the 1970s. Without the widespread anger in the American heartland, we would never have been able to tap into this wide financial base."[73]

By the late stages of the monetarist assault on the Federal Reserve, the monetarists' and supply-siders' emphasis on controlling inflation and taxes was having an impact outside the Republican party as well. But by 1978, the Carter administration had discovered for themselves just how independent the Federal Reserve could be. Once again, the corporate culture surrounding the chairman was at work. The former Fed governor Sherman Maisel once predicted "how dangerous it would be for the economy if in the future, a new Chairman of the Federal Reserve was not well trained in economics."[74] This remarkable possibility came to pass when Arthur Burns was replaced in early 1978 by G. William Miller, a businessman with no previous experience in banking or economics and, as it turned out, a marked indifference to monetary policy theory. Had this taken place in Germany, it would have been regarded as a clear violation of the Bundesbank's requirement for expert qualifications. As it was, the

Fed staff was not inclined to a favorable estimate of the new chairman's skills or attitudes. One senior staffer contrasted Miller with his successor by noting, "Volcker asked to see the money supply numbers three times a day. Miller asked for them every third day."[75] While Miller may have disdained current economic debates, his staff did not; and the staff members, together with some more economically minded governors, were increasingly of the mind that the Fed needed a dramatically different approach. The very procedures that chairman Volcker would employ in his monetarist reversal were finalized by the senior staff months earlier, during Miller's reign.[76] So although the senior staff had a much clearer concept by 1978 (and certainly by early 1979) of the technical steps necessary to bring the money supply under control, Miller's aloofness left this knowledge untapped. As one staffer lamented, "We had the tools, but Miller didn't know what to do with them."[77]

As William Niskanen observed, "not since the Depression had the Federal Reserve seemed so demoralized."[78] In the spring of 1979, the Fed had taken the unprecedented step of loosening at the peak of the business cycle. Both Treasury secretary Blumenthal and CEA chairman Schultze expended much energy attempting to persuade chairman Miller to tighten money, but to no avail.[79] The presidents of several more regional banks—Atlanta, San Francisco, and Richmond—had become monetarist. The staff, now augmented with rising monetarist stars like Tommie Thompson, Bernie Monk, Bill Poole, David Lindsay, and Tom Simpson, was pressing for a change. Even Paul Volcker, the president of the New York Federal Reserve Bank, whose own respect for the consensual culture of the Federal Reserve generally prevented him from opposing the chairman, found himself obliged to register a number of unprecedented dissenting votes with Miller's policy.[80] Thus numerous sources of pressure on the Federal Reserve chairman—the administration, Congress, dissident FOMC members, and his own senior staff, to say nothing of the growing tide of monetarist academic work—were unable to turn the Federal Reserve toward greater monetary discipline. The Federal Reserve's corporate culture had shown that it could shelter even the most vulnerable of chairmen.

POLITICIZED MONETARISTS IN POWER, 1979–1985

By the turn of the decade, a relatively broad agreement had emerged around several of the key planks of the monetarist–supply-side agenda. On the monetary side, this consensus stressed gradually reducing monetary growth to curb inflation without producing recession and unemployment. These sentiments were shared by the new chairman of the Fed, the administration, and Congress, whose House Banking Committee, in July

1979, passed a resolution (by 42 to 1) criticizing the Federal Reserve for stabilizing the federal funds rate instead of the money supply.[81] On the fiscal side, the consensus sought reduced government outlays and taxes and a more balanced budget. Yet none of these things came to pass as envisioned: above all, the money supply shrank not in the medium term but in the short term; and federal deficits exploded over both the short and the long term. The next pages will explain these events by showing how the Fed's long exclusion of monetarists from effectual power came back to haunt it. Monetarists who had been politicized and radicalized by their wilderness years in the 1970s were the same monetarists who were mobilized into power by the events at the dawn of the 1980s and whose efforts to press their agenda on the Fed contributed directly to these unintended—or at least unarticulated—outcomes.

Paul Volcker and the "October Revolution" of 1979–1980

In the summer of 1979 the Carter administration at long last "elevated" the Federal Reserve chairman G. William Miller to the post of Treasury secretary and replaced him shortly thereafter with Paul Volcker. The White House wanted someone at the Fed with enough credibility to do something "fairly conventional" to rescue the economic situation before the election.[82] Volcker, a longtime monetary policy insider (unlike Miller), was believed, by those who thought they knew him, to be a "practical monetarist," though there was considerable ignorance in the White House about what this might imply.[83] Volcker's testimony at his confirmation hearing that summer was almost a textbook summary of monetarists' policy prescriptions. Contending that "there is no substitute for monetary discipline," Volcker maintained that a short recession would be insufficient to curb inflation; only four to five years of slow growth could accomplish this.[84]

Within weeks of his taking office, events served notice to Volcker that a serious move against inflation would require more than the usual measures. An unusual split vote at the board meeting of September 18th led many observers to believe that the Fed still lacked the will to fight inflation. This further weakened the markets. So, aided by Stephen Axilrod, the board's staff director and chief economist, Volcker put the finishing touches on new monetarist-inspired operating procedures that would control the reserve base more closely than ever before. These measures were informally agreed to by the board and the FOMC on September 28th but were held in readiness for the appropriate time. This date is significant, because of a widespread perception—actually a misperception—that the switch to monetary targeting was driven by international market pressures. European governments, so the theory goes, had been propping up the imperiled dollar throughout 1979 (because of its impact on oil prices) but now felt betrayed by the Fed's recent laxness. This currency crisis came to a head during the Belgrade meeting of the IMF the following week. There the Europeans reportedly told the American delegation, led by Volcker, that artificial props like Carter bonds and half-measures on interest rates no longer sufficed.[85] But in fact, the new consensus had already been achieved. At home, an editorial in *Business Week* expressed the business community's strongest demand yet for a switch to a hard-line monetarist approach: "If the Federal Reserve simply decided what rate of money growth it wanted and metered out reserves to support that amount of expansion and no more, the Federal Reserve, the banks, and the nation would all be much better off."[86]

And so Volcker decided to act. On October 6, 1979, he convened the FOMC for an extraordinary Saturday meeting, after which it announced its unanimous decision in favor of a broad package of measures that included another full 1 percent hike in the discount rate and special surcharges on certain forms of credit. Most important, the Fed announced that it would henceforth steer monetary policy with direct reference to its targets in M1 (after 1980, M1-B) and would deemphasize other variables, such as the federal funds rate. Controlling nonborrowed reserves now meant that the FOMC would not have to decide on specific levels for short-term interest rates but would instead let these be determined by market forces as banks accommodated themselves to the quantity of reserves available. Beginning the following morning, these changes yielded record interest rates (an increase of 3.75 percentage points in the federal funds rate alone) and the biggest stock market loss in 6 years. These resulted in a higher rate for the dollar (at least until interest rates abroad moved up to cut the differential, toward the end of the year) and brought M1 to within the top of its target band for the year.

Unusually for monetary policy, which is typically conducted in obscurity, Volcker's "October revolution" generated banner Sunday headlines and a remarkable amount of interest among nonspecialists. Official Washington's skepticism was in marked contrast to the reception elsewhere. Although most liberals were silent, Miller at the Treasury and McGovern in the Senate expressed reservations. Lane Kirkland of the AFL-CIO called it "the wrong move at the wrong time," and warned that it put the Carter administration's "national accord" in jeopardy. At the same time, Carter told union members in San Francisco that he would not let the Fed fight inflation with their jobs.

But as the measures appeared to restore confidence in the dollar and the inflation rate, the Fed began winning back the support of Wall Street economists.[87] Allan Meltzer, the prominent academic monetarist and member of the SOMC, endorsed the switch but reiterated that the new policy would not end inflation in less than three to five years.[88] Although the SOMC would later attempt to downplay the significance of the October switch in control procedures, its first official evaluation was very favorable.[89] And the St. Louis Federal Reserve president, Roos, long the toughest critic of the FOMC within the system, heralded the switch as the long-awaited advent of monetarism.

Yet there was, and is, considerable controversy as to exactly what Volcker's October revolution had wrought. John Woolley is probably correct in denying that it represented an "intellectual conversion" of the board to monetarist principles.[90] Scholars and pundits have identified numerous reasons for the FOMC to collectively adopt a set of practices in which it did not wholeheartedly believe. Monetarists themselves would soon find cause to identify all the ways Fed practice deviated from their prescriptions.[91] And certainly the perception of significant and lasting change was slow to percolate to the outside economy, where it mattered most. Nonetheless, it can be shown that the switch was real, lasting, and of a decidedly monetarist character. One major factor which impeded its recognition as a "policy regime change" originated not so much with the Fed's program as with the nature of the audience in the Fed's policy environment.

As with the arrival of monetarism in Germany, Volcker understood that monetary aggregates served the interests of discipline both internally and externally, and that these were interrelated. Internally, the Fed needed a new mechanism, giving a truer reading, that would permit FOMC policymakers to agree upon intermediate targets more closely related to their ultimate policy objectives. Continued reliance on interest rates as the indicator of Federal Reserve policy had become seriously compromised. More important, the monetary system as a whole needed an anchor in a post–gold standard world: "In a sense, this role in stabilizing expectations was once a function of the gold standard, the doctrine of the annually balanced budget, and fixed exchange rates. . . I view the 'monetary targeting' approach as an effort to adopt a new and in many ways more sensible and comprehensible symbol of responsible policy."[92]

Volcker's analysis of the need for an internal policy anchor pointed to a weakness in the Fed's corporate culture. Volcker recognized that the emphasis on consensus within the FOMC was really procedural and that it masked a lack of intermediate policy objectives. Procedural consensus of this sort created compromise positions around merely incremental changes in the federal funds rates that were simply too ineffectual to carry the necessary impact on the real economy. Over the previous 3 1/2 years the board of governors and the FOMC generally had slowly come to the belief that inflation was a serious problem. Even so, some members were still loath to push interest rates high because once the rate was elevated, the same inertial forces would make it difficult to reduce—thus making the Fed excessively deflationary. The new operating procedure, by deflecting the FOMC's attention away from setting specific federal funds rates, turned it into a more flexible decision-making body, whose consensus would now be focused on ends, not means. For some governors, Volcker's new system seemed to hold the prospect of a more rapid and automatic switch from fighting inflation to fighting recession as circumstances warranted. This is an important fact, for it reveals just how much central banks rely on the politics of a fait accompli. The Fed believed it was in its self-interest to have enough flexibility to switch later to "fighting the recession" and demobilize slow-to-organize opposition in Congress and elsewhere.[93]

But the other, and perhaps more immediate, function of targets was external. As Volcker wrote in 1978, "Monetary targeting is first of all a useful tool of communication with the public."[94] Clearly, the SOMC was not the only group of policy experts who had been watching the German experience with targeting: some senior staffers hoped, in the spirit of apparent German practice, that the new targets would signal to labor that it should moderate its wage demands and achieve what the unsuccessful "national accord" of the Carter years had been unable to obtain.[95] Volcker's view, however, was more sanguine:

> I make no claims that the "announcement effect" of monetary targeting is nearly so effective or precise as some of my German friends interpret the experience in their own country, where the claim is sometimes heard that wage negotiations, for instance, are directly affected. But I do believe the strategy of public monetary targets aiming at gradual reduction in inflation can [have] and has had some value in calming and stabilizing inflationary expectations.[96]

But *whose* inflationary expectations? As soon as this question is asked, the impact of the Fed's policy environment on its unique experience of monetarism becomes clear. Volcker, who "knew the financial markets like the back of his hand" was extraordinarily frustrated by the reception given his first experiment with monetarism.[97] Despite many weeks of speechmaking, and despite the fact that federal funds rates had climbed into the high teens by the first quarter of 1980, the real economic situation remained unchanged for months, which caused much consternation at the Fed.

One possible explanation for the failed announcement effect was the accelerating transformation of American finance. As noted earlier, the Fed had for some time been concerned about the growing erosion of its monetary control caused by the defection of member banks from the Fed to state regulators. Now the high interest rates entailed by monetary targeting accelerated this erosion. At first, congressional support for traditional bank regulations precluded the Fed from obtaining the legislation that would fix this problem. But by 1980 both the administration and Congress were themselves worried by the failure of demand to decline, and so the Fed obtained the passage of the Depository Institutions Deregulation and Monetary Control Act (MCA) of 1980.

MCA's contributions to Volcker's monetarism were both external and internal. MCA ended the two-tier membership system, brought the Euromarkets into the Fed's purview, and eliminated that pillar of the New Deal in banking, regulation Q. These were its external objectives. MCA also helped entrench monetary targeting internally by reorganizing the management responsibilities of the staff and the board. Previously, the Fed's staff had been organized into two divisions, domestic and international; and board members had been kept apart from the day-to-day administration. Henceforth, there would be a third division, the monetary division, headed by the staff director and chief economist of the board. MCA also reorganized the board into distinct management committees, which did not confer line administrative responsibilities on the governors but did enhance their supervisory functions. Although the Fed saw the MCA as a necessary step to complete its monetarist switch, it did not anticipate that this assault on the New Deal order would handicap the new monetarist order. Overlooked was the fact that monetarist theories had measured, not money in the abstract, but money as defined by populist banking regulations. When these regulations began to disappear, the old empirical relationships began to disappear with them.

Volcker's experiment with practical monetarism was also unable to alter the Carter administration's political imperatives. Volcker may have had a medium-term strategy for lowering inflation, but the Carter administration had a short-term electoral deadline. So on March 14, 1980, the president authorized the implementation of strict credit controls through the Credit Control Act of 1969, which produced the single biggest drop in GNP, 10 percent, since the war, and sent unemployment climbing to 7.5 percent. In the second quarter of 1980, the money supply actually *dropped* 2.4 percent, primarily because of a 17 percent drop in April alone. The credit controls, coming on top of many months of tight money, sent the real economy into cardiac arrest. Among the worst-hit sections was, as usual, the housing sector. The housing market came to virtually a complete standstill—and this prompted outraged home builders to deliver piles of unused lumber to the Fed's doorstep.[98] Carter lifted credit controls in July; and this, coupled with steep declines in short term interest rates in May and June, caused the money supply to rebound at an astonishing 17 percent rate in the next quarter. In order to bring the growth of the money supply back within target, the Federal Reserve again raised money market interest rates, to the point where they were actually higher at the end of the year than they had been in the spring.

If a chief aim of a monetarist policy is medium-term economic stability, observers had grounds for asking whether the United States was farther from this goal than ever. The evidence of the last few months seemed to suggest that this was the case and elicited multiple alternative interpretations. One view pointed to Carter's reelection campaign. The dramatic rebound in the money supply in 1980, courtesy of the Federal Reserve, could easily be consistent with a partisan interpretation, in the spirit of Burns and Nixon. The SOMC certainly believed that the Fed's actions were otherwise inexplicable. But this view is not persuasive; a more plausible view is that the Carter White House "never got hold of the monetary policy machinery."[99] Carter may not even have known what direction he wanted the machinery to go in. Had he gotten hold of it, he might not have found himself, in the late stages of his campaign, calling the "strictly monetarist approach" of the Federal Reserve "ill-advised."[100] These comments, and perhaps the outcome of the election itself, suggest that Volcker may not have been pursuing Carter's first-choice policy.

Alternatively, the new and more complicated relationship between the Fed's actions and interest rates led some to conclude that the switch to targeting was no more than a way for the Federal Reserve to camouflage its responsibility for a painful recession. Charles Schultze, for example, thought that the Federal Reserve was using the new operating procedure for "deniability," to say to Congress and the public that interest rates were really determined by the market. Even some Federal Reserve officials have endorsed this view. As one former senior staff member observed, "No central bank can take responsibility for 20 percent interest rates politically. . . . We knew there was going to be pain and suffering, but we felt this was the only way we could get the job done."[101] Yet Volcker and Axilrod, the architects of the switch, believed that the new system was far too transparent to be effective political camouflage.[102] They fully expected the new system to produce higher interest rates, and they did not expect it to reduce the intensity of political assaults on such rates. This view is corroborated by the dramatic increase in the number of bills introduced in Congress directing the Fed to reduce interest rates.

In fact, despite Carter's interference, the Volcker Fed's monetary actions in its first year were remarkably consistent with its announced targeting regime. First, the yearly growth in the money supply, as measured by M1B, exceeded its target by less than 1 percent. Second, this growth in late 1980 was clearly intended by several key FOMC meetings that year, when even the monetarist hawks among the regional bank presidents voted to allow the money supply to rise back up to the year's target. Third, the greater variability and greater volatility in interest rates seen in the nation's money markets would never have been permitted by the old regime, but both were consistent with prioritizing monetary aggregates over the federal funds rate. From a strictly internal perspective, then, the Volcker revolution was true to its intentions.

Nonetheless, Volcker would later describe the rebound in the money supply in late 1980 as his greatest mistake.[103] The problem was that observers in the American private sector wielded a different, more precise set of monetarist measuring devices from those of their German counterparts. When Volcker's Fed hoped to imitate the Bundesbank and use annually announced targets—play by the monetarist's rules—it neglected to note that the American and German rules were different because the policy environments were different. In America, the central bank in Washington didn't control the statistics. The "enormous appetite for data" in American financial markets elevated the weekly St. Louis numbers into the Fed watchers' litmus test for monetarist purity. Despite his public plea for a longer-term view of growth in the money supply, the chairman was forced to concede in the end that what one might call the "big M" definition of monetarism had trumped his own more "small m" definition. Conflicting measurement criteria turned Volcker's gradualism into a credibility problem. Lost credibility, Volcker felt, made the next round of fighting inflation all the tougher.[104] Not least significantly, the Fed's credibility problem alienated its own potential allies among the monetarist–supply-side coalition that was about to sweep into the White House.

The Reagan Monetarist Ascendancy, 1981–1982

Ronald Reagan's inaguration as President in January 1981 brought into power in Washington an ill-blended amalgam of politicized monetarists and supply-siders on the one hand and traditionalist Republican budget-balancers on the other. This internal Republican cleavage shaped the policy environment for Paul Volcker and the Federal Reserve in such a way that an abandonment of monetarist gradualism, if not of monetarism altogether, became highly likely. Montarists were unwilling to oppose, on anti-inflationary grounds, the supply-siders' massive tax cuts; and this, combined with their political assault on the Fed, produced the sharp reduction in inflation, recession, and the growth of deficits that no one in Washington claimed to want.

David Stockman's memoirs illustrate that in the hands-off policymaking style that trickled down from the Reagan White House, personnel was indeed policy: "If you got a consensus among the key advisers, it was a done deal." The most formal grouping of the monetarist–supply-side advisors was the new President's Economic Policy Advisory Board (PEPAB), a kind of quasi-CEA convoked specially for the occasion and chaired by George Schulz. Its members included Arthur Burns, Milton Friedman,

Alan Greenspan, Arthur Laffer, James T. Lynn, Paul McCracken, William Simon, Thomas Sowell, Herbert Stein, Charles E. Walker, and Walter Wriston. PEPAB was "truly the board of directors for the development of Reaganomics" and would meet with Reagan six times during the critical first year's battle over the money supply and tax cuts.[105] At Treasury, Reagan appointed Donald T. Regan, a Wall Streeter with pronounced supply-side instincts and a willingness to study and accommodate himself to Reagan's policies. Regan in turn recruited Beryl Sprinkel (Harris Trust, SOMC member) as his undersecretary for monetary affairs because he shared Regan's "supply-side belief in the slow, steady certain growth of the money supply."[106] (It was Sprinkel who would utter the infamous motto of American monetarism, "Control the money supply and everything else falls into place. Thank you, and good night.") Paul Craig Roberts, perhaps the leading supply-sider from the congressional staff, joined Regan as his principal assistant, and Allan Meltzer was appointed as an outside consultant. Jerry Jordan, of Pittsburgh National Bank and the SOMC, was appointed to the CEA, where he was later joined by Bill Poole (a monetarist staff member from the Federal Reserve Board); and Beryl Sprinkel was later named chairman of the CEA. Not least among the enthusiastic monetarists and supply-siders was Ronald Reagan himself. Tutored by Friedman, Reagan had long before learned to trace twenty years' worth of the money supply, and he knew all about the Fed's tendency to "zoom" the economy. The monetarist–supply-side coalition was arrayed against an ill-defined set of Republican traditionalists, budget-balancers, Republican Keynesians, and "eclectics."

The key to sorting out the "sects within sects" turned out to be their views about inflation, whose evils all Republicans seemed agreed upon but about whose causes they differed. These causes were understood as either monetary or "fiscal-social." The case of David Stockman, erstwhile congressman and champion of Kemp-Roth, illustrates how important it is to pursue the different players' views about inflation down to their (often implicit) economic first premises. As budget director, David Stockman was a self-professed combination of supply-side and monetarist economics who, because he considered himself "more of an anti-inflationist than anything else," was in reality, a budget-balancing traditionalist. Ultimately believing that "political demands" entailed by government spending programs determined Federal Reserve policy, Stockman at first argued that the deficit had to be strengthened during the upcoming budget battles "as a symbol of what had to be radically changed."[107] Upon discovering later in 1981 that Republicans would not trim those programs, Stockman followed the remorseless logic of his own economic syllogisms about inflation and moved over to the anti–supply-side Republican camp, forsaking both his tax-cutting credentials and his long association with Kemp's circle. Stockman's onetime supply-side ally Paul Craig Roberts observed with uncharacteristic understatement about his defection, "It didn't occur to us that Stockman was not really committed to the program."[108]

The first battleground for the sects was over precisely what the new administration's program was, which involved proposing a new budget and an accompanying economic forecast. The forecast was a deceptively important device for signaling to the Fed the administration's preferred policies and selling Congress on its Economic Recovery Act (the heir to the Kemp-Roth tax reduction plan). The intramural battle lines in the economic forecast concerned which numbers to assign to real GNP growth plus inflation to equal current dollar or "money" GNP. Supply-siders (Roberts) wanted the highest possible real GNP growth, while the monetarists (Sprinkel) quite uncharacteristically wanted the lowest possible money GNP. Inevitably, "the inflation number took it in the neck." The OMB initially forecast inflation as dropping to 2 percent per annum within three years.[109] This reduced the projected 1985 money GNP forecast by $400 billion relative to Carter's CBO forecast, leading to a $100 billion decline in revenues. Together with the increased defense expenditures, this produced a $150 billion dollar deficit. But Stockman fully expected that the threat of a budgetary shortfall would force his colleagues to cut at least $100 billion in expenditures, or "face national ruin."[110]

This "purist" forecast instantly ran into opposition from Republican eclectics, represented by Murray Weidenbaum, Reagan's first chairman of the CEA. Weidenbaum had famously popularized the hidden costs of government regulation but proved to be something of an unknown quantity when it came to inflation and the budget. He simply refused to accept the figure of 2 percent for inflation for the next year, and so a much higher rate of inflation was restored to the budget.[111] Weidenbaum's intervention rescued monetarist gradualism for the forecast. Whether his action was due to his support for the monetarist ideal or, as others suspect, his belief in the very unmonetarist notion of "core inflation" is uncertain. But certainly there was a political necessity in those early days to pay lip service to balanced budgets: "Any more fussing [about the forecast] and we would have been painted in the media as people who thought deficits unimportant, and our own party would be causing difficulties at our confirmation hearings."[112] The final forecast of February 18th, nicknamed the "rosy scenario," assumed "that the growth rates of money and credit are steadily reduced from the 1980 levels to one-half those levels by 1986" and forecast 5 percent real GNP growth.

But Washington knew that the real battles were not about forecasts but about policies. As Roberts observed in a memo to the Treasury secretary in March, "The economy and forecasts of its performance might interact in decisive ways with the success of the President's economic policy package in Congress."[113] The "consensus forecast" was supposed to smooth the way for the next item on Reagan's agenda, the enactment of the Economic Recovery Act, the heir to the Kemp-Roth tax-cutting bill of the 1970s. As Roberts correctly observed, Stockman's "hiding of the deficit" inadvertently made a balanced budget the ultimate yardstick of the Reagan administration's first year in office. This gave Stockman license to pursue his "draconian" program cuts and made Congress and the media fear that tax cuts would be "wildly inflationary." Little wonder, then, with signals like these emanating from the White House, that Bob Dole, chairman of the Senate Finance Committee, and the Senate majority leader Howard Baker—Republican traditionalists—doubted that tax cuts were economically sound.

Thus the tax cut proposals were delayed and reduced (5 percent in the first year, for example, instead of 10 percent). Volcker intimated in a speech in February that spending should be cut first, and that Stockman's suggestion of a "trigger" for tax cuts would allow the Fed to lower interest rates. Stockman believed that he could browbeat the cabinet into major program rollbacks by holding out tax cuts—and Volcker's reductions in interest rates—as a reward for pruning spending. But as spring became summer, and cabinet members successfully defended their turf against Stockman's cuts, the tax-cut bill languished in Congress. Alan Greenspan's briefing to the Fed at this time asserted that relative to fiscal policy, "monetary policy was the junior partner, and could do nothing other than a weak rear-guard action."[114] The essential monetarist framework—that monetary policy, not fiscal policy, determined inflation—had still not been accepted by many Republicans.

To sell tax cuts to traditionalist Republicans in Congress, it therefore became imperative for the administration's monetarists to show that fears of inflation were unfounded. Working from their "bureaucratic politics" assumptions about the Fed's behavior, Friedman and other academic monetarists argued vigorously from the sidelines that the deficit was not the real issue; the real issue was the institution of the Federal Reserve and its commitment to fighting inflation.[115] Led by Beryl Sprinkel, the White House put intense private and even public pressure on the Fed over the next few months to "be monetarist."

Indeed, the monetarist–supply-side coalition questioned whether the Fed as currently designed even could be monetarist. But instead of calling for greater political independence, the monetarists called for greater *dependence*. The SOMC wanted the president to become more formally responsible for monetary policy and hold the Fed accountable for its actions:

> Much weight is occasionally attached to the presumed independence of the Federal Reserve System. We also hear voices raised in defense of the Fed's

"institutional integrity." But the fact of this "integrity" means that we must suffer any consequences produced by the Federal Reserve Authorities. We must suffer Great Depressions and permanent inflations without recourse or accountability. But it is time for a change, and change NOW.[116]

These sentiments were echoed in the White House. Privately, Treasury secretary Regan and undersecretary Sprinkel discussed abolishing the Fed. Sprinkel later revealed publicly the lengths to which the monetarists' skepticism of the Fed might run when he said, "There is, on the one hand, an argument to keep the Federal Reserve independent to avoid the problem of an administration running away on an inflationary policy. But on the other hand, the president is elected by all the people, and he has a right to put his policies into being and to be held accountable for them."[117] "The Administration's monetarists," Roberts recalled with frustration, "were worried that the Federal Reserve would overshoot its targets. . . . An old-fashioned Keynesian belief in the predominance of fiscal policy combined with politics and Washington competitiveness to whip up an inflation hysteria even while the economy was plummeting into recession."[118]

If bureaucratic resistance at the Federal Reserve—which monetarists believed accounted for the Fed's failures on inflation—was to be overcome, monetarists believed they would need the support of the president. Their campaign culminated in a series of meetings between Reagan and Volcker, beginning in the spring of 1981. These meetings cleared up in Volcker's mind any lingering ambiguity about the timeliness—and opportuneness—of "really hitting the targets."[119] This was the new element. As Ed Meese would write, "While control of the money supply and hence inflation is vested in the Federal Reserve Board, the President was steadfast in supporting the Fed's stance of monetary restraint—too much so, in the thinking of some of his staff."[120] Volcker would later recall that the Reagan administration was like all the others—which is to say, hostile to tight money—"except in the beginning."[121]

And so in May, Volcker announced that he would err on the side of restraint, and the FOMC increased the discount rate and its surcharge by a full 1 percent. These moves produced even higher and more variable interest rates than those of 1980, and ultimately the beginning of a second economic downturn, which would prove even deeper, by some measures, than that of 1975. "There can be little doubt," Roberts observed, "that the inflation hysteria encouraged Volcker to overreact by clamping down too tightly on money growth." [122] The federal funds rate, after dropping by more than 6 percent in the first quarter, attained near record-levels in the spring. For the first four months of 1981, M1 increased at a rate of 14.2 percent; in the next four months it declined 1.5 percent; and in the last three months it again increased 7 percent. The Fed managed to bring growth of M1 down so that it ended the year slightly below target, but with a high price in unpredictability and volatility. High interest rates in 1981 also helped the dollar to soar some 27 percent on world markets.

The change in the economic climate after the crucial "encouragement" of monetarism in May forced the budget balancers and the monetarist–supply-side coalition into a long-postponed showdown. High interest rates implied a reduction in economic growth, with negative implications for government revenue and expenditures. At long last it was clear that a balanced budget could not be squared with tax cuts. One of them would have to give, and the choice was made in a crucial cabinet-level meeting chaired by the White House chief of staff, Jim Baker. All the departmental heavyweights were in attendance, except for Stockman, who was represented by his deputy, Larry Kudlow. As reported by Kudlow, the question of the significance of high interest rates for the deficit was raised by Meese, who wanted to know whether, as "a friend's theory" had it, "large government deficits were absorbing available savings, and this was pushing up interest rates." Stockman believed that this was no theory but a "stark reality," testified to by the financial markets. He thought that there were probably only "five human beings alive who disagreed with Meese's friend. Unfortunately, two of them—the Treasury Secretary and his principal assistant [Roberts]—were in Jim Baker's office." Roberts argued that "interest rate increases were strictly a monetary problem, and had nothing to do with deficits and government borrowing."[123] Thus reassured, the cabinet decided to push ahead with the tax cuts in the modified form and not seek the major spending cuts that Stockman had wanted. The fate of the budget was sealed, and the Republicans made their unprecedented break with decades of budget-balancing tradition.

"Once again," Stockman claimed, "the truth had been buried, and this time the White House had done it deliberately, in order to win the tax battle."[124] But any implication that Roberts's view of inflation as a monetary phenomenon was an isolated or minority position in the White House, or was not taken on good faith, is mistaken. In fact, the monetarists had disseminated it widely in the Reagan administration, even among those who would not be expected to follow economic policy debates closely. Thus Ed Meese, the president's counsel, probably spoke for a new and largely sincere White House consensus when he argued in favor of tax cuts as curtailing outlay growth (the Friedman strategy) and distinguished the deficit from total expenditures. As Meese catechized, "The ultimate burden on the economy is precisely the total amount of government spending. Fixation on the deficit tended to ignore this crucial fact. If the government spends it, then one way or another, it has to be paid for—either through taxes or through credit markets. *Agitation on how the burden is to be financed distracts attention from this larger point.*"[125] Many Reaganite Republicans may have been taught to think like this by the actual events, rather than in a graduate seminar, but one risks overlooking the historical significance of the monetarist break with Republican traditionalism by insisting upon too large role for deception and bad dealing in accounting for its origins.

By 1982, the Fed's tight money policies had plunged the U.S. economy into full-fledged recession. Output declined over 1.5 percent, resulting in a level of real GNP that at the end of 1982 was actually lower than its level of three years earlier, an unemployment rate that reached 10.8 percent, and a consumer price index of 4.5 percent—half the rate of the year before. Political efforts by the White House to demonstrate that inflation was purely a monetary phenomenon had scuttled monetarists' cherished gradualism. "The policy we requested [in February 1981] from the Federal Reserve Chairman Paul Volcker," wrote Roberts, "was a gradual 50 percent reduction in the growth rate of the money supply spread over six years. . . . [But] instead of evenly spreading the reduction in money growth over a six year period, the Federal Reserve delivered 75 percent of the reduction in the first year."[126] Milton Friedman, testifying to Congress in 1982, claimed, "If this be monetarism, then I am no monetarist."[127] The SOMC's criticism of overly rapid deceleration in the growth of monetary aggregates was vociferous.[128] The basic problem for critics on both the left and the right was the cost imposed by the Federal Reserve in switching so rapidly from one path of monetary growth to another. Both sets of opponents argued that slower change, as in Germany, and as Volcker intended, would certainly have produced less controversy, possibly less economic dislocation, and possibly less inflation in the long run. Perhaps none expressed the essence of monetarism's misfortunes better than the Treasury secretary himself:

> As for monetary policy, nobody argued with Paul Volcker's desire to drive inflation out of the economy. . . . At our weekly breakfast, I argued with Volcker for a steady, predictable monetary policy that would assure an adequate and dependable supply of money for the private sector. Volcker is a brilliant and dedicated man, and there is no doubt that his actions did, indeed, cauterize inflation, but the burn cost the patient the use of his right arm for nearly two years.[129]

Congressional reaction to the Federal Reserve's "burn" reached a crescendo between the spring and early autumn of 1982. Monetarism and monetary targeting had neither diminished the political importance of interest rates for congressmen, nor, as events would show, convinced many of them that deficits and inflation were unrelated issues. Congress demanded lower interest rates and was prepared to fight hard to get them. The complicated tax-cutting dramaturgy of 1981 among the White House, Congress, and the Fed unspooled in 1982 like a film run backward. Stockman, Dole, and others told the president that restoring lost tax revenue would "encourage the Federal Reserve to lower interest rates."[130] Supply-siders and monetarists, who saw the economy plunging deeper into recession, found this logic of tax hikes "Orwellian." PEPAB, the intellectual conscience of Reaganomics, "personally reassured the President that he, and not his advisors who wanted to raise taxes, was right. Milton Friedman and William Simon, two of Reagan's favorites, were very eloquent and persuasive on this point."[131]

Eloquent or not, Reagan could not resist the pressure to raise taxes forever. Donald Regan reported to the president a breakfast meeting that spring during which Volcker assured the Treasury secretary that he would "try to be accommodating to the Administration—he would ease money to bring interest rates down if he could see some movement by us on the deficits."[132] The next month, Reagan authorized negotiations with Congress through the so-called "gang of 17." Their agreements raised hundreds of millions of dollars in social security taxes and closed tax loopholes, restoring much, but not all, of the revenues that Reagan's measures of 1981 had cut. Years later, many Reaganites still regarded this agreement as the "debacle of '82."

Members of Congress also introduced a flurry of bills attacking the Federal Reserve more directly. These culminated in the Democrats' "Balanced Monetary Policy Act," a "shot across the Fed's bow."[133] When the Republican leadership returned to Washington in 1982 after the summer recess, electoral calculation led the Senate majority leader, Baker, to propose making the bill bipartisan. The "Balanced Monetary Policy Act" proposed to change the monetarist orientation of the Federal Reserve by mandating lower real interest rates. Though Volcker lobbied hard against it, Congressional staffers claimed that the bill never represented a serious threat to the Federal Reserve or the Fed's policies, not least because it stood little chance of success without presidential support, which was not forthcoming.

With regard to the retreat from monetarism, like its arrival, it is difficult to draw sharp distinctions between politics and economics. The Federal Reserve finally began to loosen in July, and this led to a 50 percent reduction in interest rates by October, at which time the FOMC announced that it was going to "deemphasize" M1B as a policy target. The Fed's switch in late 1982 to a more expansionary approach also appeared to herald the abandonment of more than a tight money supply. Deregulation in the financial sector had begun with NOW accounts, had accelerated with MCA, and now included the Garn-St. Germain Act (which sought to ameliorate the thrifts' problems by allowing them to engage in activities previously reserved for commercial banks) and the introduction of new financial products. Dismantling the New Deal banking-sector firewalls began to irrevocably alter the financial environment, so that M1B no longer behaved as predicted by monetarist economists. Growth in M1B reached 13 percent for the year as a whole, overshooting the target by 3 percent. Yet inflation abated, thanks to an unanticipated change in the velocity of the aggregates.[134] Henceforth, the Federal Reserve would rely more heavily on the broader aggregates. As one congressional staff member put it, Congress's deregulatory initiatives "destroyed the monetarist system almost before we had a chance to use it."[135] But as a senior Federal Reserve economist, himself a monetarist, expressed the intellectual imperatives of 1982: "To persist in using targets at that time would simply have been intellectually pigheaded."[136]

Monetarist Aftermath: Consequences and Lessons, 1983 – 1985

In his *Triumph of Politics*, published in 1986, David Stockman contemplated America's burgeoning deficits and prophesied, "The clock is ticking away inexorably toward another bout of inflationary excess. If we stay the course we are now in, the decade will end with worse hyperinflation than the one with which it began."[137] Yet ten years later, while Washington was still playing politics with America's enormous deficits, inflationary catastrophe was nowhere in sight. Even at the time it was penned, Stockman's prediction was almost certainly wrong. Beginning in 1983, the U.S. recovery produced what the OECD, no friend of Reaganomics, called "an exceptionally good" trade-off between unemployment and inflation.[138] By contrast with Germany, where unemployment was rising above 11 percent, the evidence suggested that in the United States unemployment and inflation were not traded off so much as reduced simultaneously. The aftermath of American monetarism seemed to produce policies of high interest rates (both real and nominal) and enormous deficits that appeared to be working at cross-purposes. This defying of the conventional wisdom forced politicians, economists, and citizens to rethink what they had previously taken for granted. But as Stockman's unreconstructed Republican traditionalism attests, changed economic realities do not necessarily renovate the myths, models, and assumptions which animate politics and policy.

From 1983 to 1985, the United States was the only major Western nation apart from Japan and Canada to register a strong recovery. Its GNP increased 6 percent per year before leveling off at 2 percent in 1985. Unemployment declined steadily until it reached 6 percent. Inflation dropped rapidly to less than 4 percent. But this prosperity was unlike that seen in the 1960s. Interest rates, both real and nominal, were much higher. From 1983 to 1985, for example, short-term rates averaged between 8.5 and 9.5 percent, compared with 3 to 4 percent a decade earlier. This was necessary if a fiscal deficit approaching $195 billion (6 percent of GNP exclusive of off-budget items) was to be financed without causing a run on the dollar. The new Reagan administration and its advisers did not believe in intervening in the exchange market, and so, from April 1981 until the time of the Plaza accord in September 1985, the United States abjured intervention in the currency markets. Thus unencumbered, the dollar attained a perch some 40 percent above its 1980 value and contributed directly to a current account deficit that reached $118 billion.

According to the OECD, the principal reason for the unusually positive recovery was the labor market's new found ability to adjust real wages downward. This was unlike the situation in Germany, and it was crucial to maintaining both employment and competitiveness.[139] As William Niskanen, of Reagan's CEA, observed, "The major conditions that led to a restructuring of wages and salaries" were due to the aftershocks of the monetarist and supply side revolution, in particular "deregulation and increasing foreign competition" driven by the strong dollar.[140] These subjected the United States' blue-collar and unionized workforce to unprecedented competitive pressures. A quarter of all 9 million workers covered by collective bargaining agreements were forced to make wage and benefit concessions.[141] Heavy manufacturing was decimated. In 1986, manufacturing accounted for only 19 percent of America's employment, compared with 27 percent ten years earlier. By far most of this decline took place in the unionized sectors, especially in the Northeast and Midwest.[142] As interest rates increased, the recession deepened, and the dollar rose, import-competing industries lost market share, transferred their production to states with antiunion "right-to-work" laws, or simply went bankrupt. As inflation declined, the U.S. strike rate dropped from 23.7 million workdays lost during 1978 to 16.9 million during Reagan's first year in office to 7 million in 1985. By the mid-1980s, the unionization rate of the U.S. workforce had dropped to less than 16 percent. The conflict and malaise of the 1970s were gone, replaced by a new, less egalitarian stability.

It is these deeper connections among the monetarist episode, the social division of economic rewards, and political stability that we must grasp if we are to understand the role of monetarism in the still ill-understood Reagan revolution, starting with the relationship between the Fed and the mobilization of labor. William Niskanen expressed the central message of the monetarist revolution as a rejection of Arthur Burns's cost-push theory:

Many observers from both the right and the left unfortunately have a cost-based theory of prices and assume that some federal intervention to limit labor costs is necessary to reduce inflation. . . . The empirical evidence is clear: changes in the growth of nominal wages generally follow, rather than lead changes in the general inflation rate."[143]

To the extent that the monetarists have proved their point—that inflation in the United States is ultimately indeed a monetary phenomenon—this fact is freighted with political implications for America's independent central bank. American monetarists had set out simply to curb money and end inflation. In the attempt, however, they found that their policies dramatically altered the balance of power between unionized workers and business, to the disadvantage of the workers. This was not a result they directly intended, but insofar as it prevented the further slide of American politics toward what they called a disabling conflict of interest groups and a "Latin Americanization" of the polity, it was not wholly unwelcome. The price-wage spiral, properly understood, points to a deeper meaning of "monetary rule" that puts the Fed squarely in the driver's seat.

Second, the monetarist episode shows that the Fed's power to deeply influence the economic contestations of everyday life also has important implications for its political power in Washington, when we recognize that those same daily economic contestations fuel the politics of the Fed's nominal overseers. In the early 1970s, Sherman Maisel wrote that the Fed's independence was not so great "that it can use monetary policy as a club or threat to veto Administration action."[144] But Arthur Burns, in his famous Per Jacobsson lecture at Belgrade in 1979, entitled "The Anguish of Central Banking," recanted any such belief on his own part. He asked why central banks such as his own let inflation get out of hand when they knew that in the long run inflation was a monetary phenomenon. His answer was that among other things, the Fed had to spend too much of its time trying to ward off Congress's efforts to mandate wage and price controls or lower interest rates. But in a clear break with the past, Burns acknowledged that many of these pressures on the Fed originated in its own policy failures, and that it had underestimated the degree of discretion at its disposal.[145] The Fed's ability to control, within the limits set by the financial system, the inflationary tempo of the economy—its control over the money supply, however loosely defined—is the source of its ability to "bend with the wind" politically: the Fed preserves its independence by altering the economic conditions which opposition forces seek to exploit against it.

Perhaps for this reason, the Federal Reserve's growing success, confidence, and prestige had helped it redefine what Americans in the wider polity believed they knew about monetary policy. By 1981, as one senior congressional staff member observed, everyone concerned with economic policymaking in the United States was "at least a little bit monetarist."[146] Even many officials in the Carter administration, who in the 1970s had opposed monetary targeting and who in the early 1980s were watching policy from the think tanks to which they had retired, were readier to concede that their "opposition to monetarism was 70 percent wrong and only 30 percent right."[147] Within the Federal Reserve itself, a new generation of staff members and officials had acquired a new appreciation of "staying ahead of the inflationary curve."[148] As Paul Volcker wrote of this great change in the intellectual climate, "It has become respectable for the first time in my conscious life-time to talk about amending the Federal Reserve Act to make its primary responsibility price stability."[149]

A more profound question is whether the monetarist episode produced a change in the Federal Reserve's corporate culture. It would be naive to think that price stability as an intermediate target for Fed policy will not itself require updating at some point in the future. There are simply too many definitional, empirical, and technical questions involved in monetary control for any single procedure to provide satisfactory answers for very long. This means that the Fed's culture will be called upon again to reexamine what the Fed does and why. By the 1980s, at least some Federal Reserve officials recognized that excessive power in the hands of the Fed chairman was clearly a problem in this regard. "The best arrangement," said Wayne Angell, a Fed governor in the 1980s, "is to have independent opinions around the table. If all members of the board or FOMC think the same thing, why have them?"[150] This recognition can be detected in the resistance to Volcker's initiatives in the mid-1980s and perhaps in the more collegial style of Volcker's successor as chairman, Alan Greenspan.[151] Such change may not be significant or permanent; very little of it has been institutionalized, except in the personalities of the individuals involved. The management reorganization of 1980 (when the governors were assigned formal committee responsibilities for the first time) appears to have done little to alter the underlying imbalance between the policy resources commanded by the chairman on the one hand and his fellow governors and FOMC members on the other. Indeed, every indication is that the chairman of the Fed is more powerful than ever, and therefore that the well-being of America's premier economic policymaking body is still excessively vested in the preferences and aptitudes of a single individual. If hope for amelioration can be found at all, it rests in drawing the lesson that the Fed is a national monetary authority, not merely a federal and still less a partisan body, especially if reinforced by the continued consolidation of American banking toward a universal model implied by the wave of mergers and deregulation after the 1980s. Only changes in the central bank's policy environment which embed the institution more firmly in the full range and scope of the nation's economic life are likely to alter the bank's policy culture over the long run.

Commenting on the Fed's implementation of monetarism, a German central banking official charitably observed, "It was a long time coming, but the Fed's stabilization of the money supply was ultimately as successful as ours."[152] But in "the long time coming," even if measured in only a dozen years, hangs an important tale. In politics, time is a crucial variable. This delay ultimately determined that the Fed's monetary stabilization, when it arrived, would look very different from Germany's. Inflation and the Fed's culture of its chairman's hegemony mobilized a monetarism which harnessed populism as a revolutionary force. Yet this populism also broadened the Fed's policy horizon. The Fed, dislodged from its obsolete focus on preserving a vanishing New Deal economic system, was taught by a new monetarist populism to stabilize a more national economic order. At least for the 1980s and 1990s, the legacy of monetarism allied populism with an anti-inflationary consensus. Congress, one of the principal engine rooms of populism, remained largely pacified by the Fed's rediscovered power. But when one recollects that over the entire sweep of American monetary policymaking populism has been not only a revolutionary but also a conservative force, it is far from clear that the monetarist episode in itself represented a solution to the problems in the Fed's policy culture. The problem of learning while governing endures.

CHAPTER 6

Central Banks as Guardians of Democracy

In 1986, the German Bundesbank struck a 5 DM coin commemorating the two-hundredth anniversary of the death of Frederick the Great. The coin bore Frederick's famous motto, *"Ich bin der Erster Diener meines Staates"* ("I am the first servant of my state"), and was often given to visitors to the central bank. The coin was minted in the year when the Bundesbank's program of monetary targeting had at last brought inflation back to zero, and this made it a kind of medal of valor the bank conferred upon itself. Indeed, it was as if the Bundesbank had taken Frederick's motto as its own. Rather later, and with rather less fanfare, the Federal Reserve's own anti-inflationary successes would win it recognition. In the space of fifteen years, these two central banks had rendered significant service to their states: they had similarly deployed monetarist techniques and mobilized economic expertise to combat inflation. In so doing, they restored a measure of economic and social stability to their polities, but with a pronounced difference of timing and with some pronounced differences in political effects. In this chapter we take a second, more comparative look at these experiences, in order to understand their significance for politics in liberal democracies.

In Chapters 3 and 5 I showed that the speed of the adoption of monetary targeting and the nature of its implementation in Germany and the United States hinged on the openness of the central bank's corporate culture to new expertise that sought to redefine how the institution pursued its mission. The degree of openness manifested itself primarily in the hierarchic or collegial patterns within the central banks' highest decision-making bodies. In the Bundesbank, a more balanced, embedded culture allowed a relatively swift "palace revolt" by the Bundesbank council against its president to mobilize monetary targeting from inside the central bank in the early 1970s. By contrast, the more hierarchical and deferential culture at the Federal Reserve led the colleagues of chairmen Burns and Miller to acquiesce in policies that increasingly lacked economic rationale. Monetarism, when it finally came, was disproportionately mobilized by economists from outside the central bank, and when implemented it proved much more politicized and contentious.

Furthermore, this patterning of corporate cultures, as I argued in Chapters 2 and 4, could be explained by the extent to which history had endowed the central banks' external policy environment with universalistic economic institutions. Foremost among these historical legacies was the nature of the banking system, for it is through this instrument that the central bank necessarily exercises its powers. In the United States, the populism of the nineteenth century combined with pluralism of the 1930s to fragment banking power by, among other things, dividing commercial from investment banking, state from national banks, and—perhaps most important—commercial banking from thrift institutions. Germany's postoccupation policymakers, by contrast, reversed the regulatory pluralism that had been imposed on them by the American military government. Thus in Germany, universal banking proved a robust instrument of monetary control. Above all, the incorporation of the household sector into the universal banking system through the growth of savings institutions created a new domestically oriented constituency within the Bundesbank's monetary system itself. These differences, I argued, when reinforced by other characteristic differences between labor and governmental actors, conditioned how the central banks defined their mission and the opportunities for theoretical balance and professional collegiality in the two central banks.

Nonetheless, for both countries the struggle over monetary targeting represented the major domestic monetary controversy of the postwar era. The coming of monetarism redefined how the central bank pursued stabilization. Monetarism, whether internally or externally mobilized, taught central banks to use money and the financial system to stabilize not international systems or particular banking sectors, but the national economy. In Germany, monetarists fought a touch-and-go battle with proponents of fixed exchange rates and dirigism who very nearly eliminated the bank's autonomy. In the United States, the debate about monetarism from 1970 to 1985 was inseparable from the rejection of Bretton Woods, the Federal Reserve's preoccupation with commercial banks and interest rates, and ultimately a rejection of political dependence for the central bank sought by American monetarists themselves. In fact, for both countries, the monetarist victory can best be understood as perhaps the decisive episode, if not the culmination, of a long-term trend. These episodes finally domesticated monetary policy. The arrival of monetarism showed that an independent central bank can successfully serve its polity by stabilizing the national economy. In Germany, the early internal mobilization of monetarism produced a new system of "monetary corporatism" in which the Bundesbank's council and its annual monetary targeting displaced the old failed quasi-corporatism of Concerted Action. In the United States, the external mobilization of monetarists into the Fed via "monetary populism" educated otherwise unaccountable Federal Reserve chairmen about the problem of inflation and the stabilization of the entire economy.

The broadened stabilizing role exercised by central banks implies a new intertwining of economics and democracy which is, however, only imperfectly grasped. I have contended that the adoption of monetarism as a "mobilization of expertise," and the subsequent patterns of monetary corporatism and monetary populism, resulted from central banks' framing their policy choices in the complex language and analysis of economics in order to manage a policy environment without surrendering power to it. Inevitably, this raises the question whether such monetary policymaking is compatible with democracy. There are several ways of posing this question. Is such politics democratic in origin? Is it procedurally democratic? Is it democratic in effect? To answer these questions, and draw whatever lessons we can from those experiences described in the four preceding chapters, I will now make several comparisons. In the first section, I compare the two cases to describe monetarism's lessons about the political power of central banks. In the second, I explore the limits to political stabilization by central banks. Drawing upon these two assessments, I will hazard a few possible proposals for reform of monetary policymaking in the two countries. In the third section, I compare monetary stabilization and certain other forms of liberal stabilization with which we are familiar in modern democracies. In the fourth section, I draw lessons in terms of comparisons with countries where monetary stabilization is less in evidence. This comparison will contrast countries that change economic policies by changing economic expertise and countries that change policies by changing their regime.

THE POWER OF CENTRAL BANKS IN LIBERAL DEMOCRACIES

One question comparative politics asks of the countries it examines is, Who rules? Who actually makes the decisions or works the levers of power? Whose interests do public policies serve? Clearly, this is not the only or even the best way of assessing the implications of monetary policy, but the argument I have presented requires such questions in this case. To answer them, we need to notice certain shared traits about the form of the debate, the participants in the decision, the process of implementation, and the outcome.

First, the form of the debate. The decision to switch to monetary targeting emerged from a highly technical discussion whose implications were intelligible almost exclusively to bankers, economists, and finance ministry officials. At its deepest levels, this debate was primarily between proponents of two theoretical perspectives—the monetarists and the neo-Keynesians—who couched their arguments in statistics and mathematical models organized around such concepts as nonborrowed reserves and CBM. Yet it is evident that, whatever the persuasiveness of monetarist concepts, they would not have been adopted simply on their merits. They required the impetus of political discontent brought about by increased inflation and deepening recession during the 1970s. In Germany, this was most keenly felt in the early 1970s when increased anxiety about the resilience of German democracy, discontent among middle-class savers, and perhaps most especially, an increase in the strike rate among workers seemed to herald a return to earlier, and potentially nastier, forms of class conflict. In the United States, political discontent lent its weight to monetarism later in the decade. Only after radicalized monetarists identified the discontent they called the "Latin Americanization" of the American polity did they successfully ally themselves with a populist antitax movement and win official favor for monetary targeting.

Second, the participants. Who is consulted, and who is ignored, always reveals important fault lines and probable biases of outcomes in any policy area. The two monetarist initiatives (in 1973 in Germany, and in 1979 in the United States) were undertaken peremptorily by central bank officials in closed-door meetings. This all but foreclosed any possibility of undesired outside influence. Even bankers and treasury officials were called on not so much to participate as to acquiesce in or applaud the decisions. To list this *dramatis personae* is to see that the shift to monetary targeting was not a showcase for democratic participation, even though the problem it sought to address—inflation—was uppermost in the minds of ordinary citizens in Germany and America. This exclusivity was no accident. Both sets of policymakers, whether in Washington or Frankfurt, feared arousing or including popular power. Not only history, but the monetarist controversy itself, taught them that disruptions to the monetary system often coincided with crises of political authority. Central bank officials took it on themselves to act on this insight, sometimes even despite legal obligations to do otherwise, as when the Bundesbank ignored its treaty obligations under Bretton Woods.

This new centrality of the central banks in domestic monetary politics reflected monetarism's renovation of their substantive cultures. In the public rhetoric accompanying the switch to monetary targeting, monetarists were careful to avoid mention of any but the broadest public interest. Instead of replacing the ultimate goal of stabilization, monetarism helped modernize intermediate policy benchmarks used by central bank officials since the 1950s that no longer corresponded to stabilization. Thus, there was no rejection of stabilizing the business cycle as a national priority, only a new strategy to achieve it. In each country, this meant jettisoning important commitments to fiscal demand management and to the primacy of the international system.

For Germany in particular it had been thought that political stability depended on export-led growth, full employment and economic integration into the Bretton Woods system.[1] The monetarists' rejection of Bretton Woods and abandonment of the commitment to full employment meant that domestic stability would thereafter be homegrown and monetary targeting would be its instrument. For this reason, the nomination of new economists to the Bundesbank council in a de facto monetary corporatism increasingly reflected new economic views and a diversity of expertise as outside groups sought to influence the Bundesbank by remote control. In the United States, of course, intellectual negotiation could not be so deeply institutionalized in the Fed's policy culture, where monetary populism revealed that the chairman's dominance was hard to dislodge, even if the chairman was henceforth committed to a broader concept of domestic stabilization, beyond the confines of the national banking system.

Third, the implementation of monetarism. Here the central lesson is the rediscovery of money's power to govern society, even in the face of concerted opposition. This lesson took some time to learn, however. During the initial experimental phases of monetarism, central bank officials in both countries advertised it widely, believing that cooperation from the public would make stabilization easier. In particular, they devised publicly announced monetary targets to provide the means for such cooperation. Bank officials believed the cooperation of certain groups to be particularly desirable. In Germany, these were the universal banks, the unions, and government budget-makers; in the United States they were primarily the fragmented financial institutions and unions, together with congressional populists. Indeed, the Bundesbank was so concerned with possible opposition that its press office orchestrated efforts to reinsert memories of the hyperinflation of the 1920s into Germany's postwar political mythology.

Yet as the monetarist experiments unfolded, compliance with stabilization turned out to owe less to central banks' public relations departments than to their high interest rates. Tight money restricted firms' ability to raise prices and increased business bankruptcies; failing firms put employment at risk; job losses reduced workers' willingness to strike; a calmed labor climate restored the appearance of social stability; social stability enhanced public confidence in government; and confident governments curbed their attacks on central banks' autonomy. Of course, recessions provoked backlashes of their own if they were too deep or lasted too long. But as central banks had rediscovered the power of money, they found they could defuse these as well. This was the lesson of Arthur Burns's famous Per Jacobsson lecture, in which he confessed that America's economic "anguish" had been due to his bank's failure to understand and exploit the weapons at its disposal. This failure was ultimately intellectual. For the majority of academics and central bankers—though by no means all—the implementation of monetarism buried the old theory that central banks were hostage to "cost-push" inflation, or that in comparison to fiscal policy, monetary policy could fight only a weak rearguard action. Keynesianism's policy contraptions of price controls or corporatist wage negotiations fell from favor. Monetarism demonstrated that money—perhaps money alone—governed. Even if central bankers never tore down the original rhetorical drapery of social consensus, it survived largely for the sake of legitimacy, not efficacy.

Finally, the consequences. Whose interests did monetary targeting serve? The beneficiaries of monetarism range from the most particular to the most general. Most obviously, the Federal Reserve and the Bundesbank emerged from their respective monetarist episodes as two of the most powerful economic institutions in the world. Their control over the most important levers that move the economy—the cost and availability of credit—is now virtually unchallenged. As their underlying financial systems have recovered from the instability of the 1970s, and the institutions have grown in professionalism and reputation, opportunities to contest their authority have correspondingly declined. Both central banks not only dictate monetary policy but also exert enormous influence on fiscal policy. Both have become the major agents for the formulation and execution of macroeconomic policy. For both countries, in fact, domestic macroeconomic policy is now for the most part monetary policy.

More broadly, however, the *timing* of monetarist stabilization greatly affected which economic interests benefited, and how. The early introduction of monetarism in Germany was perhaps most notable for its broadly beneficial consequences for the Sparkassen and their large middle-class clientele of depositors. For middle-class democracies, it may not be a bad thing for the general populace to have a large and growing financial stake in stability. Perhaps more surprisingly, however, early monetarism was comparatively beneficial for labor and the German welfare state as well. Although German labor became less militant during the mid-1970s, the moderate character of German monetarism meant that it was not used roll back wage gains (which were quite substantial during the early years of the decade), still less to break the unions. Rates of unionization actually increased after 1973, as did the size and generosity of the German welfare state. This trend continued even during the relaunching of monetarism after 1981. German monetarists, having won early internal access to their central bank, never mobilized externally to the extent that their American colleagues did. Consequently, they never helped to radicalize German conservatism, either through political engagement or by propagating radical tax-cutting ideology. German monetarists supported the Bundesbank's pressure to reduce government deficits by raising taxes, something scarcely imaginable among American monetarists.

Conversely, the later arrival of American monetarism meant that stabilization would take place in an environment in which the New Deal was already under widespread attack. By 1978, anti-inflation sentiment had mobilized radical critiques of the state and state spending from the grassroots in California to the congressional "class of 1978," the most conservative group of congressional freshmen elected in decades. The two years of tight money under Reagan certainly added to this ferment, but it must be recognized how much the social and economic landscape had already been changed by a decade of inflation. The forces that would bring about the greatest decline in the power of American labor were already well under way during the late 1970s. Moreover, American commercial banks, heavy industry, and exporters were severely compromised by monetary stabilization. The commercial banks alone had to write off hundreds of billions of dollars in nonperforming debt after 1982, and several years after that, the thrift institutions would be devastated by their botched response to this crisis. By 1984, with inflation essentially defeated, the steam went out of the Reagan revolution. Reagan's second administration looked very different from his first. With an earlier adoption of monetary targeting, and with fewer radical monetarists to drive the political agenda, Ronald Reagan might never have been elected at all; and if he had, his policies might have resembled nothing so much as Helmut Kohl's.

In the most general sense, however, one can say that monetarism benefited everyone with a vested interest in economic stability. Monetarism, as was once said of Keynesianism, helped save the economic system from itself, with all the advantages that implies for those who benefit from capitalism. In societies in which the democratic franchise exists alongside capitalist economic organization, stabilizing the latter may be entailed by stabilizing the former, and vice versa.

From the foregoing comparisons we conclude that the answer to the question "Who rules?" is that the politics surrounding central banking are unusually determinative of the political system as a whole. Like a formal constitution, the politics of monetary policy confers on certain social actors, but not others, the ability to make political claims. It does so both directly, by restricting who makes monetary policy decisions, and indirectly, by affecting the balance of economic power elsewhere. This ensures that monetary policymaking will be exclusionary in ways that are not typical of other areas of policymaking in either country. But monetary policy has far wider consequences than almost all other policy areas. Precisely because money is the ocean in which all social and economic actors swim, monetary policy cannot be made like fisheries policy. Those who make monetary policy—the narrow elites that include economists of high professional standing and the officials of treasuries and central banks— must do so with at least one eye toward preventing broad monetary dislocations that could mobilize the public to question the "institutional integrity"—the vaunted independence—of the central banks.

The stabilization that monetary policy can provide for democracy is thus not so much altruistic as, perhaps, an unintended consequence of the central bank's self-interested desire to minimize the public's voice in the determination of policy. All told, the combination of negligible public supervision of central banks and the unrivaled power of money to govern economic behavior implies that the privileged roles of the Bundesbank and the Federal Reserve make their respective political systems substantially less democratic than is generally acknowledged. One is tempted to paraphrase the monetarist economist Beryl Sprinkel and say, "Control the central bank and everything else falls into place."

LIMITS TO STABILIZATION BY CENTRAL BANKS

This conjuncture of monetary policy and political stabilization, powerful though it is, nonetheless requires qualification. I do *not* wish to suggest as a universal rule that to control the price level is necessarily to control the political thermostat. Monetarists have attempted to argue over the years that monetary policy could be reduced to a simple mechanical exercise—a simple monetary rule—by which a fixed amount of money would be counted up and fed into the economy year in, year out. Steady behavior by the central bank would produce, they claimed, steadiness in the economy. But precisely as our cases of monetarism demonstrate, stabilization is not necessarily achieved quickly or easily. Of our two cases, the Federal Reserve's experiences are most illustrative of this fact. When provided with the right leadership by the chairman, it can be quite effective in stabilizing the economy around a steady growth path of about 3 percent per year. During the 1950s and 1960s, and again in the 1980s and 1990s, the Federal Reserve achieved a record of stabilization that made it the equal of any of its peers. But in the 1970s, it was poorly led, and its corporate culture failed to compensate. In this cultural failure we find an important qualification to the monetarist experience: monetarists are right in saying that money matters but wrong in saying that it can always be controlled mechanistically from an Archimedean point called a central bank. Instead, as I have argued, monetary policy depends on how expertise is mobilized into the central bank to mediate between the state and society. Certain challenges to the central bank particularly constrain its ability to use money to stabilize its environment. These challenges come from three sources: the state (especially foreign policy); the institutionalization of money in society; and the mobilization and deployment of expertise by the monetary authorities

Limits by States and Wars

The absolute limit of independent monetary policy and monetary stabilization may be defined by war. In both the United States and Germany, the first central banks originated in anticipation of war or in response to war. Their unequivocal purpose was to assist the government with war finance. In this sense they were pure servants of the state. Later, when they had won political independence in peacetime, they would lose it again during subsequent hostilities. As was once said of the press, central banks may be independent in peace but slavish in war. War or the threat of war is probably the most compelling reason why national states might be considered the real source of swings in monetary policy, even in those interludes between war that we call peace. In World War II, the Fed was compelled to stabilize low rates of interest in the market for government war debt. Perhaps only the shift from "hot" to cold war gave the Fed its independence. Some observers attribute the loss of monetary control in the early 1970s to international military conflict. In 1965, as the Vietnam War escalated, chairman Martin was summoned to Lyndon Johnson's ranch for a lecture about the Fed's policy on interest rates. Nixon's authority to impose wage and price controls was granted as a title to a defense spending bill in 1970, and both explosions in oil prices in the 1970s were ignited by military conflict in the Middle East. Similarly, the turn to monetarism might be said to reflect the termination of the Vietnam War. By contrast, the Bundesbank's success in stabilizing prices may simply reflect that in 1945 Germany was forced to sheath its sword. In both cases, therefore, evidence can be found to suggest that the state's foreign policy may prevent central banks from using monetary policy to stabilize their societies in ways that monetarists have not recognized.

While there can be no denying that total war on the magnitude of the conflict of 1939–1945 will impose itself on a central bank, the evidence from monetarism suggests that the limits imposed by smaller wars are actually more relaxed than might be thought. First, as shown in Chapters 4 and 5, the monetary "abdication" of the Vietnam years in the United

States had much less to do with the war than with worries about the banking system and a fear that unemployment would make an already volatile social climate even worse. Martin's Fed raised interest rates despite Johnson, and forced the White House, belatedly, to raise taxes. In 1969, at the height of the war, the federal budget was still in balance. Had Burns been less fearful of threats to housing finance or the market for corporate debt, his Fed might have moved more aggressively against inflation and forestalled the congressional politicking that gave Nixon so many interventionist powers. Absent such powers, the president is hampered in influencing monetary policy by his lack of control over its personnel, and by his own lack of knowledge. Apparently, so long as the Federal Reserve avoids major policy moves during presidential election years, it can avoid presidential supervision.

The second fact suggesting that warfare may not be highly constraining is the connection between monetarism and the United States' military posture in the late twentieth century. Reagan's military buildup, though vast, was accomplished while reducing the inflation rate and while keeping the federal government's share of national GDP at a level lower than that of virtually any other major government. This suggests that for large modern economies, even major defense expenditures mean that inflation is merely a mistake, not a necessity. In fact, this was the conclusion reached by President Nixon's Advisory Commission on an All-Volunteer Armed Force in 1973, of which Milton Friedman was a member. The commission concluded that foreseeable military requirements—even two simultaneous regional wars—could best be met through an all-volunteer professional army that would reduce the demands on American society and its economy. In its recommendations, the commission concluded that the financial and political strains of national defense would be most easily reduced through low inflation. Such arguments led the United States to abolish the draft.

Finally, however, sovereign states represent boundaries which economic activity must necessarily traverse. The prosperity of all economies today involves individual economic entities and individual states in an international division of labor. If this international division of labor is imperiled by individual state actions, leading to another round of beggar-thy-neighbor policies of tariff-raising or currency-dumping, there may not be much that monetary policy can do to cushion the impact of such external shocks.

Limits by Financial Systems

In the absence of sustained foreign policy constraints, the real obstacle to central banks' stabilization policies may be not their political accountability but their control over money, and money's reach into society. One important lesson to be drawn from our study of monetarism is that the central bank's capacity to conduct stabilization policy writ large may turn on the role of money in society. Money cannot be used effectively if it only partially penetrates the economy. The growth of what Marxists quaintly call the "cash nexus" in market societies has been long but uneven. For decades, commercial banking, the conveyor belt of the monetary system, figured in the lives of only the largest businesses and a wealthy minority of the population. Recall that Federal Reserve governor Young, in the 1920s, refused to identify Fed policy with any broader goal than the stabilization of the big commercial banks. The story of domestic monetary stabilization is in many ways the story of broadening the central bank's goals by broadening the banking system, especially through those institutions, such as the Sparkassen and the thrifts, that promoted the formation of savings among middle- and lower-class households.

This historical broadening and deepening of financial institutions extends the central bank's reach into all corners of society, but this extension has taken different forms. These different forms can affect the strength of the banking system through which money and monetary policy flow. Simply put, it is impossible for central banks to implement stabilization policy if doing so imperils the financial system itself. Monetarism's technicalities in Germany and the United States suggest that the financial system influences the central bank as both object and executor of policy.

The first impact of the financial system was on the output side of monetary policy. Germany's universal banking system, like the automobiles that roll out of showrooms in Stuttgart or Munich, lends itself to easier, more precise steering. In the United States, fear of compromising fragile specialized financial institutions colored individual Fed decisions to raise or lower interest rates. Yet both central banks are aware that financial collapse and bank runs can never be entirely ruled out. It is the nature of banking to take risks and the nature of money to panic. Central banks' duties as lenders of last resort mean they must always offer hostages to fortune.

The second influence of the financial system on monetary policy was on the input side. The character of the banking system affected monetarists' ability to know what money is. Ironically, because the U.S. banking sector bore such a heavy imprint of Keynesian regulation, monetarists' ability to define, measure, and analyze money's influence on the economy depended on a system they wished to abolish. And indeed, once money became deregulated in the mid-1980s, measuring and controlling money became much harder. Schumpeter's dictum that capitalism is a system of creative destruction applies no less to finance than any other sector. New forms of money appear; the boundaries of the financial system shift; new markets spring up; economic agents learn new lessons and forget old ones. Given such dynamism, knowledge comes at a growing premium.

Limits by Expertise

That central banks' actions may stabilize politics imposes certain intellectual responsibilities on central bankers and their advisers. Much depends, therefore, on the character and evolution of economic theory as the vehicle for thinking about what monetary policy should do and why. The question necessarily arises of how effectively central banks and economists interact.

One of the first conclusions we can draw from both our cases is that the appointment of professional economists to leadership positions at the central bank seemed to coincide with monetary policy which was markedly worse than what had been produced by the old-fashioned bankers they displaced. While the arrival of professional economists in the Bundesbank's council was probably more an effect than the cause of the greater policy instability of the 1970s relative to the 1960s, the evidence from the Federal Reserve is not so reassuring for those who are inclined to put faith in doctorates. Arthur Burns's underestimation of the Fed's room for maneuver almost certainly had something to do with his academically fashionable theory of cost-push inflation. And the willingness of central bankers to defer to finance ministries' fiscal leadership may depend on whether they accept the theoretic claim that monetary policy by nature can play only a rear-guard role, as even Alan Greenspan once claimed, behind fiscal policy. So it is far from self-evident that economic expertise per se assists with monetary stabilization; only expertise that starts from the premise that "money matters" seems to play this role.

Despite Germany's successful monetary stabilization, it is not clear that this lesson has been fully digested in Germany itself, which is especially apparent when one considers the Bundesbank's attitude toward Europe's new central bank. It has already been decided that Europe's central bank, like the Bundesbank, will be independent. But largely at the Bundesbank's insistence, European officials have formally agreed that all national governments must keep an extremely tight rein on their deficits. This decision appears to misread Germany's own history of monetarism. Not only did Bundesbank monetarists demonstrate that price stability could be achieved by a central bank acting alone, but one of the consequences of reduced inflation is likely to be higher deficits. Given the political legitimacy that a relatively free hand for fiscal policy can win for governments during anti-inflation fights, the insistence that governments make drastic cuts in spending programs to fulfill the Maastricht criteria seems likely to impose unnecessary burdens on the monetary integration of Europe and make economic and monetary union less, not more, popular.

A second limitation drawn from our history of monetarism pertains to the institutional design of the central banks as employers of expert knowledge. For both central banks, the coming of monetarism enhanced their responsibility to the domestic economy. Monetarists' mechanistic prescriptions notwithstanding, this necessarily implied a significant augmentation of the central banks' capability to gather and analyze information. In fact, this heightened need for research derives partly from monetarists' success in promoting financial and economic deregulation. As modern economies and financial systems have grown more dynamic, such steps as defining and measuring money, inflation, growth, and output, so fundamental to a central bank's policymaking, have grown more problematic. Both institutions, with their hundreds of professional staff members processing reams of economic reports, are now think tanks which also set interest rates.

Perversely, the increased independence and research-orientation of central banks heightens the risk that economists, whether among the staff, the directors, or their academic colleagues, will view monetary policy as an apolitical, technocratic, or scientific exercise. Previously, the risk was, perhaps, that central banks and economists might underestimate what central banks can do; now the risk is overestimation, hubris. This points to an issue for economists beyond pure intellectual capacity—the issue of philosophical attitudes and values. As Paul Volcker expressed it, "The reality is that printing money is a very profitable activity. . . . When an institution has that privilege, it must be controlled and disciplined by an inner professionalism, and that inner professionalism may be far more important to the success of a central bank over time than any of the technicalities of monetary policy."[2] Here the most important professional virtues may be intellectual curiosity, openness, and a willingness to be proved wrong. Especially in the American context, with the increasing abstraction of the discipline and the spread of theories of public choice into social sciences, economics risks erecting a deductively rigorous yet empirically naive neoconservative rationalism to replace a now discredited naive, universalizing Keynesian rationalism. Deductive theorizing and model-building, no matter how mathematically sophisticated, are no better than the validity of their assumptions and the rigor with which they are put to real-world tests. This is true no matter whose paradigm builds the models. Absent an openness to empirical verification and real-world grounding, economic advice risks marginalizing itself, or harming public policy, or both.[3] The central banks of both the United States and Germany have potent examples of independence misused and theory pursued in the face of inconvenient facts.

Ironically, American monetarists were among the first to recognize that American monetary policy must confront the problems of the real world, especially, they believed, the undemocratic biases of the Fed's bureaucracy. Bureaucratic incentives, they thought, explained why the Federal Reserve was so reluctant to surrender its Keynesian economic philosophy. Hence the birth of the monetarist-inspired "new political economy," the founding of the Shadow Open Market Committee, and the monetarists' call for greater accountability by the Fed. By positing the phenomena of rent-seeking behavior and bureaucratic self-interest, monetarists restored a measure of "political" preference as a variable in economic thought. Even if this insight about rent-seeking was ultimately wrong as an explanation of Fed policymaking, it was a long overdue rediscovery that neoclassical economics was about *political* economy. Friedman and Schwartz's monumental study *A Monetary History of the United States* has an empirical, historical, and inductive gravity quite unlike the glib neo-Keynesian rationalism that preceded it or much of the rational choice theory that is popular today. It is not going too far to suggest that economic thinking in the United States exhibits the solipsistic tendency of any debate in which one party is too long in power and its opponents too long out.

In contrast, German economics never quite fell into such a trap. An earlier switch by the Bundesbank to monetary targeting helped demonstrate that monetary stability did not require a radical critique of the central bank's independence. But also, the more effective and more balanced integration of economists into the Bundesbank deprived German academia of some of the most radical influences of whatever stripe. German monetarists never forgot—because direct exposure to the Bundesbank's policymaking wouldn't let them forget—that there was more to economics than money. Nor were German Keynesians permitted to overlook money.

We are confronted, in the end, with two possibly irreconcilable views of the proper use of monetary policy expertise by central banks in a democratic society. The first, articulated by Sherman Maisel, is that advances in economic knowledge have made monetary policy purely a technocratic exercise:

> I strongly favor the suggestion that the Board cease to be thought of as representative of regions or special interests. . . . It should be recognized as composed largely of technicians and spokesmen for the public at large. The idea of representation assumes that policy-making is based primarily on value judgment rather than knowledge, an interpretation I think wrong.[4]

The alternative view, voiced by the monetarist economist Richard Timberlake, is that:

In point of fact, monetary norms are extremely varied and highly controversial. Nothing is gained by pretending otherwise. To do so simply denies
the majority faction the ability to get its will into action and thus subverts a
fundamental principle of the democratic process.

Giving independence to a central bank, he concluded, "is no more logical than giving the same status to the State Department."[5]

If, as I have been contending, monetary policy is intrinsically complex
and requires sensitivity to democratic interests, how then may central
banks best utilize expertise? This issue seems most pressing in the case of
the Federal Reserve, where the policymaking culture is to this day still too
dependent on the chairman. To modernize the Federal Reserve, to make
it more collegial, more open, and more solicitous of the long-term good of
the economy, a number of reforms of its nomination procedures are in
order. First, and most important, the role of the states should be enhanced. Federal Reserve district bank presidents should be selected by the
state governors in each district, not by representatives of commercial
banks. Second, with this new democratic legitimacy, Federal Reserve district presidents should be offered the same lengthy terms of tenure as Fed
governors. Third, the selection of the chairman should not be left to the
president; at most, the chairman should be nominated from among sitting
Fed governors. Fourth, Fed governors should be given enhanced management responsibilities. Finally, a new and genuinely national economic advisory body should be established to provide economic advice that stands
apart from Washington partisanship. To ensure such a dispassionate, national perspective, appointments to this body should be shared by the federal government and state governments. These reforms, if implemented,
would likely move the Federal Reserve toward a broader and more consistent appreciation of the public good without sacrificing either independence or technical competence. Indeed, even some of the Fed's own officials think that it is in the Fed's interest to move in this direction, toward
the corporate culture of the Bundesbank or, as I will suggest in the next
section, toward a "supreme court" model of decision making.[6]

LIBERAL STABILIZATION: CENTRAL BANKS AND SUPREME COURTS

At the outset of this chapter I suggested that monetary stabilization by independent central banks mobilizing special professional expertise can be
compared with other, familiar phenomena in liberal democracies. Now I
will suggest that stabilization by way of epistemic politics is essentially
what is accomplished by the highest judicial bodies in the United States
and Germany. That these two countries have both kinds of autonomous,

expert institutions reflects, I maintain, similar political forces and objectives. Most significant, however, is that court systems and banking systems share fundamentally similar organizational properties as what I call "inductive bureaucracies," which make them similar in their workings for liberal stabilization.

The essential features of court and banking systems as liberal stabilizers are defined by the unique properties of the power resources they manage, the "inductive" (empirical or observational) mode of analysis they use, and the bottom-up decision-making hierarchy that this naturally promotes. These shared properties have important implications for both democratic sensitivity and limits on state power.

First, courts and banks as inductive bureaucracies stand the logic of ideal-typical Weberian bureaucracies on its head. The Weberian bureaucracy is characterized by a top-down, command-and-control logic of administrative standardization and instrumental rationality. At its heart, it is "deductive" and "plan rational."[7] Fundamental policy initiative rests with officials at the top of the hierarchy, who use their superior information to direct subordinate bureaus toward predetermined objectives. By contrast, in inductive bureaucracies, fundamental policy initiative originates at the bottom of a loosely connected hierarchy. Both the administration of law and the allocation of credit are characterized by a decentralized application of abstract norms followed by delayed, centralized review. Lower court judges apply the law as it currently stands (or contracts as negotiated) to the vast range of public activity, with an independent hierarchy of appeals courts reviewing their work after some delay. The equivalent of the court of first instance is the loan officer at a bank, whose adjudication of economic behavior (the granting or denying of loans) is reviewed by more senior credit committees within the bank and ultimately, if indirectly, by policies established by the central bank. Policymaking moves upward as regional or national bureaus observe the consequences of decisions made by local bureaus, then ratify or reject them.

Liberal stabilization by courts and banks is further characterized by their allocating such abstract power resources as money or legal norms. These power resources have common properties that Talcott Parsons called "media of interchange."[8] The management of money and law by banks and courts is a passive, reactive form of social control in which the institutions do not create social organization so much as provide the *means* for it. They provide the framework for that "spontaneous organization" that F. A. Hayek, Walter Lippman, and other classical liberals have argued was the most liberal feature of modern society. Liberal stabilization does not put a premium on a priori perfect knowledge and objectivity by state managers as the Weberian bureaucracy does. Instead, by allocating media of interchange, inductive bureaucracies promote, accumulate, and adjudicate the experiments of innumerable social actors. Successful experiments may then be diffused throughout society by being elevated from local to national policy.

There is a final parallel in liberal stabilization between the role of jurisprudence and economic theory in influencing policy. This reflects the similar complexity, diffusion, and embeddedness of law and money which generate research and intellectual controversy. In analogous ways, debates about jurisprudence and economic theory permit the forces of conservatism and liberalism to consider alternative policies without disturbing the fundamental framework of law and markets to which they are all committed.

These arguments suggest that macroeconomic and constitutional politics are linked at the highest levels. If this intuition is correct, monetary stabilization in Germany and the United States should find parallels in their judicial politics. Some initial corroborating evidence for an overlap between efficient mobilization of expertise in the judicial and monetary arenas can be found by comparing the flexibility of the Roosevelt administration's response to the Depression with the inflexibility of the Weimar Republic in Germany. As we noted in Chapter 2, Germany's first independent central bank was not well embedded in its democratic society, and it refused to undertake those reflationary measures which might have saved the Weimar regime. A crisis of policy became a crisis of the republic, and Hitler won enormous popularity by sweeping away the autonomy of the Reichsbank and reflating the economy.

The contrast with Roosevelt and macroeconomic policy in the United States is extremely revealing. Originally elected on a balanced-budget platform, Roosevelt soon reversed course and promoted economic activism, inspired in part by the ideas of Hansen and other American Keynesians. But all was not easily changed. Roosevelt's proto-Keynesianism encountered a significant obstacle in the Supreme Court. For many decades, until the 1930s, the American judiciary had been routinely denying the federal government the authority to regulate the economy. So long as this jurisprudential framework remained in force, Keynesian economic reforms remained beyond the legitimate powers of the federal government. However, after his landslide reelection in 1936, Roosevelt threatened to "pack the court" with justices sympathetic to his program. Prudently, however, the Supreme Court's "switch in time that saved nine" both preserved the independence of the judiciary and permitted the government to implement its economic program.

Yet this far-reaching reversal in judicial attitudes toward government activism would not have been sustainable if prior intellectual developments had not first prepared the ground. More specifically, Oliver Wendell Holmes, Jr., had for years been arguing in eloquent dissents from the bench and in learned articles, for a new and revolutionary approach to interpreting the law and the Constitution. The reigning school of thought—"property above all"—taught that law resembled "axioms and corollaries of a book of mathematics." By contrast, Holmes argued that "the life of the law has not been logic; it has been experience."[9] With the doctrine of the "felt necessities of the times," Holmes and his followers sought to unshackle government and public policy. The famous Lochner case initiated a Holmesian regime change in law that opened the door to a Keynesian regime change in American economic policy.

Postwar reforms of the policy systems in both countries now mean that America and Germany seem to exhibit further similarities in their judicial politics which parallel their monetary politics. Germany's post-war *Bundesverfassungsgericht* (Constitutional Court) seems to act in many ways like the Bundesbank. Similarly independent, with a high degree of intellectual prestige, the court has been an important bulwark for the Federal Republic's postwar political stability. Intrinsic to its stabilization capacity has been a kind of "judicial corporatism" akin to the distribution of economic theories in the Bundesbank after 1973. As Donald Kommers argued in a survey of Germany's constitutional court, three major legal traditions—classical-liberal, socialist, and Catholic—have played an important role in the life of the court. "Each of these traditions . . . was powerfully represented at the Constitutional Convention of 1949, finds many of its central values represented in the text of the Basic Law, and today is well represented in German political life."[10] Consequently, the politics and jurisprudence of the court resemble the Bundesbank's collegial and pragmatic negotiation of stabilization doctrine: "When . . . the court is faced with a dispute involving competing constitutional values, it often resorts to ad hoc balancing. Indeed, the rhetoric of conceptual jurisprudence belies the 'pragmatic, flexible, and undogmatic' approach to constitutional interpretation that often characterizes the court's work."[11] Collegiality within the court produces a lower level of ideological conflict in the policy environment: "There is no debate in Germany, as there is in the United States, over whether the Constitution is primarily procedural or value-oriented. Germans commonly agree that the Basic Law is a constitution of substantive values."[12]

By contrast, the politics of the United States Supreme Court and American jurisprudence in the 1980s witnessed increased ideological conflict, just as American macroeconomics was more divided by the rivalry between neo-Keynesians and monetarists. A new legal theory, derived from the ideas of Friedman and his Chicago colleagues, aimed to make judicial decisions promote free-market efficiency. These neoconservatives were accused of "packing the courts"[13] while liberals responded by contesting their judicial appointments to an unusual degree. The most infamous instance of this politicization was the nomination of Robert Bork to the Supreme Court, and his subsequent defeat. As with monetarism, such epistemic political struggles were not confined to the formal institutions themselves. Neo-conservatives' efforts to mobilize new norms into the judicial system also encompassed teaching and publishing. Robert Bork, Richard Epstein, and Richard Posner not only won appointment to important appellate positions but have also influenced a new generation of law students. Despite important disagreements between jurists such as Richard Posner and Robert Bork, their shared "economic analysis of law"[14] poses the biggest challenge to liberals who favor "taking rights seriously."[15] In Germany, a higher degree of formality and institutionalization in the judicial arena, especially for judicial appointments, makes it clear what social interests promote stabilization by way of laws; not so in the United States, where the risk is of arousing democratic ire. The politics of the Bork nomination sheds light on why, with important exceptions, the Supreme Court is more susceptible than is the German constitutional court to such external expert mobilizations.

Yet, as we saw with monetary policy, the United States and Germany may be more alike than different. Both have independent judiciaries and high courts deeply embedded in their societies through extensive networks of lawyers; powerful bar associations; multiple and consultative appointment procedures to the bench; and widespread discussion of legal precedents through law journals, law schools, and the regular media. These institutions, together with those of the financial system, mean that major issues of adapting the legal and economic framework to new circumstances can be debated and resolved by way of autonomous policy change. In other countries, this is not the case. To see the significance of such arenas for the politics of democratic stability, it is useful to consider countries where stabilization has not relied to the same extent on changes in paradigms concerning law and money.

Monetarism by Other Means: Illiberal Stabilization

The wide variety of experiences among countries with respect to the role of central banks in adjusting the problems of international competitiveness or openness suggests the hypothesis that regime change and expert politics are inversely related. Where governmental institutions are unable to efficiently mobilize expertise to cope with new economic problems, a state may run the risk of dramatic, even destabilizing regime changes. This theme provides a larger normative background for one last set of comparisons of the institutions of monetary policy in economic stabilization.

A survey of some other countries' responses to economic dislocation reveals a continuum between those which rely on some degree of efficient mobilization of expertise through central banks (in the manner of Germany and the United States), and those which rely on economic adaptation by regime change. Essentially, both strategies attempt to stabilize economic relations within society while simultaneously adjusting those relations to new circumstances or challenges. Efficient mobilization of expertise does so indirectly, through administrative changes that redirect institutions' missions but do not destroy their fundamental structure. Regime change, on the other hand, is an abrupt alteration of the institutions or laws by which the society is governed. It usually represents the replacing of one set of governing elites by another, sometimes violently, and often by creating or destroying institutions. The differences between these two processes are not neat. Nonetheless, they do represent opposite poles of response to economic adaptation and stabilization. As we shall see, both are explicable by considering the autonomy of central banks and the character of their external policy environment. The cases of Britain and Chile help illustrate the variety of experiences with monetary policy in the last few decades.

Britain seems to be an intermediate case between countries (such as Germany or the United States) with independent central banks, and the vast multitude of countries (such as Chile) whose monetary authorities were traditionally quite dependent. For centuries, the Bank of England was the central bank par excellence, independent and formidable. After World War II it was nationalized. From then until 1997, it was understood that "the Bank of England executes the monetary policy of the government." But while article 4 of the Bank of England Act permitted the chancellor of the exchequer to give instructions to the bank, in practice the bank was said to wield a considerable influence within government. But to what effect?

Much of the policy of the British government during the 1950s and 1960s, regardless of party, was broadly Keynesian, with pronounced corporatist features of tripartite planning and consultation, especially through the National Economic Development councils (the "Neddies") and later, through national-level corporatist wage accords. Both Conservatives and Labour tried valiantly to reconcile the objectives of demand management and full employment with episodic sterling crises. During the 1970s, however, a gap widened between the demands of an increasingly militant labor movement and the lagging growth of the British economy. Consensus Keynesianism broke down with the manifest failure of the Heath, Wilson, and Callaghan governments to sustain full employment without inflation inducing sterling crises. As inflation, unemployment, and the strike rate mounted, the advocates of neoconservatism grew increasingly militant. Monetarism was tentatively introduced during Denis Healey's residence at 11 Downing Street, then was fully implemented by Margaret Thatcher in the early 1980s. Thatcher, of course, waged a campaign to remake the British economy as a "shareholders' democracy." She abolished the Neddies and scorned consultation with the unions. Her tight-money policies promoted a restructuring of both labor relations and business productivity. Thatcherism represented the most profound reorientation in postwar British political life. Its effects are still very much under scrutiny, but it illustrates in a dramatic though still democratic case the implications of insurgents' mobilizing politically to sweep out the old policy managers and restructure economic institutions in pursuit of low inflation and social stability.

By contrast, Chile in the 1970s and 1980s represents the most extreme example of the opposite type of policy innovation—a change in regime in order to restructure the economy. Until the military coup of 1973, the Bank of Chile was little more than the passive note-issuing agent of the treasury.[16] Unchecked inflation fanned the flames of rampant social dissension. The military coup of 1973 brought a professional, nationalistic military cadre to power with the aim of restoring national unity and social stability. But the initial means chosen, apart from military repression, amounted to economic authoritarianism. An extensive series of edicts covered wages and prices, and the military regime subsidized and protected sectors of the economy it deemed of "vital" national interest. There was, however, an inherent flaw in the military's response to the crisis of economic stabilization. The initial neglect of monetary policy institutions failed to provide either the autonomy or the capacity for efficient stabilization. This military dirigisme achieved some momentary success in suppressing popular demands and curbing inflation. But this did not last. The regime failed to modernize the banking system that would have permitted the softer, more indirect methods of stabilization afforded by the discipline of money. Only after several years of failure did the regime turn to monetarists for advice on how to reconstruct the economy.[17]

Guillermo O'Donnell's seminal contributions to the literature on "bureaucratic authoritarianism" help explain why Latin American authoritarianism represents a major alternative to the expanded model of liberal stabilization I am describing. Essentially, bureaucratic authoritarianism is a regime that follows a military coup in certain kinds of (formerly) democratic countries. Bureaucratic authoritarianism is government by the coercive apparatus of the state (chiefly the military), which, by excluding representatives of the popular elements of society, severely restricts their ability to make claims on the state.[18] As the case of Chile suggests, bureaucratic authoritarianism is usually preceded by populist regimes of a particular pathology. In such populist regimes, stimulative economic policy (usually marked by rapidly rising inflation) leads to the emergence of what certain state elites—chiefly the military—consider "sectoral egotism" and a "threatening symbolism of class identification."[19] When these policies reach their fiscal limits, the state's initial response is often to increase dirigisme, which usually increases inflationary pressures. Unabated social discontent leads to further calls for wage and price controls, rationing, quantitative controls, centralized coordination—in brief, allocative decisions become displaced from the arena of economics and markets to political processes internal to the state apparatus. The legitimacy of the state then becomes dependent on its ability to placate ever more politically mobilized economic interests, and the economic success of interest groups depends on increasing levels of political agitation. The rough separation of economics and politics characteristic of liberal democracy now collapses entirely. In such circumstances the state will find it increasingly difficult, if not ultimately impossible, to reconcile economic allocation with political legitimacy and stability. Denied the use of money, central banks, or market forces to stabilize social conflict, the state eventually finds itself vulnerable to more drastic instruments of social control, such as the police or the military. Indeed, this is precisely what happened with Latin America's bureaucratic authoritarian regimes. The military intervened to impose order by limiting access and depoliticizing issues by making policy according to norms of "technical rationality." But as O'Donnell makes clear, such regimes achieved only tacit support at best. They are neither very good at solving the economy's problems nor ensuring their own survival. And in the meantime, stabilization is achieved through court martials, curfews, and curbs on civil liberties.

As O'Donnell has said, while the state is ultimately based on coercion, it usually is also based on consensus, which both "encompasses and conceals coercion. . . . This tension is the key to the theoretical analysis of the state."[20] The coercion characteristic of the bureaucratic authoritarian state is concealed or obviated in Germany and the United States by recourse to the management of law and money. Liberal stabilization not only makes military stabilization superfluous, but actively ensures the continued success of democratic states.

CONCLUSION: GUARDIANS OF THE GOVERNMENT OF MONEY

In conclusion, it is remarkable that O'Donnell should choose "sectoral egotism" as the immediate cause of bureaucratic authoritarianism, for sectoral egotism was the very term used by the future Bundesbank director Wilhelm Gaddum to describe the social conflict in Germany in the 1970s that Bundesbank policies sought to contain. Gaddum's Bundesbank successfully coped with this problem at arm's length, with monetary policy aimed at stabilization writ large. An earlier, no less independent institution, however, refused comparable service to his country's first experiment with democracy.

The interlaced implications of monetarism—the governing power of money, the politics of economic expertise, and central banks as "guardians of democracy"—involve a central dilemma verging on a contradiction: those who sympathize with democracy must also sympathize with the survival of democracy, or the phenomenon of democratic stability. Where the contributions of central banks to democratic stability are concerned, neither simple institutional independence nor simple political accountability resolves this dilemma. Even if, as Friedman conceded, the independence of central banks is justified only if it is used to take unpopular measures, democracy is too important to be left to central banks. The role of the Reichsbank in the collapse of Weimar and the mobilization of Nazi Germany illustrates for all time the vulnerability of democratic institutions to economic forces. Unpopular measures in realms such as monetary policy are occasionally the means to democratic stability, and as such must be judged superior to the alternatives—hyperinflations, depressions, and juntas. The unpopular measures of independent central banks may in the end prove less drastic and more democratic than other forms of stabilization. But if the banks' ultimate responsibility to democratic stability is to be ensured, we may have no means apart from the expertise and norms embedded in the theories of the economists who run them. Even in the government of money, the guardian of the guardians is a good education.

Notes

1. The Problem of Economic Policy Innovation in Democracies

1. Concepts such as M1, M1-B, M2, M3 (in the United States) and *Zentralbankgeldmenge* (central bank money, in Germany) are measures of the money supply. M1 defines money most narrowly (cash and checking accounts), the others define it more broadly. Measures of the money supply such as these are the main tools by which central banks execute a program of monetary targeting.

2. Milton Friedman, cited in *Monetarism and the Federal Reserve's Conduct of Monetary Policy*, Joint Economic Committee, U.S. Congress (Washington, D.C.: USGPO, 1982).

3. *Financial Times*, December 7, 1981.

4. Indeed, money is often described generically as "media of exchange." The literature on what money is and how it fulfills its mediating role is vast and specialized, and most of it is generated, not surprisingly, by economists. For an introduction for nonspecialists, see James S. Coleman, *Foundations of Social Theory* (Cambridge: Harvard University Press, 1990), p. 119.

5. Claus Offe, "The Attribution of Public Status to Interest Groups," in *Disorganized Capitalism: Contemporary Transformations of Work and Politics*, ed. John Keene (Cambridge: MIT Press, 1985), p. 230.

6. David M. Jones, *The Politics of Money: The Fed under Alan Greenspan* (New York: New York Institute of Finance, 1991), p. 53.

7. Jay Lorsch, *Pawns or Potentates* (Cambridge: Harvard University Press, 1992).

8. Donald F. Kettl, *Leadership at the Fed* (New Haven, Conn.: Yale University Press, 1986), p. 13.

9. James Q. Wilson, *Bureaucracy: What Government Agencies Do and Why They Do It* (New York: Basic, 1989).

10. Andrew Shonfield, *Organized Capitalism* (Oxford: Oxford University Press, 1965); John Zysman, *Governments, Markets, and Growth* (Ithaca, N.Y.: Cornell University Press, 1986).

11. Paavo Uusitalo, "Monetarism, Keynesianism, and the Institutional Status of Central Banks," *Acta Sociologica* 27 (1984), 31–50.

12. *Financial Times*, July 12, 1981.

13. Cited in David Smith, *The Rise and Fall of Monetarism* (Harmondsworth: Penguin, 1987), p. 132. The rest of the passage reads: "Now I know a few people in Washington who would love an intellectual justification for fiscal irresponsibility. Someday they are going to discover the most important usage of the monetarist view. And then we will see some fireworks."

14. See, for example, A. Cukierman, S. Webb, and B. Neyapti, "Measuring the Independence of Central Banks and Its Effects on Policy Outcomes," *World Bank Economic Review* 6, no. 3 (September 1992).

15. On the Bundesbank's self-concept, see Ellen Kennedy, *The Bundesbank: Germany's Central Bank in the International Monetary System* (New York: Council on Foreign Relations Press, 1991).

16. Sylvia Maxfield, *Gatekeepers of Growth: The International Political Economy of Central Banking in Developing Countries* (Princeton, N.J.: Princeton University Press, 1996).

17. Fritz W. Scharpf, *Sozial Demokratische Krisenpolitik in Europa* (Frankfurt: Campus Verlag, 1987).

18. Peter A. Hall, ed., *The Political Power of Economic Ideas: Keynesianism across Nations* (Princeton, N.J.: Princeton University Press, 1989), p. 376.

19. Leon N. Lindberg, Fritz W. Scharpf, and Guenther Englehardt, "Economic Policy Research: Challenges and a New Agenda," in *Comparative Policy Research: Learning from Experience,* ed. Meinolf Dierkes, Hans N. Weiler, and Ariane Berthoin Antal (New York: St. Martin's, 1987), p. 369.

20. Christopher S. Allen, "The Underdevelopment of Keynesianism in the Federal Republic of Germany," in Hall, *The Political Power of Economic Ideas.*

21. Robert Solomon, *The International Monetary System, 1945–1981* (New York: Harper and Row, 1982).

22. Manfred G. Schmidt, "West Germany: The Policy of the Middle Way," *Journal of Public Policy* 7, (1987), 135–177.

23. Thomas Mayer, ed., *The Political Economy of American Monetary Policy* (New York: Cambridge University Press, 1990).

24. Douglas A. Hibbs, Jr., "Inflation, Political Support, and Macroeconomic Policy," in *The Politics of Inflation and Economic Stagnation: Theoretical Approaches and International Case Studies,* ed. Leon N. Lindberg and Charles S. Maier (Washington, D.C.: Brookings, 1985).

25. Kathleen Thelen and Sven Steinmo, "Historical Institutionalism in Comparative Politics," in *Structuring Politics: Historical Institutionalism in Comparative Analysis,* ed. Steinmo, Thelen, and Frank Longstreth (New York: Cambridge University Press, 1992).

26. Sybille Oesterlin, "Zwischen autoritärer und marktwirtschaftlicher Zentralbankpolitik," *Kredit und Kapital* (1982), 179.

27. John T. Woolley, *Monetary Politics: The Federal Reserve and the Politics of Monetary Policy* (New York: Cambridge University Press, 1984), p. 154.

28. Milton Friedman, "Should There Be an Independent Monetary Authority?" in *In Search of a Monetary Constitution,* ed. L. B. Yeager (Cambridge: Harvard University Press, 1962); Friedman, "How to Give Monetarism a Bad Name," in *Monetarism, Inflation, and the Federal Reserve,* Joint Economic Committee, Congress (Washington, D.C.: USGPO, 1985), p. 51. See also Mark Toma, "Inflationary Bias of the Federal Reserve System: A Bureaucratic Perspective," in *Central Bankers, Bureaucratic Incentives and Monetary Policy,* ed. Eugenia Froege Toma and Mark Toma (Dordrecht: Martinus Nijhoff, 1986), pp. 37–66.

29. Keith Acheson and John F. Chant, "Bureaucratic Theory and the Choice of Central Bank Goals," *Journal of Money, Credit, and Banking* 5, no. 2 (May 1973). Reprinted in Toma and Toma, *Central Bankers,* p. 109.

30. Richard H. Timberlake, "Federal Reserve Policy since 1945," in *Money in Crisis: The Federal Reserve, the Economy, and Monetary Reform,* ed. Barry N. Siegel (San Francisco: Pacific Institute for Public Policy, 1984), p. 185.

2. THE ORIGINS OF THE BUNDESBANK'S CORPORATE CULTURE

1. Howard S. Ellis, *German Monetary Theory, 1905–1933* (Cambridge: Harvard University Press, 1937).

2. Helmut Müller, *Die Zentralbank—eine Nebenregierung: Reichsbankpräsident Hjalmar Schacht als Politiker der Weimarer Republik* (Opladen: Westdeutscher Verlag, 1973), p. 57.

3. Gerald D. Feldman, *The Great Disorder: Politics, Economics, and Society in the German Inflation, 1914–1924* (New York: Oxford University Press, 1993), p. 853.

4. Müller, *Die Zentralbank*, pp. 103–118.

5. Heinrich Irmler, "Bankenkrise und Vollbeschäftigungspolitik (1931–1936)" in *Währung und Wirtschaft in Deutschland, 1876–1975*, ed. Deutsche Bundesbank (Frankfurt a.M.: Fritz Knapp Verlag, 1976), p. 289.

6. Feldman, *The Great Disorder*, p. 854.

7. *"Der Nationalsozialismus ist, wie wir wissen, der schärfste Gegner der liberalistichen Auffassung, dass die Wirtschaft für das Kapital da sei, und das Volk für die Wirtschaft"* (author's translation). Quoted in Lothar Gall, Gerald D. Feldman, Harold James, Carl-Ludwig Holtfrerich, and Hans E. Büschgen, *Die Deutsche Bank, 1870–1995* (Munich: Verlag C. H. Beck, 1995), p. 320.

8. Gall, *Die Deutsche Bank*, p. 323.

9. Müller, *Die Zentralbank*, pp. 57ff.

10. Gall, *Die Deutsche Bank*, p. 318.

11. Feldman, *The Great Disorder*, p. 845.

12. Karl Hardach, *The Political Economy of Germany in the Twentieth Century* (Berkeley: University of California Press, 1980), p. 63.

13. "Das Bankensystems eines Landes ist ebenso stark wie seine schwächste Aktienbank." Cited in Gall et al., *Die Deutsche Bank*, p. 505.

14. In 1960. Andrew Shonfield, *Modern Capitalism: The Changing Balance of Public and Private Power* (Oxford: Oxford University Press, 1978), p. 249.

15. Thomas Alan Schwartz, *America's Germany: John J. McCloy and the Federal Republic of Germany* (Cambridge, Mass: Harvard University Press, 1991), pp. 62–63.

16. Michael Kreile, "West Germany: The Dynamics of Expansion," in *Between Power and Plenty*, ed. Peter J. Katzenstein (Madison: University of Wisconsin Press, 1978).

17. Interview with former German industry association official "KK."

18. Interview with German Trade Union Federation officials "OO" and "PP."

19. Christopher S. Allen, "The Underdevelopment of Keynesianism in the Federal Republic of Germany," in *The Political Power of Economic Ideas: Keynesianism across Nations*, ed. Peter A. Hall (Princeton, N.J.: Princeton University Press, 1989).

20. David Ricci, *The Tragedy of Political Science* (New Haven, Conn.: Yale University Press, 1984).

21. Interview with German economist "B."

22. T. W. Hutchison, "Walter Eucken and the Social Market Economy," in *The Politics and Philosophy of Economics* (New York: New York University Press, 1984).

23. Herbert Giersch, Karl–Heinz Paque, and Holger Schmieding, *The Fading Miracle: Four Decades of Market Economics in Germany* (New York: Cambridge University Press, 1992), p. 19.

24. Interview with former German finance ministry official "SS."

25. Henry Wallich, "The American Council of Economic Advisers and the German Sachverstaendigenrat: A Study in the Economics of Advice," in *The Economic Approach to Public Policy*, ed. Ryan C. Amacher, Robert D. Tollison, and Thomas D. Willett (Ithaca, N.Y.: Cornell University Press, 1976), pp. 490–498.

26. Cited in Shonfield, *Modern Capitalism*, p. 288.

27. Helmut Schlesinger, Bundesbank vice president, cited in Heinz-Peter Spahn, *Bundesbank und Wirtschaftskrise* (Regensburg: Transfer Verlag, 1988), p. 55.

28. Deutsche Bundesbank, *Monetary Policy and Instruments* Special Series No. 7 (Frankfurt: Deutsche Bundesbank, 1987).

29. Karl-Otto Pöhl, "Widersprüche und Gemeinsamkeiten in der Politik der Bundesregierung und der Deutschen Bundesbank in der Zeit von 1978–1982," in *Kämpfer ohne Pathos*, ed. Helmut Schmidt and Walter Hesselbach (Bonn: Verlag Neue Gesellschaft, 1985).

30. Interview with federal finance ministry official "C."

31. Interview with Bundesbank official "N."

32. Shonfield, *Modern Capitalism*, p. 286.

33. Interview with former Federal Reserve official "T" and former Bundesbank official "R."

34. Interview with "R."

35. Ibid.

36. Interview with former SPD official "U" and with Bundesbank officials "R" and "G."

37. Interview with "R."

38. Interviews with Bundesbank officials "G," "J," and "R." Cf. Sherman J. Maisel, *Managing the Dollar* (New York: Norton, 1973); interview with former Federal Reserve official "F."

39. Interview with LCB official "Y."

40. Wilhelm Vocke, *Memoiren* (Stuttgart, 1973); Otmar Emminger, *D-Mark, Dollar, Währungskrisen: Erinnerungen Eines Ehemaligen Bundesbankpräsidenten* (Stuttgart: Deutsche Verlags-Anstalt, 1986), p. 94.

41. *Jahresbericht*, Bank Deutscher Länder, 1955.

42. Shonfield, *Modern Capitalism*, pp. 274–286.

3. THE BUNDESBANK'S MONETARIST REGIME CHANGE, 1970–1985

1. Otmar Emminger, *D-Mark, Dollar, Währungskrisen: Erinnerungen eines ehemaligen Bundesbankpräsidenten* (Stuttgart: Deutsche Verlags-Anstalt, 1986), p. 20.

2. Interview with former Bundesbank official "G."

3. Arnulf Bäring, *Machtwechsel: Die Ära Brandt-Scheel* (Stuttgart: Deutsche Verlags-Anstalt, 1982), p. 143.

4. "Nur über seine Leiche." Bäring, *Machtwechsel*, p. 143.

5. Helmut Schlesinger, "Die Geldpolitik der Deutschen Bundesbank, 1967–1977," *Kredit und Kapital* 11, no. 1 (1978), 3ff.

6. Cited in E. C. M. Cullingford, *Trade Unions in West Germany* (Boulder, Colo.: Westview, 1976), p. 34.

7. Ibid., p. 30.

8. "Victory for Friedman," *New York Times*, July 12, 1971.

9. Emminger, *D-Mark, Dollar,* chap. 4.

10. Interview with former SPD official "U."

11. Robert Solomon, *The International Monetary System, 1945–1981* (New York: Harper and Row, 1982), pp. 179–180.

12. Interview with "U."

13. Interview with former Bundesbank economist "B."

14. See the Proceedings of the First Konstanzer Seminar, *Kredit und Kapital*, Beiheft 1, 1971.

15. Interview with Sparkassen und Giroverband official "HH."

16. BDI *Jahresberichte*, 1970–1971; interview with the former BDI official "KK."

17. Interviews with "U" and former SPD cabinet minister "A." Cf. Otmar Emminger, *D-Mark, Dollar,* chaps. 4 and 5.

18. Interviews with "U" and the former SPD cabinet minister "A." See also Fritz Scharpf, *Sozial Demokratische Krisen Politik in Europa* (Frankfurt: Campus Verlag, 1987).

19. Helmut Schmidt, *Men and Powers: A Political Retrospective,* trans. Ruth Hein (New York: Random House, 1989), p. 156.

20. Interview with Sparkassen official "HH."

21. *"Mehr Macht der Bundesbank is noch längst nicht mit mehr Preisstabilität gleichbedeutend"* (author's translation). "Zuviel Macht für die Bundesbank?" *Wirtschaftswoche*, February 16, 1973.

22. "I was and still am in principle a supporter of pegged exchange rates." Schmidt, *Men and Powers*, p. 153.

23. Emminger, *D-Mark, Dollar,* p. 231ff.

24. *"Wir waren bereit, dies letztere der Öffentlichkeit zu erklären, mit allen daraus folgenden Konsequenzen."* ("We were prepared to release this to the public and to accept all of the consequences that followed." Author's translation.) Emminger, *D-Mark, Dollar,* p. 234.

25. *Handelsblatt*, March 2, 1973.

26. Deutsche Bundesbank *Annual Report*, 1973.

27. Helmut Schlesinger, "Die Geldpolitik als Mittel der Inflationsbekämpfung," *ifo Schnelldienst*, Munich, July 18, 1973.

28. *"Wenn das Wirtschaftsministerium und die Bundesbank einer Meinung sind, dann wird es wohl so richtig sein"* (author's translation). Emminger, *D-Mark, Dollar,* p. 241.

29. Deutsche Bundesbank *Annual Report*, 1973.

30. Georg Bleile, "Die Neue Geldpolitik der Deutschen Bundesbank," *Zeitschrift für das Gesamte Kreditwesen* 1. Heft (1975), 23.

31. Deutsche Bundesbank *Annual Report*, 1972.

32. Horst Bockelmann, "Quantitative Targets for Monetary Policy," in Banque de France, *Cahiers économiques et monétaires. VI: Actes du séminair des Banques Centrales et des Institutions Internationales*, April 1977, p. 11.

33. Bockelmann, "Quantitative Targets," p. 15; Joint Economic Committee, U.S. Congress, *Monetary Policy, Selective Credit Controls, and Industrial Policy in France, Britain, West Germany, and Sweden* (Washington, D.C.: USGPO, June 1981); Otmar Emminger, "Deutsche Geldpolitik im Zeichen des Monetarismus," *Sparkasse* 99 (September 1982), 288ff.

34. Bockelmann, "Quantitative Targets," p. 22.

35. Interviews with German commercial bank economist "Q" and German banking official "II."

36. *"Rückfall in die naive Quantitätstheorie."* Cited in "Hessen-Bank rüstet sich für die grosse Staatsverschuldung," *Handelsblatt*, February 7, 1973. See also "Helaba und die Baufinanzierung," *Frankfurter Rundschau*, November 23, 1973; "Growth—at almost any price," *Financial Times*, December 11, 1973.

37. *Frankfurter Allgemeine Zeitung*, December 18, 1973.

38. Deutsche Bundesbank *Annual Report*, 1973.

39. Dieter Duwendag, ed., *Macht und Ohnmacht der Deutschen Bundesbank* (Frankfurt a.M.: Athenaeum Verlag, 1973).

40. See the Bundesbank's comments on this in Deutsche Bundesbank, *Annual Reports* for 1973 and 1974.

41. Scharpf, *Sozialdemokratische Krisenpolitik*.

42. Interview with German union official "NN."

43. Interview with German union official "PP."

44. Deutsche Bundesbank *Annual Report*, 1973, p. 40.

45. Interview with "PP."

46. *"Reprivatisierung des Beschäftingungsrisikos"* (author's translation). WSI *Mitteilungen*, Heft 12, 1974.

47. *Handelsblatt*, December 23, 1974.

48. *"Bestürzende Entgleisung der Währungshüter"* (author's translation). *Handelsblatt*, May 12, 1975.

49. *Wirtschaftswoche*, October 24, 1974.

50. *"Inflation schrittweise abzubauen"* (author's translation). *Handelsblatt*, December 7, 1974.

51. *Financial Times*, April 19, 1974.

52. *Wirtschaftswoche*, November 1, 1974.

53. Interview with German economist "VV."

54. *"Versteckte einkommenspolitik."* Interview with the Bundesbank official "R."

55. Interview with "R."

56. Interview with German economist "B."

57. *Frankfurter Rundschau*, May 21, 1975.

58. *Tagesspiegel*, December 19, 1975.

59. *Frankfurter Rundschau*, December 16, 1975.

60. *"Regimewechsel."* Helmut Schlesinger, "Zehn Jahre Geldpolitik mit einem Geldmengenziel," in *Öffentliche Finanzen und Monetaere Oekonomie*, ed. Wolfgang Gebauer (Frankfurt: Fritz Knapp Verlag, 1985), p. 127.

61. Emminger, *D-Mark, Dollar*, p. 418; cf. his note 15.

62. *Handelsblatt*, February 19, 1974.

63. J. Wilhelm Gaddum, "Die Inflation—ihre wirtschaftlichen, sozialen, moralischen, und politischen Wirkungen aus der Sicht des Staates." In *Die Inflation: Ursachen, Wirkungen, Folgerungen*, ed. Heinrich B. Streithofen (Stuttgart: Seewald Verlag, 1975), pp. 32–33.

64. *Frankfurter Allgemeine Zeitung*, December 18, 1975.

65. Interview with Economics Ministry official "G."

66. Interview with Economics Ministry official "C."

67. Interview with former BDI official "KK."

68. *Die Zeit*, March 23, 1974; see also *Handelsblatt*, May 31, 1974.

69. *Die Zeit*, July 23, 1976.

70. *"Prominente Vertreter der Volkswirtshaftlichen Lehre und erfolgreiche Verwaltungsbeamte sind zahlreicher geworden, während Experten des praktischen Bankgeschäfts immer seltener neu in den Zentralbankrat gekommen"* (author's translation). *Rheinischer Merkur*, May 12, 1978. On Klasen's long-standing "campaign" about this issue, see *Welt am Sonntag*, June 6, 1976.

71. *Frankfurter Rundschau*, February 21, 1974.

72. *Der Spiegel*, July 19, 1976.

73. Interview with former SVR official "P."

74. Interview with former DGB official "PP."

75. Interview with former Bundesbank officials "X" and "R."

76. Interview with "X."

77. Interview with "PP."

78. Interview with union official "NN."

79. Interview with union official "OO."

80. Ibid.

81. Interview with "NN."

82. Private poll for the Deutsche Bundesbank, conducted in 1986.

83. *"allzu mechanistische," "unsichere Prämissen," "mehr Schaden . . . als Nutzen." . . . "Die Gefähr einer Überschätzung alter und neue Instrument der Geldpolitik scheint uns in erster Linie darin zu liegen, dass die eigentlichen Ursachen der Inflation und Rezession Verkannt und ihre Träger von der ihnen zukommender Verantwortung entlastet werden"* (author's translation). Dresdner Bank, "Geldpolitik ein Jahr nach der 'Deklaration von Frankfurt.' "

84. *"Operation Geldmengenziele geglückt, Konjunktur tot"* (author's translation). Dresdner Bank press release, 1977.

85. Interview with German economist "B."

86. Ibid.

87. Shadow European Economic Policy Committee, "Europe Enters the Eighties," *Banca Nazionale del Lavoro Quarterly Review* 129 (June 1979), 124.

88. Ibid., p. 125.

89. Interview with "B."

90. Martin Hellwig and Manfred Neumann, "Germany under Kohl," *Economic Policy* (October 1987).

91. Interview with former Bundesbank official "R."

92. Hellwig and Neumann, "Germany under Kohl," p. 112.

93. Interview with SPD official "A."

94. Interview with "A" and former SPD official "C."

95. German Federal Statistics Office, cited in Peter Trapp, "Labor Market Barriers to More Employment: Causes for an Increase in the Natural Rate in Germany," *Kiel Working Paper*, 1987.

96. Herman J. Dudler, "Financial Innovation," *Kredit und Kapital* 19 (1986), 472ff. Cf. Deutsche Bundesbank, "Zur längfristigen Entwicklung und Kontrolle des Geldvolumens," *Monatsbericht* 37, no. 1 (January 1985).

97. OECD *Economic Survey* (Paris, Organization for Economic Co-operation and Development, 1985), p. 50.

98. Hellwig and Neumann, "Germany Under Kohl," p. 140.

4. THE ORIGINS OF THE FEDERAL RESERVE'S CORPORATE CULTURE

1. David Vogel, "Why Businessmen Distrust Their State: The Political Consciousness of American Corporate Executives," *British Journal of Political Science* 8 (January 1978), 70.

2. Cited in John T. Woolley, *Monetary Politics: The Federal Reserve and the Politics of Monetary Policy* (Cambridge: Cambridge University Press, 1984), p. 38.

3. Murray N. Rothbard, "The Federal Reserve as a Cartelization Device: The Early Years, 1913–1930," in *Money in Crisis: The Federal Reserve, the Economy, and Monetary Reform,* ed. Barry N. Siegel. (San Francisco: Pacific Institute for Public Policy Research, 1984), p. 135

4. Gabriel Kolko, *The Triumph of Conservatism* (Glencoe, Ill.: Free Press, 1963), p. 186.

5. "The main difference between the draft and the eventual legislation is that in the former national board of directors was largely chosen by the banks themselves rather than by the president of the United States. This provision was so blatantly cartelist that it was modified for political reasons to have the President name the board." Rothbard, "The Federal Reserve as a Cartelization Device," p. 101.

6. Woolley, *Monetary Politics,* pp. 30 ff.

7. Cited in Richard H. Timberlake, Jr., "Politics, Economists, and the Central Bank," in *Money, the Market, and the State,* ed. Nicholas A. Badles and L. Aubrey Drewery, Jr. (Athens: University of Georgia Press, 1968), p. 46.

8. Timberlake, "Politics, Economists," pp. 47–48.

9. Ibid., p. 49.

10. *Journal of the American Banking Association* 31 (October 1928), p. 281.

11. Interview with an American Bankers Association official "J."

12. American Bankers Association, *Compendium of Banking Issues,* various years.

13. Florence Peterson, *American Labor Unions,* 2d rev. ed. (New York: Harper and Row, 1963), pp. 21–22.

14. Robert Solomon, *The International Monetary System, 1945–1981* (New York: Harper and Row, 1982), p. 32.

15. Nathaniel Beck, "Domestic Sources of American Monetary Policy: 1955–1982," *Journal of Politics* 46 (August 1984).

16. See Douglas A. Hibbs, Jr. "Inflation, Political Support, and Macroeconomic Policy," in *The Politics of Inflation and Economic Stagnation: Theoretical Approaches and International Case Studies,* ed. Leon N. Lindberg and Charles S. Maier. (Washington, D.C.: Brookings Institution, 1985.)

17. I. M. Destler and C. Randall Henning, *Dollar Politics: Exchange Rate Policymaking in the United States* (Washington, D.C.: Institute for International Economics, 1989).

18. Henry Wallich, "The American Council of Economic Advisers and the German Sachverständigenrat: A Study in the Economics of Advice," in *The Economic Approach to Public Policy,* ed. Ryan C. Amacher et al. (Ithaca: Cornell University Press, 1976), pp. 490–498.

19. Interviews with former CEA officials "D" and "E."

20. Interviews with Congressional staff members "G," "H," and "I."

21. Morris Fiorina, *Congress: Keystone of the Washington Establishment* (New Haven, Conn.: Yale University Press, 1989).

22. Interviews with "G," "H," and "I."

23. Interview with "H."

24. Ralph Nader Congress Project, *The Money Committees* (New York: Grossman, 1975).

25. Interview with "I."

26. Woolley, *Monetary Politics,* p. 142.

27. G. L. Bach, "The Federal Reserve and Monetary Policy Formation," *American Economics Review* 57 (December 1949); Marriner Eccles, "The Climax of the Treasury Federal Reserve Dispute," in *Money and Economic Activity,* ed. Lawrence S. Ritter. (New York: Houghton-Mifflin, 1961); L. W. Mints, "Monetary Policy—Discussion," AER *Proceedings* 43 (May 1953); M. Friedman, "Monetary-Fiscal Framework for Economic Stability," *American Economic Review* (1948).

28. Timberlake, "Politics, Economists," p. 56.

29. Interview with former CEA official "E."

30. Interview with former Federal Reserve officials "T" and "K."

31. Board of Governors, Federal Reserve System, *Membership of the Board of Governors of the Federal Reserve System, 1913–1988.*

32. Interviews with former Federal Reserve officials "V," "T," and "W."

33. Interview with former Federal Reserve official "S."

34. Interview with Federal Reserve official "CC."

35. Author's calculations for 1945–1985.

36. Interview with former Federal Reserve official "F."

37. Interview with Federal Reserve staff member "BB."

38. Interview with Federal Reserve official "K."

39. Minutes of the meetings of the FOMC and board of governors, 1970 to 1975; interviews with Federal Reserve staff member "S," and former Federal Reserve officials "T" and "V."

40. Interview with "F."

41. Interview with "T."

42. Interviews with "T," "V," "F," and "S."

43. David M. Jones, *The Politics of Money: The Fed under Alan Greenspan* (New York: New York Institute of Finance, 1991), p. 53.

5. THE MONETARIST REVOLUTION AND THE FED, 1970–1985

1. Arthur Burns, *The Anguish of Central Banking*, Per Jacobsen Lecture (Washington: International Monetary Fund, 1979).

2. Herbert Stein, *Presidential Economics: The Making of Economic Policy from Roosevelt to Clinton*, 3d rev. ed. (Washington, D.C.: American Enterprise Institute, 1994), p. 134.

3. Wyatt C. Wells, *Economist in an Uncertain World: Arthur F. Burns and the Federal Reserve, 1970–1978* (New York: Columbia University Press, 1994).

4. Cited in Kevin Phillips, *Post-Conservative America: People, Politics, and Ideology in a Time of Crisis* (New York: Random House, 1982), p. 126.

5. Wells, *Economist in an Uncertain World*, p. 55.

6. Arthur F. Burns, *Reflections of an Economic Policymaker* (Washington, D.C.: American Enterprise Institute, 1978), p. 95.

7. Ibid., pp. 98, 126, 177.

8. Stein, *Presidential Economics*, pp. 169–174.

9. Ibid., pp. 168, 135.

10. Ibid., p. 157.

11. Gallup Opinion Index, cited in Donald J. Devine, *Reagan Electionomics* (Ottawa, Ill.: Green Hill, 1983), p. 15.

12. Ralph Nader Congress Project, *The Money Committees* (New York: Grossman, 1975), p. 315.

13. Ibid., p. 317.

14. Donald F. Kettl, *Leadership at the Fed* (New Haven, Conn.: Yale University Press, 1986), pp. 123ff.

15. In May of 1971, Burns said, "We should not close our minds to the possibility [of] an incomes policy, *provided it stopped well short of direct price and wage controls." Reflections*, p. 99 (italics added).

16. Nader Congress Project, *Money Committees*, p. 322.

17. Stein, *Presidential Economics*, p. 179.

18. David A. Stockman, *The Triumph of Politics: How the Reagan Revolution Failed* (New York: Harper and Row, 1986), p. 31.

19. John T. Woolley, *Monetary Politics: The Federal Reserve and the Politics of Monetary Policy* (Cambridge: Cambridge University Press, 1984).

20. Kettl, *Leadership at the Fed*, chap. 5.

21. FOMC minutes for August 1972.

22. Interview with American economist "AA."

23. Interviews with CEA officials "D" and "E."

24. Sherman Maisel, *Managing the Dollar* (New York: Norton, 1973), pp. 110ff.

25. Interview with Federal Reserve official "CC."

26. Allan H. Meltzer, "The Fed at Seventy-five," in *Monetary Policy on the 75th Anniversary of the Federal Reserve System*, ed. Michael T. Belongia. (Boston: Kluwer Academic Publishers, 1991), pp. 21–35.

27. Interview with former Federal Reserve staff member "S."

28. Henry C. Wallich and Peter M. Keir, "The Role of Operating Guides in U.S. Monetary Policy: A Historical Review," *Kredit und Kapital* 11 (1978), 42.

29. Interview with former Federal Reserve official "V" and the former CEA official "D."

30. Interview with "V."

31. Interview with American economist "Z."

32. Sidney Blumenthal, *The Rise of the Counter-Establishment: From Conservative Ideology to Political Power* (New York: Times Books, 1986).

33. Interview with "Z."

34. Interview with American economist "AA."

35. Shadow Open Market Committee (SOMC) proceedings of September 1974 (Rochester: Carnegie-Mellon Conference Series).

36. Ibid.

37. Ibid.

38. Ibid., September 1977.

39. Ibid.

40. Interview with "Z."

41. SOMC documents, September 1977.

42. Ibid., March 1979.

43. Ibid., September 1978.

44. Ibid.

45. Ibid.

46. Ibid., September 1979.

47. Ibid., February 1980.

48. Ibid., September 1980.

49. Ibid., February 1980.

50. Ibid., September 1980.

51. Interview with former CEA official "E."

52. James L. Pierce, "The Myth of Congressional Supervision of Monetary Policy," *Journal of Monetary Economics* 4 (1978), 363.

53. See the introduction to HR 133 (Washington, D.C.: USGPO, 1975).

54. Pierce, "The Myth of Congressional Supervision," 364.

55. A senior staff member of the Fed, who helped prepare Burns's reports and testimony before Congress, indicates that congressional monetarism probably affected him more than anyone else; it obliged him to phrase Burns's presentations in the monetarist terminology that Congress had mandated, but the mandate did not extend to the substance of the policy decisions. Interview with the Federal Reserve staff member "AA."

56. Interviews with congressional staff members "D," "I," and "H." Cf. Robert Weintraub, "Congressional Supervision of Monetary Policy," *Journal of Monetary Economics* 4 (1978), 341–362.

57. Interview with American economist "Z."

58. "There weren't five people on the Hill who knew M1 from Adam's ox." Interview with Congressional staff members "H" and "J."

59. SOMC documents, September 1978.

60. Phillips, *Post-Conservative America*, pp. 131–132.

61. Milton Friedman, "The Kemp-Roth Free Lunch," *Newsweek*, August 7, 1978.

62. Milton Friedman, personal correspondence with author, September 1996.

63. See Milton Friedman, "Two Economic Fallacies," *Newsweek*, May 12, 1975.

64. Phillips, *Post-Conservative America*, p. 126.

65. Milton Friedman, "The Message From California." *Newsweek*, June 19, 1978.

66. Stockman, *Triumph of Politics*, p. 53.

67. Ibid., p. 39.

68. Friedman, "Kemp-Roth Free Lunch."

69. On these intramural battles, see Paul Craig Roberts, *The Supply-Side Revolution: An Insider's Account of Policymaking in Washington* (Cambridge, Mass: Harvard University Press, 1984), p. 7ff, 20ff, 94ff.

70. James Allen Smith, *The Idea Brokers: Think Tanks and the Rise of the New Policy Elite* (New York, Free Press, 1991), p. 177ff.

71. Ernest W. Lafever, Raymond English, and Raymond S. Schnettinger, *Scholars, Dollars, and Public Policy* (Washington, D.C.: Ethics and Public Policy Center), p. 12.

72. Quoted in Smith, *Idea Brokers,* p. 197.

73. Interview with Heritage Foundation Official "A."

74. Maisel, *Managing the Dollar,* p. 123.

75. Interview with former Federal Reserve staff member "S."

76. Ibid.

77. Interview with Federal Reserve staff member "DD."

78. William A. Niskanen, *Reaganomics: An Insider's Account of the Policies and the People* (New York: Oxford University Press, 1988), p. 158.

79. Interview with former CEA official "E."

80. Interview with "S" and the Federal Reserve official "T."

81. *Business Week,* August 13, 1979.

82. Interview with "E."

83. Paul A. Volcker, "The Role of Monetary Targets in an Age of Inflation," *Journal of Monetary Economics* 4 (1978), 329–339.

84. *Economist,* August 4, 1979.

85. For a very detailed reconstruction of these events written from a left populist perspective, see William Greider, *Secrets of the Temple: How the Federal Reserve Runs the Country* (New York: Simon and Schuster, 1987), pp. 128ff.

86. *Business Week,* October 8, 1979.

87. *Economist,* October 27, 1979.

88. *New York Times,* October 14, 1979.

89. SOMC documents, March 1980.

90. Woolley, *Monetary Politics,* pp. 100–106.

91. Karl Brunner, "Has Monetarism Failed?" *Cato Journal* 3 (Spring 1982).

92. Volcker, "Role of Monetary Targets," p. 334.

93. Interviews with "S" and "T."

94. Volcker, "Role of Monetary Targets," p. 332.

95. Interview with former Federal Reserve staff member "S."

96. Volcker, "Role of Monetary Targets," p. 332.

97. Interview with Federal Reserve staff member "DD."

98. Greider, *Secrets of the Temple,* p. 189.

99. Interview with former CEA official "E."

100. *New York Times,* October 3, 1980.

101. Interview with former Federal Reserve official "V."

102. Interviews with "T" and "S."

103. Interview with "T." Cf. Greider, *Secrets of the Temple.*

104. Interview with "T."

105. Martin Anderson, *Revolution* (Stanford: Hoover Institution, 1988), p. 267. PEPAB was abolished by the Bush administration in 1989.

106. Donald T. Regan, *For the Record: From Wall Street to Washington* (New York: Harcourt Brace Jovanovich, 1988), pp. 157–161.

107. Stockman, *Triumph of Politics,* pp. 54, 58–65, 96.

108. Roberts, *Supply-Side Revolution,* p. 92.

109. Stockman, *Triumph of Politics,* p. 93.

110. Ibid., pp. 68–69.

111. Ibid., p. 95.

112. Roberts, *Supply-Side Revolution,* p. 97.

113. Ibid., pp. 116–117.

114. Ibid., p. 114.

115. See, for example, Friedman's *Newsweek* columns of 1981: "Deficits and Inflation," February 23; "Whose Money Is It Anyway?" May 4; "Monetary Instability," June 15; "Closet Keynesianism," July 27; "Churning at the Fed," August 31; "Reaganomics and Interest Rates," September 21; and "Which Budget Deficit?" November 2.

116. SOMC documents, March 1981.

117. *Economist,* June 26, 1982.

118. Roberts, *Supply-Side Revolution*, p. 115.

119. Interview with Federal Reserve official "T."

120. Edwin Meese III, *With Reagan: The Inside Story* (Washington, D.C.: Regnery Gateway, 1992), p. 156.

121. Interview with "T."

122. Roberts, *Supply-Side Revolution*, p. 114.

123. Stockman, *Triumph of Politics*, p. 331.

124. Ibid., p. 332.

125. Meese, *With Reagan*, p. 160.

126. Roberts, *Supply-Side Revolution*, p. 116.

127. Joint Economic Committee, United States Congress, *Monetarism and the Federal Reserve's Conduct of Monetary Policy* (Washington, D.C.: USGPO, 1982).

128. SOMC documents, March 1982.

129. Regan, *For the Record*, p. 172.

130. Meese, *With Reagan*, p. 144.

131. Anderson, *Revolution*, p. 268.

132. Regan, *For the Record*, p. 178.

133. Interview with former Congressional staff member "EE."

134. Stephen Axilrod, "U.S. Monetary Policy in Recent Years: An Overview," *Federal Reserve Bulletin* 71 (January 1985), 18.

135. Interview with Congressional staff member "J."

136. Interview with Federal Reserve staff member "DD."

137. Stockman, *Triumph of Politics*, p. 380.

138. *Economic Survey* (Paris: Organization for Economic Cooperation and Development, 1986).

139. OECD *Survey*, 1986, p. 74.

140. Niskanen, *Reaganomics*, p. 194.

141. OECD *Survey*, 1986, p. 77.

142. Ibid., p. 76.

143. Niskanen, *Reaganomics*, p. 194.

144. Maisel, *Managing the Dollar*, p. 136.

145. Burns, "Anguish of Central Banking."

146. Interview with Congressional staff member "I."

147. Interview with former CEA official "E."

148. Interview with Federal Reserve staff member "BB" and the Federal Reserve official "D."

149. Paul A. Volcker, "The Human Factor and the Fed," in *The Art of Monetary Policy*, ed. David C. Colander and Dewey Daane (Armonk, N.Y.: Sharpe, 1994), p. 27.

150. Interview with author.

151. "Greenspan's Authority on Rates Is Said to Have Been Diminished," *New York Times*, April 18, 1991.

152. Interview with former Bundesbank official "D."

6. CENTRAL BANKS AS GUARDIANS OF DEMOCRACY

1. Michael Kreile, "West Germany: The Dynamics of Expansion," in *Between Power and Plenty*, ed. Peter J. Katzenstein (Madison: University of Wisconsin Press, 1977), p. 193.

2. Paul A. Volcker, "The Human Factor and the Fed," in *The Art of Monetary Policy*, ed. David C. Colander and Dewey Daane (Armonk, N.Y.: Sharpe, 1994), p. 25.

3. Cf. George P. Schultz, "Reflections on Political Economy," in *The Economic Approach to Public Policy: Selected Readings*, ed. Ryan C. Amacher et al. (Ithaca: Cornell University Press, 1976), p. 482.

4. Sherman Maisel, *Managing the Dollar* (New York: Norton, 1973), p. 156.

5. Richard H. Timberlake, "Federal Reserve Policy since 1945: The Results of Authority in the Absence of Rules," in *Money in Crisis: The Federal Reserve, the Economy, and Monetary Reform*, ed. Barry N. Siegel (San Francisco: Pacific Institute for Public Policy Research, 1984), p. 185.

6. Interview with Federal Reserve official "W."

7. Cf. Bernard Silberman, *Cages of Reason* (Chicago: University of Chicago Press, 1993).

8. Talcott Parsons, *Politics and Social Structure* (New York: Free Press, 1969), pp. 404–437. For a discussion of Parsons's work on this point, see Jean L. Cohen and Andrew Arato, *Civil Society and Political Theory* (Cambridge: MIT Press, 1992), pp. 130–137.

9. Oliver Wendell Holmes, Jr., quoted in Bernard Schwartz, *The New Right and the Constitution* (Boston: Northeastern University Press, 1990), p. 251.

10. Donald P. Kommers, *The Constitutional Jurisprudence of the Federal Republic of Germany* (Durham, N.C.: Duke University Press, 1989), p. 36.

11. Ibid., p. 50.

12. Ibid., p. 37.

13. Herman Schwartz, *Packing the Courts: The Conservative Campaign to Rewrite the Constitution* (New York: Scribner's, 1988).

14. Richard A. Posner, *Economic Analysis of Law* (4th ed.) Boston: Little, Brown, 1992).

15. Ronald Dworkin, *Taking Rights Seriously* (Cambridge: Harvard University Press, 1977).

16. Sebastian Edwards and Alejandra Cox Edwards, *Monetarism and Liberalization: The Chilean Experiment* (Chicago: University of Chicago Press, 1991), pp. 9–22.

17. Ibid., pp. 35–49.

18. Guillermo O'Donnell, "Tensions in the Bureaucratic-Authoritarian State and the Question of Democracy," in *The New Authoritarianism in Latin America,* ed. David Collier (Princeton, N.J.: Princeton University Press, 1979), p. 292.

19. Ibid., p. 296.

20. Ibid., pp. 288–290.

Index

INDEX

Cornell Studies in Political Economy

A SERIES EDITED BY PETER J. KATZENSTEIN

CORNELL STUDIES IN POLITICAL ECONOMY